NUTTS CORNER

STATIONS OF
COASTAL COMMAND
THEN AND NOW

Like a breath of wind gone in a fleeting second only the memories now remain.

MEMORIAL INSCRIPTION AT PREDANNACK

STATIONS OF
COASTAL COMMAND
THEN AND NOW
David Smith

Credits

ISBN: 9 781870 067874

© *After the Battle* 2016

Edited and designed by
Winston Ramsey, Editor-in-Chief

PUBLISHERS
Battle of Britain International Ltd
The Mews, Hobbs Cross House,
Hobbs Cross, Old Harlow, Essex CM17 0NN

Telephone: 01279 41 8833.
Fax: 01279 41 9386
E-mail: hq@afterthebattle.com
Website: www.afterthebattle.com

PRINTERS
Printed by Ozgraf S. A., Olsztyn, Poland.

FRONT COVER
A publicity shot purporting to show the captain of Coastal Command holding a final conference with his crew. The photograph was taken at Lagens in the Azores in front of a Fortress Mk II, FL462 'W' of No. 220 Squadron. The 'crew' were in fact an ad hoc group drawn from No. 206 Squadron RAF, and the 'captain' (third from right, wearing SD cap) was Flying Officer L. W. Taylor, RAAF, an Air Ministry public relations officer.

REAR COVER
Flight Lieutenant J. T. 'Jake' McCutcheon, one of the Flight Commanders of No. 404 Canadian Squadron in front of his Blenheim on October 2, 1942.

FRONTISPIECE
The busy scene at the Coastal Command base at Pembroke Dock, home of No. 461 Squadron of the Royal Australian Air Force.

PAGES 20-21
Sunderlands of Canadian No. 422 Squadron based at Castle Archdale in Northern Ireland.

PAGES 72-73
November 21, 1941. Members of No. 415 Squadron, stationed at Thorney Island, watch as Sergeant Pilot Ted Briggs takes off on his first solo flight in a Bristol Beaufort.

PAGES 110-111
The crew of a Beaufighter (T4712) of No. 248 Squadron pictured at Dyce.

PAGES 180-181
A Wellington and crew of No. 304 Polish Squadron at their base in south Wales — the photograph could have been taken either at Dale or Talbenny.

PAGES 250-251
North Front airfield at Gibraltar with an assortment of aircraft on the tarmac.

Acknowledgements

Although I wrote the main text, this book is really a team effort and owes much to friends and colleagues who undertook the task of producing many of today's comparison photographs. Aldon Ferguson tackled Scotland and many sites in England with Squadron Leader Colin Pomeroy, a former Shackleton and Nimrod captain, and Ernie Cromie, with the aid of fellow Ulster Aviation Society member David Hill, covered the bases in Northern Ireland. Apart from labouring on the index, Peter Gunn helped out with photography of the three bases in his patch of the world in Norfolk, and David Thompson, another friend of long standing, concentrated on his local aerodrome at Thornaby.

A number of former Coastal Command stations are still under military control and I am indebted to Wing Commander Jim Beldon of the Ministry of Defence for securing permission for us to visit them, particularly the Command's old headquarters at Northwood. I would like to thank at Benson, Mick Prendergast and Nikki Hamilton; at Brawdy, Major George Hume; at Chivenor, Major Gil Pelly and Flight Lieutenant Tamsyn Ryall; at Leuchars, Squadron Leader Nobby Clark, Karen Clayton, WO1 Alan O'Loughlin and Andy Waterton; at Northwood, Lieutenant Daniel Drew; at Portreath, Flight Sergeant A. L. Williams; at Predannack, Lieutenant-Commander Graeme Stringer, Tim Gibb and Peter Wearne; at St Eval, Flight Lieutenant Jeff Spencer; at Tain, Major A.G.P. Hay and William Livingstone, and at Thorney Island, Tim Kenealy.

I also appreciate the hospitality given us at many of the other airfields and would specially like to thank at Banff, Colin Jeffrey and Ally Rennie; at Beaulieu, John Levesley of Friends of New Forest Airfields and Gareth Owen and Joan Shergold; at Carew Cheriton, John and Deric Brock; at Dale and Talbenny Malcolm Cullen; at Dallachy, the Fochabers Folk Museum and Heritage Centre; at Davidstow Moor Mr D. C. Keast; at Dyce, Brian Harwood, Kellie Heath and John Donald; at Hamworthy, Aimée Alexander, Harry Alexander and Ken Sanson; at Holmsley South, John Levesley; at Milltown, Joe McDermott; at Mount Batten, Laura Whinney; at Pembroke Dock John Evans; at Perranporth, David Evans; at Warmwell, Anthony Cooke and Rick Penbearthy; at Wick, William Sutherland, and at Woodhaven, Gerd Garnes, Einer Garnes, David Winch and Scott Williamson.

My thanks also go to the following who helped with the supply of information and/or photographs: Denis Chick, Vauxhall Motors; Pam Clark, the Royal Collection; Andrew Davies; Nicky Deering, Beaulieu Parish Council; Tom Dolezal; Peter Elliott, RAF Museum; David Green; Cato Guhnfeldt; Marc Hill, Liverpool Air Traffic Control; John Hooton; Jonathan Howard and Colin Schroeder, Hooton Park Trust; Neil Owen; Ken Pearson; Gail Ramsey; Chris Ransted; George Rhind; Brian Stafford, North Coates Flying Club; Samuel Sjoberg; Ed Storey; Les Taylor; Bob Truman; Mark Thomas, and Mark Unsworth of Islay Studios.

I am equally indebted to the many contributors to the Airfield Information Exchange, the public online forum of the Airfield Research Group, in particular Graham Crisp and Paul Francis. The AIX Archive is an enormous and fascinating resource that grows by the day. The Airfield Research Group publishes an excellent quarterly magazine that covers all aspects of the subject (see below for contact details).

Special thanks go to Russell Boyd for his help with Squadron Leader Bill Mullen's *Memories of RAF Dallachy*. Russell is in touch with the late Bill Mullen's family and they are happy for me to quote from the unpublished manuscript of his evocative reminiscences. Peter Clare whose researches focus on No. 120 Squadron, Coastal Command, and the anti-U-Boat war during World War II, in remembrance of his father, Sergeant Seymour Clare, missing from operations on August 13, 1942. Peter willingly allowed me to quote from his researches. Also my good friend George Jones for encouragement and help with sources. Another long-time friend is Don Stephens who alerted me to the evocative memoirs of Liberator pilot Jim Glazebrook, whom Don knew well. Pavel Vancata for help relating to No. 311 Squadron.

Finally, my late friends Dr Atholl Duncan, several of whose pre-war photographs grace the Leuchars entry, and John Finch-Davies who accompanied me on a 1980s research trip round many of the far flung Scottish airfields.

SOURCES
Much of the raw material for this book was extracted from files in The National Archives, principally the AIR 27 and 28 classes covering Coastal Command squadrons and stations. Other records consulted were in the WORK and AIR 10 classes, notably AIR 10/4039. Publications which proved invaluable included *Coastal, Support and Special Squadrons of the RAF and Their Aircraft* by John D. R. Rawlings and *RAF Coastal Command Losses 1939-1941* by Ross McNeill. Most volumes of the original Action Stations series. *Airfield Focus No. 12 North Coates* by Bill Taylor. *Airfield Focus No. 25: Oban and Connel Ferry* by Neil Owen and Phil Jones. *Airfields and Landing Grounds of Wales* by Ivor Jones. *Banff Strike Wing at War* by Les Taylor. *Beaufort Special* by Bruce Robertson. *British Military Airfield Architecture* by Paul Francis. *Chronicles of a Nervous Navigator* by John A. Iverach. *Cloud Cover* by Derek Gilpin Barnes. *Evidence in Camera - the Story of Photographic Intelligence in World War II* by Constance Babington Smith. *Fields of Deception - Britain's Bombing Decoys of World War II* by Colin Dobinson. *Flying Boat Haven* by John Evans. *History of Beaulieu Airfields* by Robert Coles. *Military Aviation in Northern Ireland* by Guy Warner and Ernie Cromie. *Mosquito* by C. Martin Sharp and Michael J. F. Bowyer. *Mudville Heights (Dunkeswell)* by David W Earl. *Ocean Sentinel, The Short Sunderland* by John F. Hamlin. *Seek and strike :The Lockheed Hudson in World War II* by Andrew Hendrie. *Someone to Watch Over Me* by Jim Glazebrook. *That Nothing Failed Them - Testing Aeroplanes in War* by Air Commodore Allen Wheeler. *The Memories Linger On - a Collection of Reminiscences of Wartime RAF St Eval* compiled by Jean Shapland. *Wellington at War* by Chaz Bowyer. *Wings Over Carew* by Deric Brock. *311 Squadron* by Pavel Van ata.

Numerous issues of *Airfield Review* which is published quarterly by the Airfield Research Group, 6 Mulberry Close, Desborough, Kettering, NN14 2JQ.

Two armourers, AC1 J. D. Ayres and LAC C. R. Watt of No. 404 Squadron, service the Brownings from a Blenheim's rear turret.

Contents

Introduction

This book covers 53 of the main airfields and marine bases used by Coastal Command for operational purposes. The total includes those in Iceland, the Azores and Gibraltar which were vital to anti-submarine coverage of the North and Central Atlantic as well as the western Mediterranean. Two airfields traditionally associated with Coastal Command — St Mawgan in Cornwall and Kinloss in north-east Scotland — will not be found in these pages because their involvement was solely post-war. Nor do the flying boat stations at Calshot, Hampshire and Felixstowe, Suffolk, because both were relegated to a support and maintenance role during the war.

A number of airfields not included in the text had brief periods where they hosted units operating under the auspices of Coastal Command. For example, No. 236 Squadron was nominally based at the Suffolk airfield of Wattisham from February to July 1942 but detached its Beaufighters to many other bases. At the beginning of the war, No. 269 Squadron's Ansons operated from Montrose in eastern Scotland for a few months. One of its sorties resulted in the first DFM award of the war when the navigator, Sergeant William Willits, flew the aircraft back after his pilot, Pilot Officer Dennis Burrell, was killed in combat with a German aircraft over the North Sea.

Other bases which saw fleeting Coastal Command use included Liverpool's Speke Airport and Hawkinge and Manston in Kent. Beccles in Suffolk was the temporary home of No. 618 Squadron's Mosquitos and its other Coastal occupants in the final months of the war were air-sea rescue squadrons supporting the USAAF and also Coastal Command Strike Wing operations. Airfields intended for the Command but never used by it included Dounreay in the north of Scotland and Eglinton in Northern Ireland, which on completion was handed over to the Royal Navy.

US Navy patrol squadrons, collectively known as Fleet Air Wing 7, operated under the control of Coastal Command No. 19 Group. Their main base was Dunkeswell, sited on a Devon hilltop, but Upottery, another airfield in that county, was used as a satellite during the final months of the war. Prior to the Navy taking over anti-submarine operations in 1943, the USAAF had operated from the Coastal station at St Eval.

Royal Air Force Operational Training Units (OTU) prepared aircrew for operations on a particular type or types of aircraft or roles. Coastal Command had its own OTUs but a detailed account of the subject falls outside the scope of this book. However, the list below is included for interest. It is not exhaustive and does not detail the sometimes very complicated

November 1941: Hudson crewmen of No. 407 Squadron take a breather around the YMCA tea wagon at North Coates.

inter-action between certain of the units, swapping of bases, etc. However, it does serve to show the impressive training machine which supported the Command.

No. 1 OTU at Silloth, Cumberland, trained aircrew on patrol aircraft types until it was disbanded in October 1943.

No. 2 OTU at Catfoss, East Yorkshire, trained aircrew on twin-engined fighter and strike aircraft types until it was disbanded in February 1944.

No. 3 OTU at Chivenor, Devon, (also used Cranwell, Lincolnshire), then Haverfordwest, Pembrokeshire, with a satellite at Templeton trained aircrew on twin-engined anti-submarine aircraft.

No. 4 OTU at Stranraer, Wigtownshire, trained aircrew on flying boats until it was disbanded when it became No. 235 Operational Conversion Unit in July 1947.

No. 6 OTU at Thornaby (also used Longtown and Silloth), trained general reconnaissance crews.

No. 8 OTU at Fraserburgh in Aberdeenshire, Dyce and then Haverfordwest, Pembrokeshire, trained aircrew on photo-reconnaissance aircraft.

No. 9 OTU at Aldergrove and then Crosby-on-Eden, Cumberland, trained long-range fighter aircrew, until disbanded in August 1944.

No. 111 OTU at Nassau, Bahamas, trained general reconnaissance crews on American-built aircraft.

No. 131 OTU at Killadeas, County Fermanagh, trained crews on the Catalina.

No. 132 OTU at RAF East Fortune trained long-range fighter and strike crews.

No. 1 Torpedo Training Unit at Turnberry, Ayrshire.

No. 2 Torpedo Training Unit at Castle Kennedy, Wigtownshire.

Coastal Command Development Unit at various airfields including Carew Cheriton and Tain.

Torpedo Development unit, later re-designated Airborne Torpedo Development Unit at Gosport, Hampshire.

Further specialised support was provided by No. 1674 Heavy Conversion Unit at Aldergrove and Longtown, Cumberland, in the form of conversion training for crews intended for long-range patrol squadrons.

Of the 49 United Kingdom airfields described in the text, nine are still active, four — Brawdy, Chivenor, Leuchars and Thorney Island — are now Army or Royal Marine bases and one — St Eval — is covered with tall radio antenna masts. Six sites have been virtually obliterated, although though one of them — Beaulieu — is easily recognisable from the air by the outlines of its torn up runways and perimeter track. The others are Bircham Newton, Docking, Holmsley South, Thornaby and Warmwell.

Coastal Command's contribution to the war effort was massive but is often overlooked compared to the more glamorous Bomber and Fighter Commands. In fact, it has been referred to as the 'Cinderella Service'. Its major success was in closing the so-called Atlantic Gap where the U-Boats had until then been operating free of aerial retribution. It was a Catalina airborne from Northern Ireland which found the battleship *Bismarck* and directly influenced its destruction. The Command's photo-reconnaissance pilots ranged all over northern Europe and discovered the whereabouts of many potential targets, from *Tirpitz* to the rocket-testing base at Peenemünde. It was a weather reconnaissance Halifax crew from a Scottish island base which sent back the vital data from which meteorologists deduced that there would be a 36-hour window of opportunity around June 6, 1944.

The dropping of a tricolour flag across the Arc de Triomphe in Paris was a tremendous morale-booster for the French and was the work of a carefully selected Coastal Beaufighter crew. Four Victoria Crosses were awarded to pilots of the Command, two of them posthumously. The above are highlights of the maritime war; most operational patrols were arduous and boring, with bad weather the main enemy. When asked what he had seen on his first operational patrol, one pilot replied, 'Water, a lot of water.'

By the end of the war in Europe, aircraft under the control of Coastal Command had accounted for 188 U-Boats out of a total of 783 lost to the Germans through various causes. They had also shared in the sinking of 21 more. In addition, the Command had sent to the bottom 343 ships with a total tonnage of 513,804. For this a high price was paid. Coastal Command casualties during the war due to hostile action and accidents, but excepting death from natural causes, amounted to 8,874 with 2,601 wounded, the figures being inclusive of Dominion and Allied personnel. However, owing to the nature of a war over water, very many of the casualties have no known grave.

This simple yet poignant memorial by Neil and Richard Talbot was dedicated in Westminster Abbey on March 16, 2004 to commemorate the airmen of RAF Coastal Command squadrons. **Carved from a block of Carrara marble, it symbolises the stormy seas and grey skies of the Atlantic ocean over which the command operated.**

EAGLE BLOCK HEADQUARTERS

Coastal Command Headquarters

Coastal Command's first headquarters was located at Lee-on-Solent, a combined land airfield and seaplane station on the south coast in Hampshire.

On April 1, 1918, the Royal Air Force came into being following the amalgamation of the Royal Flying Corps and the Royal Naval Air Service. The following year the RAF was organised into four area commands covering the Southern, Northern and Coastal areas of Britain. Then in July 1936, in response to the expansion plans for the service, the RAF was reorganised into four new commands reflecting a specific function rather than the area of responsibility. These were Bomber, Fighter, Training and Coastal Command, the latter created simply by renaming Coastal Area. Coastal Command headquarters remained at the Area HQ at Lee-on-Solent but was moved to north London on August 7, 1939.

Eastbury Park was an estate in Northwood purchased in 1857 by David Carnegie of Lochearnhead, Perthshire

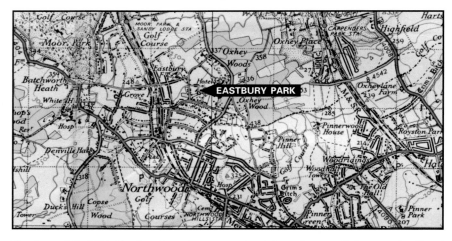

EASTBURY PARK

On August 7, 1939 the headquarters moved out from Lee-on-Solent to the Hotel Château de Madrid, located in Eastbury Park, Northwood, in north London.

8

Today Northwood is the headquarters for the Allied Maritime Command of NATO with high security and restricted access. This still, showing a US Navy vehicle entering the base during wartime, was lifted from the 1944 film *RAF Coastal Command*.

With the help of the station adjutant Lieutenant Dan Drew, we established that this did not depict the current main entrance on Sandy Lane but a rear gate which is now only used as an emergency access.

who later became the High Sheriff of Hertfordshire. The following year he built a mansion on the estate in the Scottish baronial style known as Eastbury, occupied one time by Lord Palmerston, which later found a new use as a girls' school. Then in the 1920s it became a country club called the Château de Madrid.

With the Fighter Command headquarters located in Bentley Priory, another stately home less than five miles to the east, Eastbury was purchased by the Air Ministry as a convenient location for the new headquarters for Coastal Command. As the command would have to work closely with the Royal Navy, a combined RAF/RN

operations room was initially located in a purpose-built — albeit wooden – building protected from blast by an earth banking, until an underground ops room could be provided.

Admiralty House on Watford Road (originally named Frithwood House) was provided for the personal residence of the Commander-in-Chief.

This shot shows staff members walking out across the front of the former hotel-cum-school, used during the war as the Officers' Mess.

Unfortunately it burned down in February 1968, the site now replaced by the Mercury Building, housing the offices of the Commanding Officer, Northwood HQ.

The Coastal Command underground operations room and command centre . . . then and now.

On the commencement of hostilities with Germany, the Air Officer Commanding-in-Chief of Coastal Command was Air Chief Marshal Sir Frederick Bowhill.

Here he escorts HM King George VI and the Secretary of State for Air, Sir Kingsley Wood, on a tour of the headquarters. They appear to be passing the early above-ground operations room.

In January 1944, Air Chief Marshal Sir William Sholto Douglas was recalled from head of RAF Middle East Command to take over Coastal Command for the forthcoming invasion of Normandy. Here he is pictured (left) with his Senior Air Staff Officer, Air Vice-Marshal Aubrey Ellwood, in the operations room at Northwood on the morning of D-Day. Three months later Winston Churchill sent him this personal message (which is now kept framed in the Madras Room): 'I send to you and to all your officers and men my congratulations on the splendid work of Coastal Command during the last three months. In spite of all the hazards of weather and in the face of bitter opposition from the armament of enemy U-boats and escort vessels, your squadrons have played a vital part in making possible the great operations now going forward in France. Working in close concord with the Allied Navies, they have protected so effectively the host of landing-craft and merchant vessels that the enemy U-boat campaign against them has proved a complete and costly failure. Many U-boats have been sunk or badly crippled in these operations, in which squadrons of the RAF, of the Fleet Air Arm, of the US Navy and of the Air Forces of the Dominions and of our European Allies have all played their part. In addtion most effective attacks have been delivered against enemy shipping and very many hostile escort vessels and merchant ships have been sent to the bottom or heavily damaged. I know that the achievement of these fine results required that careful plans by Commanders and staff should be executed with the utmost skill and determination by the aircrews, who, in their turn, depend upon the tireless efforts of all who work for them on the ground. All have been united in carrying out a most successful summer's operations, of which you and your men may feel justly proud.'

Air Marshal Sir Arthur Longmore was the first commander appointed on July 14, 1936 but he was succeeded six weeks later by Air Marshal Philip Joubert de la Ferté, and on August 18, 1937 Air Chief Marshal Sir Frederick Bowhill became AOC-in-C of RAF Coastal Command. Air Marshal Sir John Slessor took over on February 5, 1943 followed by Air Chief Marshal Sir William Sholto Douglas on January 20, 1944, relinquishing command on June 30, 1945.

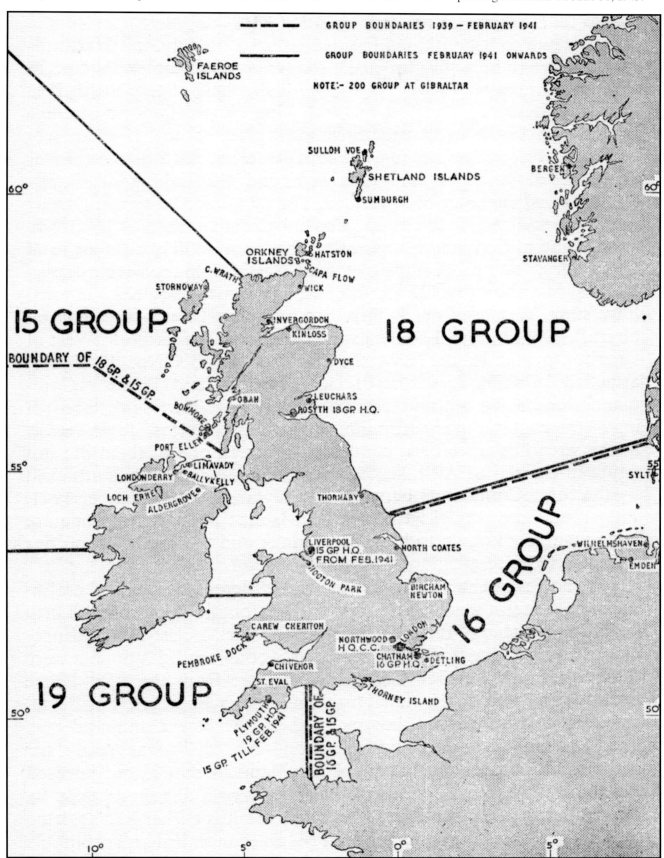

Reproduced with acknowledgement from *Royal Air Force 1939-1945* **by Denis Richards, published by HMSO in 1953.**

While RAF Bomber Command (and from 1942 the US Eighth Air Force) targeted the U-Boat bases in France, Coastal Command extended the battleground into the North Atlantic. Here the *U-258* under Kapitänleutnant Wilhelm von Mässenhausen noses its way slowly across the basin towards the U-Boat pens in the background at La Pallice — the base of the 3. U-Flotille. The submarine (a Type VIIC from Bremer Vulkan) only had six months to live when this picture was taken at the end of 1942: she was depth-charged by No. 120 Squadron based at Reykjavik on May 20 the following year.

Bases for Coastal Command

Before the Second World War, Coastal Command occupied only a handful of airfields and flying boat bases. They were, predictably, spaced around the coast but there were huge gaps in coverage, namely south-west England and, apart from Pembroke Dock and its nearby landplane base at Carew Cheriton, the entire coasts of Wales and north-west England. Northern Ireland had but one RAF station — Aldergrove. In Scotland, Leuchars and Montrose on the east coast were the only established RAF airfields. German occupation of France and Norway in 1940 would soon reveal the glaring inadequacies of this situation. Suddenly, there were U-Boats ranging into the North Atlantic from bases in western France or via the North Sea round the tip of the Shetland Isles.

Going back to 1934, RAF Expansion was part of a political decision for rearmament as a result of the looming threat from Nazi Germany. The RAF was given higher priority in terms of rearmament plans than the other services. Its major requirement was for new airfields in Yorkshire, Lincolnshire and East Anglia and a vast programme of construction was set in motion. The emphasis was on bombers and fighters, with aircraft for maritime patrol being given a very much lower priority. The new stations were built to a very high standard with well-designed permanent buildings and massive C Type hangars well able to accommodate very much larger aircraft than those in service at that time.

There was no attempt at dispersal of accommodation, the technical buildings being located immediately to the rear of the hangars. The airmen's quarters were normally grouped around an open area behind the technical buildings, with officers' and sergeants' messes provided as separate groups, somewhat more isolated but still in close proximity to both the technical and airmen's buildings. In the case of training stations, instructional buildings were constructed so as to be equally convenient to the technical and domestic sites. The actual flying field was grass-surfaced and roughly circular, with the hangars sited in a curve along part of the boundary.

Although not strictly an Expansion station, Bircham Newton was upgraded to those standards in 1936. Detling was selected as an Expansion site but, as was customary with establishments intended for training, it was not built on the usual grand scale and buildings consisted mainly of hutting.

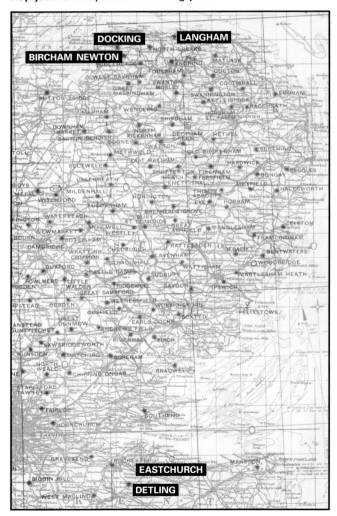

All these bases were part of No. 16 Group.

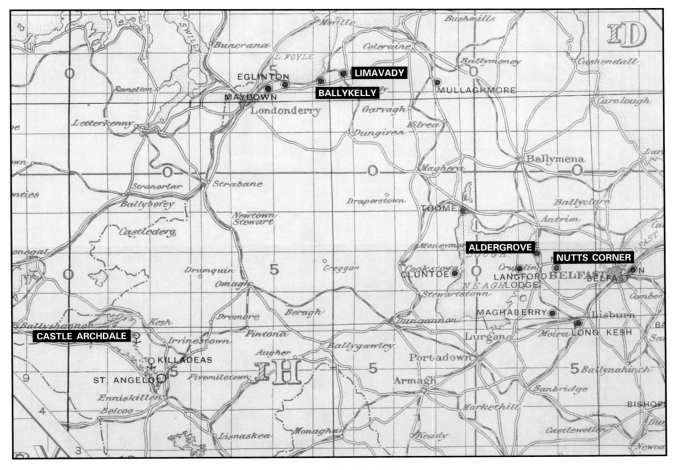

The Coastal Command stations in Northern Ireland all came within No. 15 Group.

The idea was that certain units deemed to be of a more or less temporary character, would be housed in non-permanent buildings. In 1939, when war appeared inevitable, the elegant buildings were abandoned for new airfields in favour of so-called austerity types which were quicker and cheaper to build. The austerity C Type hangar was a typical example, with roof clear height reduced from 35ft to 30ft, and the brick-work replaced by asbestos sheeting and reinforced concrete, thus saving on manpower and raw materials.

At certain locations — St Eval and Wick being Coastal Command examples — the concrete was deleted, leaving only the asbestos cladding. With predictable results, hangars at both these vulnerable stations were very badly damaged by bombing. All technical and living accommodation now con-sisted of wooden huts. Thereafter, standards fell even further with corrugated metal hangars, notably the Bellman and the T2, along with Nissen huts for communal and living accom-modation, as well as operational buildings. Battle of Britain experience showed that dispersal of living and other sites into the surrounding countryside was highly desirable.

Thorney Island was perhaps Coastal Command's most comfortable station, with Benson a close second. Otherwise, by the very nature of its operations, the Command had to make do with some very rudimentary airfields in far-flung regions of the United Kingdom as far apart as Cornwall, Northern Ireland, the Hebrides and Shetland. Necessity forced the use of some very unsuitable sites from which to launch anti-submarine operations. Pre-war landing grounds in Scotland and its islands were rapidly expanded, Cornish moorland and New Forest heaths were over-laid with runways, as were boggy stretches of Irish countryside.

Captain Ernest E. Fresson, a well-known pilot flying on Scottish internal services before the war, had been instrumental in founding some very basic landing grounds both on the islands and mainland. His shrewd choice of sites proved a major influ-ence on the decision to develop many of them into major air-fields for Coastal Command. They included Wick, Sumburgh, Tiree, Dyce and Stornoway, all of which have since evolved into community-serving airports. At Kirkwall Airport, Orkney, in wartime a Royal Naval Air Station, there is a fine memorial to Fresson, topped by a model of a de Havilland Dragon Rapide.

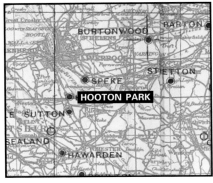

No. 15 Group.

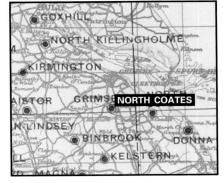

No. 16 Group.

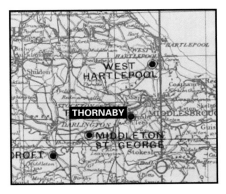

No. 18 Group.

13

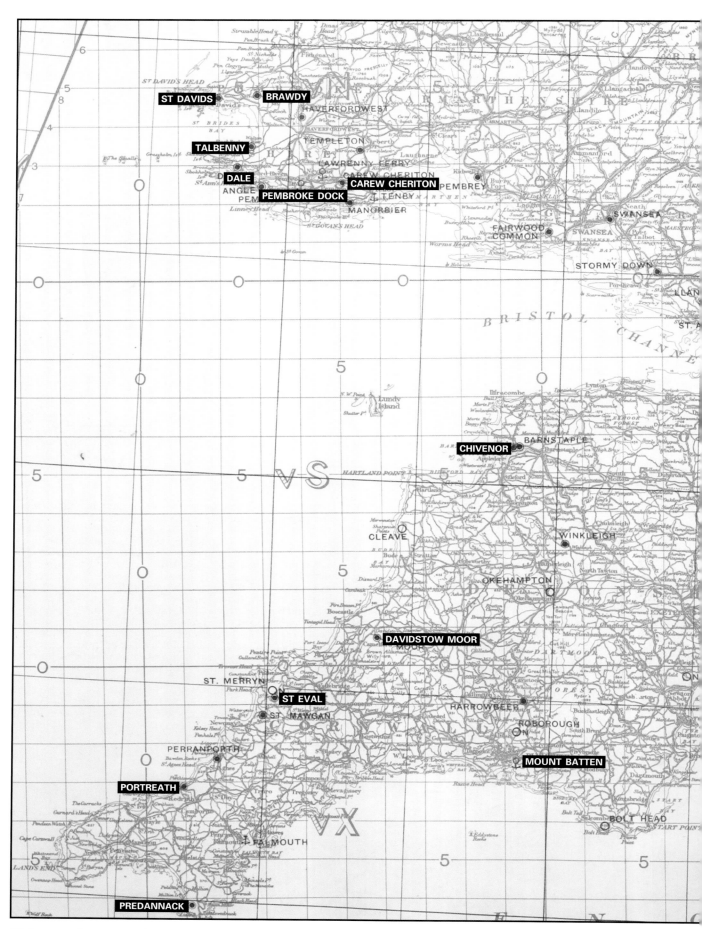

All these stations came within No. 19 Group save that Warmwell was in No. 15 Group; Beaulieu, Benson and Thorney Island in

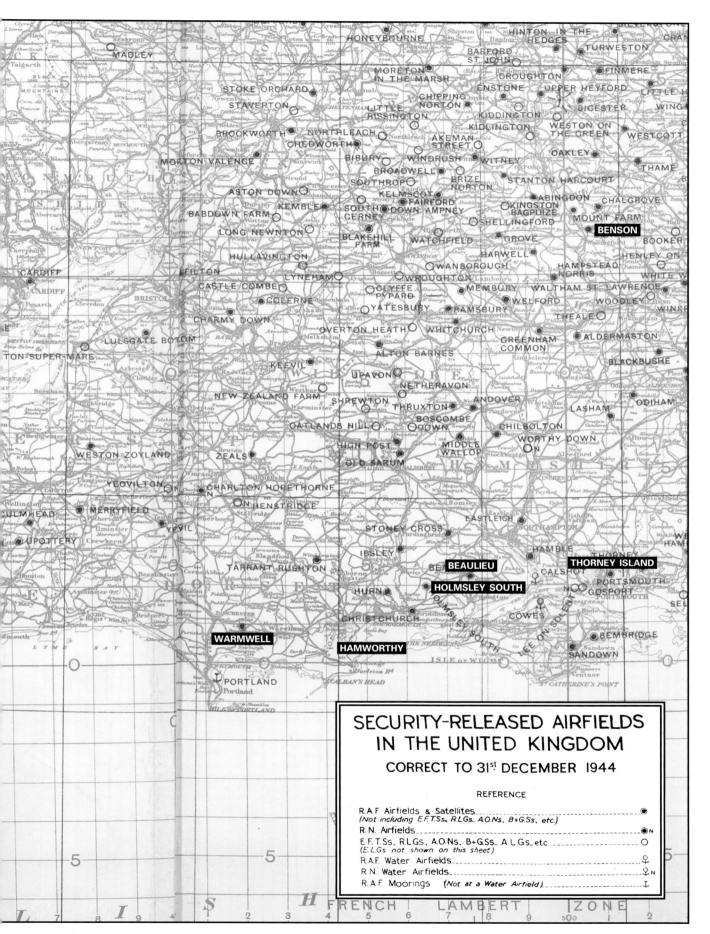

MADLEY

HONEYBOURNE
HINTON IN THE HEDGES
TURWESTON
BARFORD ST JOHN
CRAN
FINMERE
LITTLE H
MORETON IN THE MARSH
BROUGHTON
UPPER HEYFORD
STOKE ORCHARD
ENSTONE
BICESTER
WING
STAVERTON
CHIPPING NORTON
KIDDINGTON
WESTON ON THE GREEN
WESTCOTT
BROCKWORTH
NORTHLEACH
LITTLE RISSINGTON
KIDLINGTON
CHEDWORTH
AKEMAN STREET
WITNEY
OAKLEY
THAME
MORTON VALENCE
BIBURY
WINDRUSH
BROADWELL
BRIZE NORTON
STANTON HARCOURT
ASTON DOWN
SOUTHROP
KELMSCOT
FAIRFORD
ABINGDON
CHALGROVE
KEMBLE
SOUTH CERNEY
DOWN AMPNEY
KINGSTON BAGPUIZE
MOUNT FARM
BABDOWN FARM
SHELLINGFORD
BENSON
BOOKER
LONG NEWNTON
BLAKEHILL FARM
WATCHFIELD
GROVE
HENLEY ON
HULLAVINGTON
HARWELL
HAMPSTEAD NORRIS
WHITE W
NETILTON
WANBOROUGH
CARDIFF
LYNEHAM
WROUGHTON
MEMBURY
WALTHAM ST LAWRENCE
CARDIFF
CASTLE COMBE
CLYFFE PYPARD
WELFORD
WOODLEY
WINK
COLERNE
YATESBURY
RAMSBURY
THEALE
READING
CHARMY DOWN
OVERTON HEATH
WHITCHURCH
GREENHAM COMMON
ALDERMASTON
LULSGATE BOTTOM
ALTON BARNES
BLACKBUSHE
TON-SUPER-MARE
KEEVIL
UPAVON
WESTON ZOYLAND
NEW ZEALAND FARM
NETHERAVON
ANDOVER
ODIHAM
SHREWTON
THRUXTON
LASHAM
YEOVILTON
OATLANDS HILL
BOSCOMBE DOWN
CHILBOLTON
ZEALS
HIGH POST
MIDDLE WALLOP
WORTHY DOWN
MERRYFIELD
OLD SARUM
CHARLTON HORETHORNE
UPOTTERY
HENSTRIDGE
EASTLEIGH
STONEY CROSS
HAMBLE
THORNEY ISLAND
TARRANT RUSHTON
IBSLEY
BEAULIEU
CALSHOT
PORTSMOUTH
HURN
HOLMSLEY SOUTH
GOSPORT
SEL
CHRISTCHURCH
COWES
WARMWELL
BEMBRIDGE
HAMWORTHY
SANDOWN
PORTLAND

SECURITY-RELEASED AIRFIELDS IN THE UNITED KINGDOM
CORRECT TO 31st DECEMBER 1944

REFERENCE

R.A.F. Airfields & Satellites...⦿
(Not including E.F.T.Ss., R.L.Gs. A.O.Ns. B+G.Ss., etc.)
R.N. Airfields...⦿N
E.F.T.Ss., R.L.Gs., A.O.Ns., B+G.Ss., A.L.Gs., etc. ....○
(E.L.Gs. not shown on this sheet)
R.A.F. Water Airfields...⚓
R.N. Water Airfields...⚓N
R.A.F. Moorings   (Not at a Water Airfield)........................⚓

FRENCH LAMBERT ZONE

No. 16 Group and Holmsley South and Hamworthy in No. 19 Group.

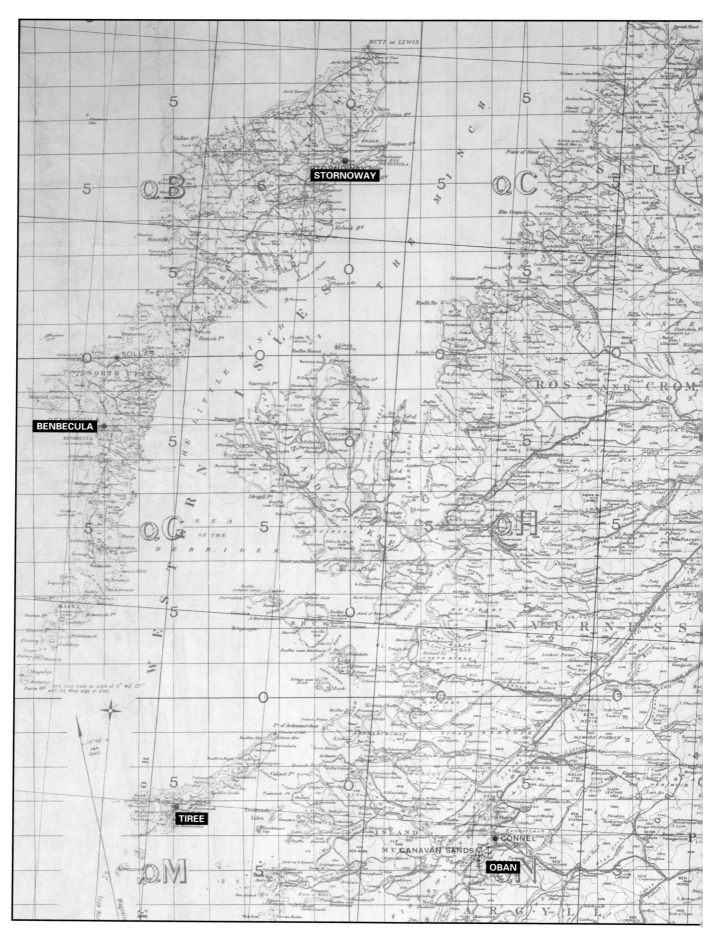

Benbecula, Stornoway and Tiree fell within No. 15 Group but Oban was in No. 18 Group.

All those stations on the east coast of Scotland were part of No. 18 Group.

17

A bitumen and sand mix devised before the war proved very useful for airfield runways in the Hebrides and a few other locations where little material was available for sub-grade (hardcore foundations). Existing wet sand was mixed with hydrated lime and a special grade of bitumen, producing a load-bearing surface which was easy to repair. This process was not only cheaper than normal methods of runway construction but could be completed in little more than half the time. Meanwhile, the few flying boat bases, such as Oban, which had been little more than convenient refuelling points for round-Britain cruises, were undergoing rapid development to render them capable of supporting offensive operations. This meant slipways, on shore servicing aprons, hangarage and bomb storage areas, as well as accommodation and technical sites.

By May 1939, the standard airfield layout consisted of four grass strips, one of 1,300 yards by 400 yards and three of 1,000 yards by 200 yards. The necessity of having paved runways for all-weather operations had now become apparent and the first runway programme was initiated at 12 RAF stations. Runways 800 yards long by 50 yards wide were laid along two of the four grass strips at each site and connected with a perimeter or taxitrack 50 feet wide. Standard runway lengths were gradually increased until from December 1940 all bomber airfields were constructed on the three-strip principle of 1,400 yards and two subsidiaries of 1,100 yards. In January 1941 the longest strip was required to be 1,600 yards and later that year it was recommended that this be increased to 2,000 yards.

The requirements of 1942 set the ultimate wartime standard for the RAF operational airfield and this was now applied to the construction of new stations and extensions to existing ones. It was known as the Class A standard and was designed for all contemporary heavy bombers. The fundamental dimensions were as follows:

Strips: (the area clear of significant obstructions). Three were planned as far as possible at 60 degrees to one another, the main strip of 2,000 yards by 400 yards and two subsidiary strips of 1,400 yards by 200 yards. Wherever possible the main strip was aligned in a north-east/south-west direction.

Runways: A main of 2,000 yards by 50 yards with subsidiaries of 1,400 yards by 50 yards with 100 yards of cleared area at both ends as an overshoot. On subsidiary runways where the differences in levels of the ends of the runways exceeded 20 feet, the runway length was, if possible, increased by 100 yards for every additional 10 feet in rise. Fillets at runway intersections were provided to enable aircraft after landing to turn onto runways not in use whenever a shorter route to their dispersal was possible than continuing to the end of the runway. Margins to a width of 75 yards on each side of the 50-yard runway were consolidated and prepared to a state suitable for emergency landing and take off. In most cases the turf was cultivated to provide normal grass airfield conditions.

Gradients: Runways and strips: Maximum longitudinal gradient 1:80. Maximum transverse runways 1:60, maximum transverse margins 1:50.

Perimeter and access tracks: Built to a standard 50 feet width. The minimum radius of curve 150 feet on the centre line when the internal angle between two sections of track or between track and runway was more than 60 degrees. When this angle was 60 degrees or less, the minimum radius of curve was 200 feet on the centre line. To prevent damage to aircraft should they run off the track, an area was cleared each side to a width of 30 feet. No buildings or other obstructions were erected within 150 feet from the centre of the track. No other track or hardstandings were within 150 feet centre to centre.

In practice, relatively few Coastal Command airfields ever aspired to these standards, mainly due to the constraints of local topography. Some examples of those that did — or at least came close to doing so — were Beaulieu, Nutts Corner, Ballykelly, Banff, Brawdy, Benbecula, Tain, Tiree and St Davids. St Eval seems to have spent much of the war years in a constant state of development to a point where in mid-1944 it was capable of housing and operating four Liberator squadrons. A few, such as Bircham Newton, Detling and Docking, remained grass-surfaced throughout their active lives.

Dispersed hardstandings in the early years of the war consisted of circles of various diameters up to 125 feet sited irregularly around the perimeter track and joined to it by a short access track. Later developments saw the introduction of the 'spectacle' or 'loop' type similarly positioned. This became the standard dispersal on bomber stations by 1943 and those of Coastal Command, especially where Liberators and Halifaxes were based. In practice, most of Coastal's stations had a mixture of circles and loops and at some, areas of metal tracking were laid as ad hoc parking areas.

The lessons learned from the Battle of Britain and the night Blitz ensured that all new stations would have living sites dispersed away from the airfield. These comprised quarters for officers, sergeants and WAAFs, some stations having up to a dozen accommodation sites. Domestic and communal sites housed messes and often had a large decontamination block to deal with the aftermath of a gas attack. This was a very real possibility at that time but fortunately never happened. There would also be sites for the operations block and station sick quarters, as well as the mundane but very necessary sewage disposal. A bomb store would be sited as far away as possible, often taking advantage of wooded areas for camouflage and also to reduce blast in the event of an explosion. Instructional sites provided for classrooms and synthetic training.

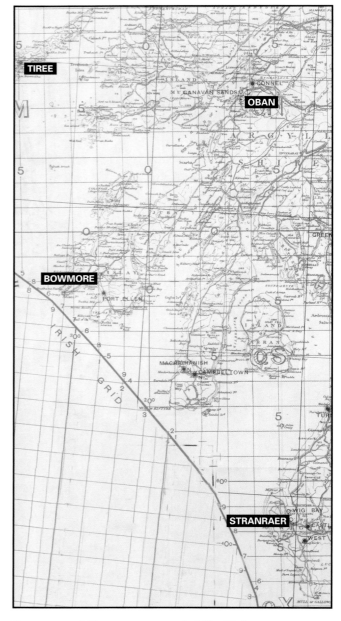

Bowmore and Stranraer were part of No. 15 Group.

The Danish-owned Faroe Islands are strategically located between Scotland and Iceland and were occupied by the British in April 1940 in order to deny them to the Germans. An airfield was built by the Royal Engineers on the island of Vaagar during 1942-43. The single runway was unusually wide, being 200 yards for its first 400 yards in length and then 100 yards for the remainder, in order to counter the effects of extremely variable wind conditions. A flying boat base was also established on the north end of Sorvaags Vatn lake just to the east of the airfield. Similarly erratic wind conditions and high ground, often cloud-covered, rendered it barely useable except in emergency. Catalinas, at least, are known to have alighted on it.

The two locations were controlled by Coastal Command and the airfield was intended to house general reconnaissance aircraft and short-range fighters. However, because of the terrain, and often poor weather, there were never any aircraft based there apart from the Station Flight's Miles Magister. The lack of direct communication with the UK mainland, apart from by radio, was another major factor. Its location was something of a mystery too as a Faroes-based airman received a letter from a friend asking him to bring some oranges when he came home on leave! In 1963, Vaagar was developed as the islands' airport and a new runway was built north of the wartime strip, the remains of which can still be discerned. Another continuing reminder of the friendly occupation is the Faroese love of fish and chips!

Of the Command's four overseas bases which are covered in this book, Gibraltar and Reykjavik were small existing airfields which were vastly expanded to accommodate large modern aircraft. Kaldadarnes in Iceland was created from nothing in a very boggy area but it served its purpose well for nearly three years until severe flooding from a nearby river forced its abandonment in November 1943. Lagens in the Azores started life as a Portuguese airstrip of packed earth that made an excellent foundation for a runway of the ubiquitous Pierced Steel Planking (PSP). It ably but noisily supported Liberator and Fortress operations until the Americans replaced it with a proper concrete runway, plus two subsidiaries, before the war ended.

Flying boats were to feature heavily in the Command's operations but in September 1939 there were a mere seven marine bases at strategic points around the British Isles. More were required as quickly as possible and the Air Ministry Works Directorate, apart from its urgent commitment to find suitable sites for land aerodromes, was also expected to survey potential flying boat stations. This involved soundings over many square miles of water and surveying sites for docks and piers, slipways and moorings. A mere handful of the new marine stations survived the war for more than a few months. The withdrawal of the Sunderland from service early in 1957 reduced those to little more than bases for the relatively few RAF rescue and other marine craft still in service.

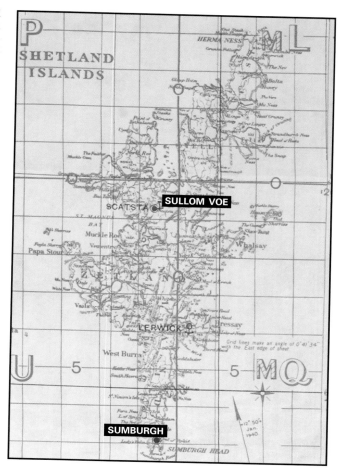

The Shetland Isle bases were part of No. 18 Group.

After the war, many of Coastal's airfields were soon abandoned because their remote positions and other factors rendered them surplus to peacetime requirements. One of the few social benefits of the conflict was represented by a number of ready-made airports in isolated parts of Scotland, especially its offshore islands. The same could be said of Northern Ireland, where Nutts Corner became Belfast's airport, later replaced by the more suitable Aldergrove, itself a product of Coastal Command expansion.

No. 407 Squadron, now equipped with Wellingtons adorned with D-Day invasion stripes. In January 1944 they were based at Limavady (No. 15 Group) in Northern Ireland, moving to Wick in Scotland (No. 18 Group) in August.

No. 15 GROUP

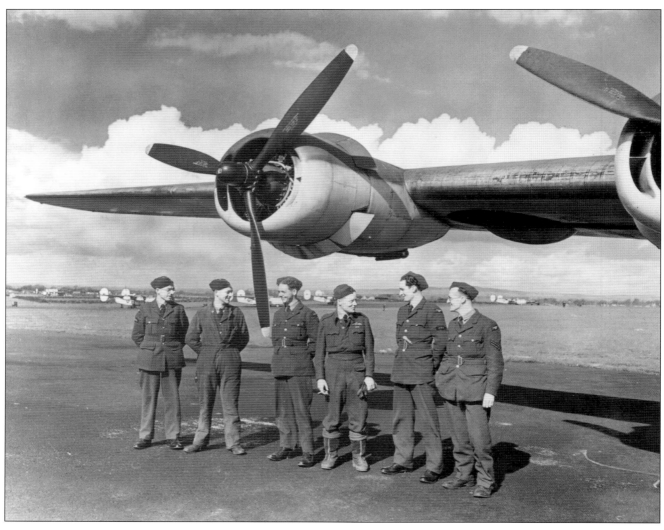

ALDERGROVE

RAF Coastal Command operated from five bases in Northern Ireland — Aldergrove, Ballykelly, Lough Erne/Castle Archdale, Limavady and Nutts Corner — all part of No. 15 Group. Aldergrove lay some 12 miles west of the capital Belfast.

In the summer of 1917 Major Sholto Douglas, a young pilot who was destined to become Marshal of the Royal Air Force, was given the task of selecting eight sites in Ireland on which flying training could take place. The specification was simple: grass fields that would give runs of 500 to 600 yards in any direction. One of the locations he found was at Aldergrove, about 13 miles north-west of Belfast. However, by the time it was prepared and opened in May 1918, requirements had changed and it was earmarked instead as an Aircraft Acceptance Park (AAP). No. 16 AAP formed there in October 1918 to handle the new Handley Page V/1500 heavy bombers being built by Harland and Wolff in Belfast, but the AAP closed in December 1919, only a few V/1500s having passed through its hands.

For the next few years the RAF retained the airfield for air exercises until No. 502 Squadron was established there in a bombing role on May 15, 1925. A succession of bomber types were then operated until November 1938 when the squadron was transferred to general reconnaissance and re-equipped with Ansons.

Aldergrove also had a separate function — that of armament training — using ranges on nearby Lough Neagh. No. 2 Armament Training Camp formed in October 1936 and after several changes of name became No. 3 Bombing and Gunnery School in December 1939. Until July 1940, Fleet Air Arm 774 Squadron was attached to the school for the

Initially, Aldergrove was grass but four runways were effective until 1942.

22

CONTROL TOWER

The four runways were then reduced to two of 2,000 yards each.

training of observers and telegraphist air gunners, using Rocs, Skuas and Swordfish. The school disbanded in July 1940 with its aircraft going to other B&GSs.

By the time the war began, No. 502 Squadron was fully operational and began patrolling and escorting convoys. Its first enemy submarine was found off the Scottish coast on September 24 and bombed but with no observed result. Generally, the Ansons shepherded their convoys with little action, apart from occasional oil slick bombings in the hope of hitting a U-Boat. In October 1940 the squadron became the first Coastal Command unit to be equipped with the

Whitley. That same month one of the Whitley crews found the liner *Empress of Britain* on fire in the Atlantic. As a result, Royal Navy ships were summoned and the crew and passengers rescued before the ship was finished off by a U-Boat. The squadron moved to Limavady in January 1941.

From July 1940 No. 245 Squadron's Hurricanes were stationed at Aldergrove for the defence of Belfast as well as carrying out convoy patrols. On May 13, 1941, a Do 17 was shot down over the Irish Sea, the squadron leaving for Ballyhalbert in June.

Aldergrove's other major function was as an Aircraft Storage Unit, along with a Repair

and Salvage Unit. This was administered by No. 23 Maintenance Unit which formed here on December 1, 1939.

No. 272 Squadron formed at Aldergrove on November 19, 1940 as a coastal fighter/reconnaissance unit with Blenheims. Its main duty was the protection of convoys entering and leaving the Clyde and Mersey ports. Although routine, the work was intensive and in February 1941 234 sorties were flown. The squadron moved to Shetland in April 1941 and was replaced by a Beaufighter-equipped squadron, No. 252, for the same convoy cover. On April 16, they shot down a Focke-Wulf Condor but later that month the squadron moved out in preparation for a reorganisation.

Hudsons of No. 233 Squadron were also based there for convoy protection between December 1940 and August 1941. Most patrols were uneventful but on May 28, 1941 a Heinkel 111 was shot down. June saw two U-Boat attacks which enable 'damaged' claims to be made and one Focke-Wulf Condor was sent down into the sea on July 28. No. 206 squadron's Hudsons took over the escort role in August 1941, with an average of one U-Boat attack per month. Results were unconfirmed but must have had a deterrent effect on their operations to keep the submarines submerged. The squadron moved to the Hebrides in July 1942.

The Air Ministry Meteorological Flight had formed at Aldergrove as early as September 1936 using four Bristol Bulldogs, but these elderly machines were replaced by slightly more modern Gloster Gauntlets in 1939. A twice-daily flight was made to 20,000 feet to take readings of temperature, pressure and humidity which were then passed via the met service to the operational stations. With the outbreak of war the weather became a matter of national security and the flights proliferated, the one at Aldergrove being re-designated No. 402 (later 1402) Met Flight on January 15, 1941. More modern and much longer-range aircraft were operated by the weather service throughout the war.

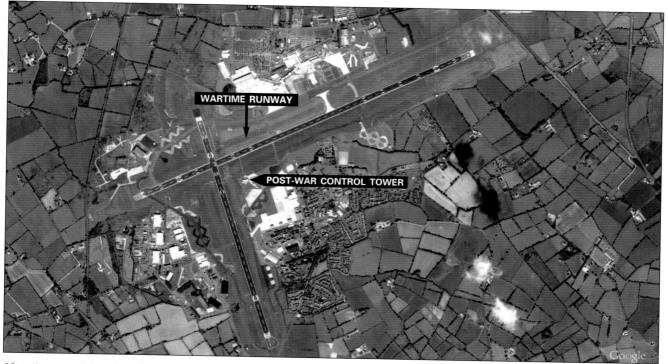

WARTIME RUNWAY

POST-WAR CONTROL TOWER

After the war, although the RAF maintained Aldergrove as their major base in Northern Ireland, in October 1963 a civilian terminal was opened on the northern side of what later became Belfast International Airport. The RAF facilities were located on the south side but in April 2008 it was announced that the remaining squadron, No. 230, was being relocated to Benson and that RAF Aldergrove would close in September 2009. So ended 91 years of RAF history in Northern Ireland but later No. 502 Squadron re-formed there in RAF Reserve and there is now even talk of a University Air Squadron being based there.

At the beginning of the war, No. 502 Squadron was equipped with Avro Ansons, seen here with armourers loading 100lb anti-submarine bombs in 1940, maximum load being 360lbs.

After having progressed through Whitleys and Halifaxes at a variety of bases, in May 1946 the squadron returned full-circle to Aldergrove, now equipped with Mosquitos.

The Czechoslovak-crewed No. 311 Squadron had transferred to Coastal Command at the end of April 1941 and required intensive training in their new role. As well as ground school at Aldergrove, low-level bombing practice took place on a dummy periscope towed by a launch and on one occasion a Wellington struck the target with its bomb doors and only skilful piloting avoided a crash! The squadron was declared operational and was based at Aldergrove in April 1942 but moved to Talbenny in southwest Wales in June.

No. 9 (Coastal) Operational Training Unit formed at Aldergrove on June 7, 1942 to train long-range fighter crews, using Beaufighters and Beauforts. It should be noted that No. 1 Armament Practice Camp had been here since December 1941, operating Lysanders for target-towing over the Lough Neagh ranges. No. 9 OTU relocated to Crosby-on-Eden, near Carlisle in September 1942. The other major training unit at Aldergrove was No. 1674 Heavy Conversion Unit, which formed here on October 10, 1943 to provide conversion training for crews intended for long-range patrol squadrons of Coastal Command. From early 1944, Halifax meteorological training was also carried out. Apart from Halifaxes, it was equipped with Fortresses and Liberators, and detachments were based at the Longtown satellite in Cumberland at various times. The HCU went to Milltown in Scotland during August 1945.

Most operational flying during 1942 and early 1943 was done by Liberator detachments of No. 120 Squadron but in March 1943 an entire Liberator unit arrived. This was No. 86 Squadron tasked for Atlantic anti-submarine escort duties. On May 4 the squadron's first U-Boat was sunk and a number of other inconclusive attacks took place until a unit move to Ballykelly in September. No. 59 Squadron was present between May and September 1943, but often much depleted as its Liberators were detached as far afield as Iceland, Cornwall and Gibraltar.

During its tenure, No. 23 Maintenance Unit's main responsibility had been for Wellingtons but it handled many other types including Corsairs, Ansons, Stirlings and Oxfords. It remained in residence after the war and did not disband until 1978, having been responsible for major servicing on such types as the Canberra and Phantom. Four of its six wartime Lamella storage hangars are still in situ.

Initially, Aldergrove had four runways but during 1942 they were reduced to two which were both lengthened to 2,000 yards. A total of 30 frying-pan hardstandings had been provided initially but many of these were replaced by loop types far more suitable for large aircraft such as the Liberator. Apart from the Lamellas already mentioned, a large number of hangars included a pre-war F Type, six C Types and three Bellmans.

By contrast, the bomb-load of a Coastal Command Liberator was up to 5,000lbs — usually made up of 450lbs depth-charges. This armourer is cleaning the four .303 Browning machine guns fitted to the rear turret of an aircraft of No. 120 Squadron.

March 1943 when No. 86 joined No. 120 Squadron. The nearest Liberator (FK228) is one of their machines whereas those in the distance belong to the new squadron. On the right work is in progress building a new control tower.

No. 502 Squadron re-formed as an auxiliary unit at Aldergrove, its pre-war base, on May 10, 1946. Mosquitos were soon given up in favour of Spitfires, later replaced by the Vampire until disbandment in March 1957. From October 1946 to July 1964, No. 202 Squadron was resident for Atlantic Met flights, equipped first with Halifaxes and then with Hastings. No. 120 Squadron returned in April 1952, its Shackletons being stationed there until April 1959.

At this point, with few military movements taking place, the Stormont government asked the Ministry of Defence if it could develop part of the site as a civilian airport. An agreement was reached, a new parking apron and terminal were built and Aldergrove Airport opened in 1963. In later years it has been renamed Belfast International. RAF Aldergrove remained as a separate entity within the airport, and during the 'Troubles' it was used as a base for helicopter support operations for the security forces. It finally closed as an RAF station on September 20, 2009. The sole military flying occupant is now 5 Regiment Army Air Corps of 38 Brigade Flying Station Aldergrove, providing support to military units and civilian agencies as required.

Ernie Cromie comments that he had to take his comparison from a slightly different angle as a new tall fence now divides the military part of Aldergrove from the international airport side. He also says that the two C Type hangars have gone and have been replaced by a new building.

Of the original hangarage, four Lamellas remain in place, as well as four C Types and the pre-war F Type. The first hangar to be built back in 1918 was around 600ft in length, but was badly damaged by hurricane winds during the 1920s and less than half of it was reinstated. This is the one immediately inside the main entrance gate to the military site. It does not appear to have been given a designation but the roof is curved and of Belfast-truss construction. It is now a Grade 'B' listed building.

The wartime control tower (left) was located on the northern side of the main runway but the one that replaced it after the war (right) was built on the southern side and is still very much in use today.

BALLYKELLY

This low-lying, farmland site on the shore of Lough Foyle to the north-east of London-derry was approved for the construction of an airfield in mid-1940. Three concrete run-ways were provided; a main of 1,600 yards and two subsidiaries of 1,400 and 1,100 yards, respectively. A small number of frying-pan hardstandings led off the perimeter track on the south-western edge of the aerodrome. Most of these were replaced later in the war by loop hardstandings better able to accom-modate large aircraft such as the Liberator. More loop types were eventually constructed on the east and north-east sides of the air-field, and hangarage reached a total of five T2s and eight blisters.

An RAF opening party arrived to take over the partially-completed facilities in June 1941, but little use was made of the aero-drome until Coastal Command Develop-ment Unit arrived from South Wales in December. It operated a number of types, chief among them being the Hudson and Whitley. CCDU was displaced to north-east Scotland in June 1942 to make room for No. 220 Squadron's Fortresses from Nutts Cor-ner. In July the squadron flew 19 convoy escorts, one anti-submarine patrol and four air-sea rescue sorties. Slowly, its North Atlantic operations built up, Benbecula and Reykjavik being used on occasion as advanced landing grounds. Two U-Boats were attacked in February 1943, one being severely damaged; the same month a move was made to Aldergrove.

Ballykelly, on the eastern shore of Lough Foyle, was under the surveillance of the Luftwaffe, even before the runways were added.

Now looking south-west, this low level oblique from 2,000 feet shows the development by August 1942.

In October 1945, Ballykelly was put on 'Care and Maintenance' and it was not until 1947 that it re-opened to become the home of the Joint Anti-Submarine School equipped with Shackletons. This was a long-range maritime reconnaissance bomber designed by Avro to replace the Lend-Lease Liberators and Fortresses and Sunderlands of the wartime period. This is Shackleton WB850 'X' of JASS Flight, displaying the definitive black stripes on the wing.

No. 120 Squadron's Liberators had been at Ballykelly since July 1942, sometimes using Predannack in Cornwall as a forward base and also detaching aircraft to Iceland to extend the range out into the Atlantic. In October 1942 Squadron Leader Terence Bulloch scored the unit's first U-Boat kill. He continued his successes in November by attacking two and damaging *U-89*. In December he attacked eight more and sank one of them. There were many more encounters with submarines but no successes were confirmed before the squadron transferred to Iceland in April 1943.

For a few months there was a gap in operational flying while the main runway was extended to 2,000 yards to enable Liberators to operate with as much fuel and armament as possible. The runway extension actually crossed the Belfast to Londonderry railway line. The control tower had a direct link with a local signal box for co-ordination, trains having priority unless there was an emergency. During this period, several Royal Navy squadrons disembarked their Swordfish and Wildcats temporarily from carriers. In September 1943, a pair of Liberator

squadrons arrived. No. 86 Squadron sank two U-Boats during October but few sightings were made before the unit departed for Iceland in March 1944. The other squadron, No. 59, continued flying the long-range escort duties for convoys inbound to the Clyde and Mersey. There were occasional attacks on U-Boats but results were unconfirmed

No. 120 Squadron returned in March 1944 and in May began to operate along the Norwegian coast, apart from the period around D-Day when it was flying night sorties over the Western Approaches. Two submarines were attacked with one being claimed as a 'probable'. From then on it settled into a regular pattern of 70-90 anti-submarine sorties per month, with very few sightings or attacks, and this continued virtually until the war ended. Disbandment came at Ballykelly on June 4, 1945, by which time No. 120 Squadron was Coastal Command's top-scoring squadron with 16 confirmed U-Boat sinkings to its credit.

Meanwhile, No. 59 Squadron had been performing similar duties off the Norwegian coast with a temporary assignment in support of the invasion. Sonobuoys — listening devices dropped in likely places to pick up submarines and transmit to the aircraft which remained in the vicinity — were now being used, and in January the squadron homed surface vessels onto U-Boats on four separate occasions.

During June the unit had, in the words of its Operations Record Book, 'a bad run of luck' when it lost three complete crews. Two Liberators flew into high ground in Donegal soon after take and within days another collided with Binevenagh, the prominent hill only a few miles to the east of the aerodrome. Despite an ever-increasing number of sorties, attacks were few as the war drew to a close and June saw the squadron move to East Anglia preparatory to disbandment. By the end of the war, Ballykelly-based squadrons are said to have been responsible for sinking 12 U-Boats, sharing with other aircraft and surface ships in the destruction of several others, and damaging many more.

Worthy of record is the use of Ballykelly during September 1944 by Liberators of the US Navy's Fleet Air Wing 7 under No. 15

In 1943 the E-W runway was extended at its western end which meant crossing the main line between Belfast and Londonderry. There was a direct link between the control tower and the local signal box giving trains the priority. In 1970, Squadron Leader Phillips pictured one of the last steam trains crossing the airfield.

Group, Coastal Command. The capture of most of their bases on the French coast forced the majority of U-Boats to leave the Bay and Channel areas. This change in the tactical situation merited more anti-submarine patrols to the north-west of Ireland and also over the Irish Sea. Aircraft were flown daily from Dunkeswell in Devon to Bally-kelly for refuelling, briefing and sometimes overnight stays. Pickings were slim, however, and only one attack was made with no visual result. At the end of the month it was decided that because of all the non-operational flying to and from Northern Ireland and lack of maintenance back-up away from base, all future patrols should be mounted from Devon.

Close up of the unusual plane-train junction, courtesy of Niall Hartley.

Stand down! It fell to No. 204 Squadron to hold the closing down parade on June 3, 1971. The following year the station was passed to the British Army. They renamed Ballykelly

Shackleton Barracks, the first Army battalion to be posted there being the 2nd Royal Greenjackets. The army vacated the barracks in March 2008.

A rescue unit, No. 281 Squadron brought its Warwicks, Wellingtons and Sea Otters over from nearby Limavady in August 1945 only to disband here towards the end of October. On the formation of NATO in 1949, the United Kingdom assumed a major anti-submarine role across the eastern Atlantic and North Sea areas. During the latter stages of the war an anti-submarine tactics school had been established at the Londonderry Naval Base, and afterwards this idea was further developed into what became known as the Joint Anti-Submarine School (JASS). Commanded jointly by RN and RAF personnel, JASS was officially opened on January 30, 1947. The unit had its own air elements, Royal Navy Barracudas based at Eglinton and the RAF's JASS Flight, based at Ballykelly, initially equipped with two Lancasters, one Warwick and one Anson. The task at JASS was to run courses to train the crews of ships and aircraft in the broader aspects of anti-submarine warfare, with emphasis on the development and application of combined tactics.

In early 1951 the airfield closed to non-essential flying for further upgrading to change it from a typical wartime aerodrome with fairly basic facilities widely dispersed, into a station equipped to support three maritime patrol squadrons. The wartime control tower was retained but heavily modified. A number of Shackleton squadrons were based thereafter and aircraft from other bases were frequent visitors for JASS courses. In the early 1960s, the east-west runway was again lengthened, this time to accommodate V-Bombers. Four Operational Readiness Platforms were constructed at its eastern end on which aircraft could be parked ready to scramble at times of international tension. The other major development was the construction during 1964-65 of a very large cantilever building, the so-called super-hangar, capable of housing six Shackletons.

The last of the Shackleton squadrons left at the end of March 1971 and in June of that year the site was handed over to the British Army as Shackleton Barracks. The Army vacated Ballykelly in March 2008 when the site was handed over to the Northern Ireland Government. The headquarters of the

Department of Agriculture has been earmarked to move from Belfast on to part of the airfield and in anticipation some buildings on the former domestic site near the main entrance have been demolished. At the time of writing (2015), all the buildings on the actual airfield remain intact.

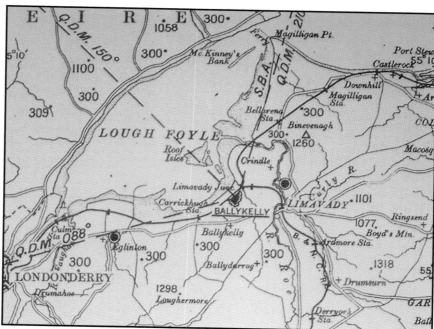

As a footnote, on March 29, 2006, an Airbus A320 operated by Eirjet on behalf of Ryanair landed at Ballykelly after the pilot on a visual approach mistook the runway for that of the nearby City of Derry Airport at Eglinton — an understandable error that gained maximum publicity! The author had cleared this aircraft to take off from Liverpool Airport but was in no way responsible for what happened later!

BENBECULA

This windswept site in the Outer Hebrides sprang from a pre-war grass aerodrome used by Scottish Airways and known as Balivanich after the nearby largest village on the island of Benbecula. Work began on upgrading the site in the autumn of 1940, even though the land was not ideal for airfield construction. However, the strategic demands of the looming Battle of the Atlantic far outweighed any objections. The need for a forward fighter base for air defence of the Western Isles was also envisaged, although this never materialised. Three runways were built using a method of construction known as 'sand carpet' which consisted of bitumen laid directly over compacted sand, resulting in a flexible surface. The eventual lengths were 2,000, 1,200 and 1,000 yards, and ten half-size T2 hangars were erected around the perimeter track. The dimensions were 135 x 117 x 25 feet and it was thought that they would offer less side area to the frequent gales. Despite this precaution, doors were sometimes blown in, damaging the aircraft inside.

Now named Benbecula, the RAF station was particularly windy due to its position directly facing the North Atlantic and only 16 feet above mean sea level. Not for nothing did the Commanding Officer of an Operational Training Unit in England (Wing Commander David Annand), threaten his pilots with a posting to Benbecula 'to pilot a balloon' if they flouted the rules! In the words of an entry in one of the squadrons' diaries, 'We learned to walk at the correct angle in the continuous gale and not to expect more than the occasional glimpse of the sun.' On the credit side, official documents stated that the prevalence of fog was nil.

The airfield had to be provided with a reliable connection to the ferry port at Lochboisdale, on South Uist. This was the sole source of fuel, armaments, spare parts and many other necessities. The answer was a single-lane bridge over South Ford, a dangerous area of shifting sands which separates the two islands. The locals had long been

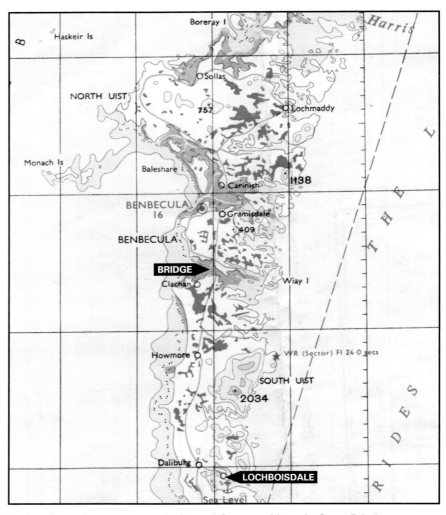

Benbecula — the most westerly Coastal Command base in Great Britain — was an isolated location, made more difficult with all supplies having to be ferried in from the mainland to Lochboisdale on South Uist, then via a bridge to North Uist.

The base was also unique in that it supported two squadrons of Fortresses — No. 206 which flew in during June 1942, initially equipped with Hudsons, later being joined by No. 220 in March 1943.

campaigning for such a link and it proved to be highly beneficial until replaced by a combined bridge and causeway in the 1980s. Dispersed living sites were built and an explosives storage area constructed to the north of the airfield. Bulk aviation fuel stowage amounted to 92,000 gallons.

The station was slow in becoming operational and there were few aircraft movements until well into 1942. The first recorded night landing occurred in May when an air ambulance arrived to ferry a serious case to the mainland. Airfields being few in these parts, Benbecula proved very useful in emergency and a 'Darkie' radio watch for lost or crippled aircraft was maintained. The first to

Benbecula's Fortresses scored two successes: first the *U-469* was sent to the bottom 80 miles south of Iceland on March 25 and then the *U-417* in the same area on June 11, 1943.

find a haven was a Wellington lost on a training flight. Another was a Boston on a transatlantic delivery flight.

At the end of June 1942, No. 206 Squadron formed here with Hudsons for anti-submarine sweeps. Several U-Boats were attacked in subsequent months but with no definite result. The squadron gradually re-equipped with Fortresses and in November one of these dropped depth-charges on a sub-

merged submarine. Despite oil seen rising to the surface, the kill remained unconfirmed. The first definite victory by a Benbecula-based aircraft took place in January 1943 when a U-Boat was sunk. The squadron spent endless hours escorting convoys, rounding up stragglers and searching for lifeboats. Often all they achieved was fleeting glimpses of oil streaks and flotsam swallowed up in rain and mist.

None of the wartime hangars survive today — it was reported that two were purchased by Royal Dutch Airlines for re-erection in Holland.

A second Fortress Squadron, No. 220, arrived from Aldergrove in March 1943. On June 11, an aircraft of No. 206 Squadron flown by Wing Commander R. B. Thomson made a successful attack and sank *U-417*. The Fortress, however, was badly damaged by return fire and had to ditch. An SOS message brought would-be rescuers to the scene but the first, a US Navy Catalina from Iceland, was wrecked landing in the heavy seas and her crew had to take to their dinghy.The Fortress crew were rescued eventually by an RAF Catalina.

The long-range squadrons — Nos. 206 and 220 — left for the Azores in October, leaving Benbecula non-operational until September 1944 when the Wellington XIVs of Nos. 179 and 304 Squadrons moved in from Chivenor. The airfield had in the meantime been considered as an Atlantic Ferry staging post but was never officially recognised as such, perhaps because of the relative proximity of Stornoway which already served this function. Two Fleet Air Arm Swordfish squadrons, 838 and 842, operated under Coastal Command from Benbecula in the autumn of 1944 for short-range patrols.

The enemy's increased use of the Schnorkel made the tracking of U-Boats even more difficult and during the whole of October, No. 304 Squadron made over 80 sorties without a single sighting. Leigh Light (airborne searchlight) tactics required a high standard of instrument flying. The pilot had to make the run in towards a radar contact and not allow himself to be distracted when the light was switched on. Only after the target had been illuminated could he glance outside the cockpit and make a definite changeover to visual flying. Considering that the run-in was made at between 50 and 100 feet, often against heavy flak, this was one of the most dangerous tasks for any aircrew.

Looking from just south of west, this shot shows the runways under construction in 1941-42. To avoid shipping in cement, a 'sand carpet' was used instead comprising bitumen laid directly over a sand base.

However, the Wellington sorties were becoming so fruitless that six aircraft from No. 304 Squadron were detached to Limavady at the end of January 1945 and the rest of the unit moved out in March. No. 179 Squadron had already left for Chivenor in October 1944 and No. 36 Squadron, again with Wellingtons, spent the last few months of the war here until disbanding in June 1945.

After a period of Care and Maintenance, the airfield was used from 1946 by British European Airways for communication with the mainland. In 1949, Royal Dutch Airlines (KLM) acquired two of Benbecula's hangars and re-erected them as a single T2 in what was then the southern corner of Amsterdam's Schiphol Airport. It was named 'Hebrides' and was capable of housing three

Unique in the annals of the Royal Air Force, and possibly unequalled anywhere in the world, is that this Polish crew of No. 304 Squadron (pictured here at Benbecula) flew with father and son together in one bomber. L-R: Flight Lieutenant L. Zeyfert, senior, the navigator; Flying Officer Zeyfert, junior, the second pilot; Sergeant Michalowski, gunner; Sergeant Naumow, gunner; Pilot Officer Karnacewicz, radar operator, and Sergeant Walentowicz, the pilot.

Douglas DC-6s. Inevitably it has succumbed to vast airport development.

In 1958, RAF Benbecula became the control centre for the South Uist Missile Range, a facility established there by the Army, and operated in conjunction with the radar-tracking station established on the island of St Kilda in 1957. The RAF presence ceased in the 1990s, leaving only an unmanned air defence radar site, and range activities are now controlled by defence technology contractor Qinetic. The longest runway, 06-24 remains in use, along with 17-35. The short runway is disused, as is the perimeter track almost in its entirety except for a short section joining the apron with the 06 threshold. Back-tracking is required if any other runway direction is in use. The sole remnant of all the original hangars are just the concrete floors.

Finally, an amusing story from the war years: several cottages around the airfield had red obstruction lamps put on their chimneys. An elderly lady lived in one with her mother; she was very sociable and enjoyed the company of young people so RAF personnel and local girls would often call in for a chat in the evening. One night two Italian PoWs turned up carrying a gift. They had misunderstood the red light on the cottage!

We cannot close this chapter without reference to the South Uist Missile Range for which the airfield is an important adjunct. It was first established on the island by the RAF between 1957 and 1958 to launch the Corporal missile — Britain and America's first guided nuclear weapon. Following on were the Sergeant and Lance tactical nuclear missiles. The facilities were updated in a £14 million facelift in 1996 and the airport also benefitted from a £500,000 upgrade in preparation for the test firing of an advanced medium-range air-to-air missile for the Eurofighter Typhoon. In 2009 it was announced that the Ministry of Defence planned to scale back operations at South Uist to save a reported £50 million, and to close the radar tracking station on St Kilda in 2014. The launch area can be accessed with few restrictions when the range is not in use, but otherwise most of the north-western side of South Uist is out of bounds. When the range is in operation, red flags are raised and red lights are displayed on access roads. As a footnote, Laima, the first un-manned aircraft to cross the Atlantic, took off from St John's, Newfoundland, on August 29, 1998 and landed successfully on the range on South Uist.

BOWMORE

In 1943 the Crown Film Unit made a film for the Ministry of Information to highlight the work of RAF Coastal Command. The participants were all serving officers, NCOs and aircrews. The film opens with a shot of a Sunderland at Bowmore.

Located on the island of Islay (pronounced Isle-a) off the Scottish coast to the west of Glasgow, Bowmore's landing area was that part of Loch Indaal to the west of two lines drawn through Bowmore Pier and Black Rock Point. Prominent landmarks included the round church at Bowmore and the substantial buildings of Bruich Laddich Distillery. A flashing buoy was moored in the centre of the Loch to mark the fact that there was one and a half miles of clear water in any direction. A flarepath was available, consisting of three power boats, a controller with Aldis Lamp being stationed on the upwind boat.

It was noted that there was good hard sand for anchorage and that there were nine flying boat moorings at Bowmore and three at Bruich Laddich. There were 18 marine craft moorings for the station establishment of two pinnaces, three seaplane tenders, four marine tenders, three refuellers, three bomb scows and two dumb dinghies, 'dumb' denoting that they were not powered but could be towed to carry small cargo. The only real disadvantage was the lack of a slipway for onshore repairs. Accommodation was provided for 44 officers and 495 men in three

As the film is a Coastal Command classic, we wanted to match stills with present day comparisons so we commissioned local photographer Mark Unsworth on the Isle of Islay to hire a boat to take the same views today on Loch Indaal.

No. 228 Squadron provided two Sunderlands which stood in for 'T'-Tommy while a Catalina from No. 413 Squadron was used for air-to-air shots with the cameraman in the nose. Some filming also took place at Port Ellen.

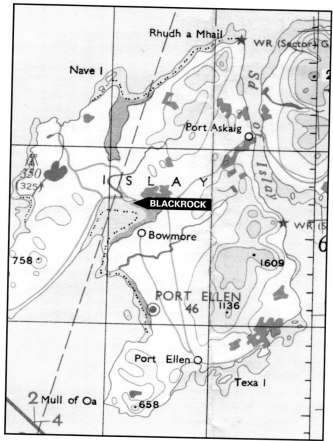

dispersed sleeping sites and one communal site, with more available by local billeting. A small bomb dump was sited to the south-west of the town.

In December 1940, 'G' Flight arrived at Bowmore from Helensburgh where it had formed to operate three Short S.26 G-Class flying boats. Named *Golden Fleece*, *Golden Hind* and *Golden Horn*, they had been built for British Overseas Airways Corporation and were now fitted with gun turrets and bomb-racks for Atlantic patrols. 'G' Flight was redesignated No. 119 Squadron in March 1941. The 'C' Class boats *Clio* and *Cordelia* were also taken on strength but soon reverted to transport duties. The Squadron moved to Pembroke Dock in August 1941.

In September 1942, No. 246 Squadron reformed at Bowmore and began to receive Sunderlands. Convoy escort duties began in December but thereafter only about 15 sorties were flown per month. For policy reasons, the squadron disbanded at the end of April 1943 and its aircraft were distributed to other units.

Bowmore was already used by Oban squadrons as an unoficial satellite and the following month No. 422 Squadron was transferred from there, its Canadian airmen promptly setting up a baseball diamond. In September one of the squadron's Sunderlands had to put down in the Atlantic after being badly damaged in a U-Boat attack, but most of its crew members were picked up by the Royal Navy.

An interesting interlude in 1942 was the use of Bowmore as 'Port Ferry Bay', the setting for much of the film *Coastal Command* made by the Crown Film Unit. Released in 1943, it was a documentary-style account of Sunderland and Catalina operations using serving aircrew rather than professional actors. A film crew were sent up to Kaldadarnes (see page 267) in Iceland and other filming took place in Port Ellen. The cinema shots were taken in the cinema at RAF Bowmore. A memorable scene at the close of the film shows a Sunderland flying low over Bowmore's distinctive church and main street.

At the end of September it was becoming increasingly evident that the running of an operational squadron at Bowmore would be

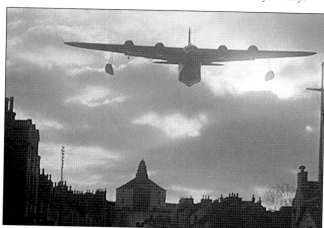

Neil Owen, who interviewed many of the airmen seen in the film, says that several of the crew of 'T'-Tommy were killed in August 1942 when the Duke of Kent's Sunderland came to grief (see page 135). Those who lost their lives included Flying Officer Sydney Smith and Flight Sergeants Edward Hewerdine, William Jones and Charles Lewis. The reason for the crash has

always been surrounded in mystery and when Neil asked Squadron Leader Joe Grunert of No. 228 Squadron about it, he replied: 'Mr Owen, I will answer any questions you may put to me about 228 Squadron but I am not permitted to answer any questions on the loss of the Duke of Kent's aircraft — so please do not continue asking'.

very difficult during the approaching winter months. A severe gale in the unsheltered mooring area would have disastrous effects and this, combined with the lack of a slipway and maintenance facilities, resulted in the transfer of the squadron to Castle Archdale at the beginning of November 1943.

Since about February 1943, Catalinas of No. 131 OTU at Killadeas in Northern Ireland had been using Loch Indaal for water landing and take-off practice which continued even after Bowmore closed down its operations in January 1944. The marine craft section, however, was retained on stand by for refuelling and flarepath duties for the OTU and any other diverted or transit aircraft.

One January night in 1944, a diverted Sunderland sank in a gale while riding at anchor. Four of the crew were on board at the time and three managed to launch a dinghy but one of the pilots was unable to reach it. He was eventually rescued from the tailplane, none the worse for his experience.

The flying boat base finally closed in July 1945 and peace returned to Loch Indaal. Today, there is little evidence of its existence apart from the station workshop buildings taken over by local businesses along the shore road just to the north-east of the town. To the south-west, almost the only trace of the wartime explosives area is its entrance road.

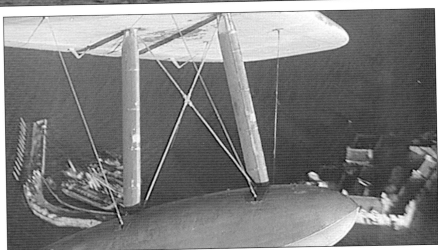

'T'-Tommy was predominately played by Sunderland P9606 which began its career with the Australian No. 10 Squadron in January 1940. In April that year it was on the strength of No. 201 Squadron and 16 months later joined the British Overseas Airways Corporation fleet before returning briefly to the RAAF. It moved to No. 4 (Coastal) Operational Training Unit at Invergordon at the end of December 1941 and was finally written off in an accident on May 11, 1944. The other Sunderland, L2160, is seen only twice in the film. It had a varied service career, moving to Singapore, the Middle East and Malta, before coming home to Mount Batten. The final entry on its record card shows it as being on the strength of No. 4 OTU.

The worst Sunderland crash on the Isle of Islay occurred on January 24, 1943 in which nine men lost their lives. That evening DV979 'F' for Freddie of No. 246 Squadron was returning to Bowmore after a long patrol over the North Atlantic. It had been an uneventful flight so its depth-charges were still on board. The crew of 12 were led by Captain Eric Lever of the South African Air Force. The gale force wind meant that the usual flare path of three illuminated pinnaces had not been deployed, the Sunderland being instructed by radio to divert to Oban. However, either the message was not received or the aircraft was low on fuel. Eyewitnesses said that the Sunderland circled several times before approaching the loch from the north over Blackrock. The flying boat's landing lights were on but suddenly they disappeared. According to the official accident report ,'the aircraft undershot the landing area and struck the ground at the water's edge'. From other reports it seems that the hull scraped across the hill above Blackrock and possibly then caught the telephone wires running alongside the road. The Sunderland ended up virtually intact and 11 of the crew managed to scramble out, with three having sustained injuries in the crash. They moved away from the aircraft towards the beach while the other eight ran in the opposite direction towards the road before they realised that one man — the rear gunner — was not with them having been trapped in his turret. All eight men returned to the machine at which point the depth-charges detonated, killing all nine men. A deep crater was blasted on the spot *(above)*, the explosion being heard up to 20 miles away. The local Home Guard commandeered a car and raced to the scene which was lit by flames from the wreckage. An RAF ambulance arrived and the three dazed survivors, Captain Lever, Sergeant George Hogg, the wireless operator/air gunner, and Sergeant John Williams, the flight mechanic, were rescued. When daybreak came, Lieutenant Bobby Hodkinson and his troop from the Kilarrow Home Guard began the awful job of gathering the remains of those who had been blown to pieces. The funeral was held in the Round Church at Bowmore, Pilot Officer Wallace Johnston of the Royal Canadian Air Force, and Sergeants Roy Jabour and Ernest Palmer of the RAAF being laid to rest in the churchyard.

CASTLE ARCHDALE/LOUGH ERNE

The Coastal Command base on Lough Erne in Country Fermanagh in Northern Ireland had the potentiial of increasing the range of its aircraft by 100 miles.

Lough Erne in County Fermanagh, Northern Ireland, is an extremely beautiful area, with many islands, coves and inlets. In wartime, it proved ideal for two flying boat bases only about four miles apart — one operational and the other for training. The former opened as RAF Castle Archdale early in February 1941 but within weeks Air Ministry renamed it RAF Lough Erne. It retained this title until January 1943 when it reverted to Castle Archdale. Operations from the Lough were detailed as follows:

'Landing area in centre of broad lake bounded on the North-East by a line joining Lustymore Island, Gay Island, South-West corner of Inis Makill and flashing light off Duress Point, and bounded on the south by a line approximately 280° from Gull Island. Landing also in channel between Inis Makill and Gay Island. Minimum runs: East-South-East — West-North-West, six miles. North — South, two miles. Six moorings east of Crevenishaughy Island. Nine moorings east of White Island. Two moorings for maintenance purposes in bay enclosed by Davey Island and Toms island. Additional moorings will be laid north and south of White island. Directions for approaching moorings: Leave red flashing buoys to port, green and white to starboard. Two standard 45ft RAF refuellers (capacity 2,000 and 2,500 gallons) maintained full and available throughout 24 hours.'

In December 1940 a survey was carried out on Lough Erne with a view to establishing a flying boat base on what was the most westerly point in the United Kingdom. From here aircraft could patrol the Atlantic and cover the convoys out to the limits of their range. The entire Castle Archdale estate was requisitioned to build the base and hundreds of ancient oak and ash trees on islands and mainland were felled because they were deemed a hazard to aircraft landing and taking off.

Today the Lough is a leading holiday centre with caravan park and purpose-built marina.

However, there was a problem. To reach the Atlantic by the most direct route, a strip of neutral territory of the Irish Free State lay in the way. The long detour around County Donegal would totally negate the advantage of a base at Lough Erne so negotiations were opened with the Irish Prime Minister to seek permission to allow aircraft to fly directly west from the base. A secret agreement, with certain provisos, was reached to establish what became known as the 'Donegal Corridor'. And to stop RAF aircraft from straying, the western coastline of Eire territory was marked with large signs together with the reference number of the nearby Look Out Post.

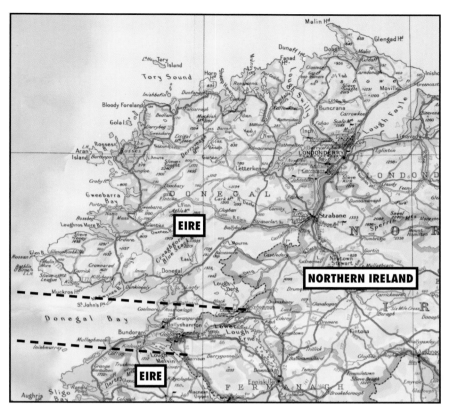

A major drawback of the new base was that military aircraft were not permitted to fly over the territory of neutral Eire. This meant that they would have first to fly northwards before heading west. With a view to removing this long detour, a meeting took place in January 1941 between Irish Prime Minister Eamon de Valera and Sir John Maffey, the British representative in Dublin. A secret agreement was reached whereby the Lough Erne-based flying boats would be permitted to fly across a short stretch of neutral territory from Belleek in County Fermanagh to Ballyshannon in County Donegal and thereby gain direct access to the Atlantic. This flight path became known as 'The Donegal Corridor'. Conditions of the concession included that flights should be made at a 'good height' and that aircraft should not fly over the military camp at Finner. In practice, these conditions appear to have been ignored by both sides. The other major condition was that aircraft should only be engaged on air-sea rescue missions, a cover story should the Germans ever discover what was going on. The agreement meant that the un-protected gap in mid-Atlantic was reduced by at least 100 miles.

This was the beginning of a pattern of co-operation with Britain that was far more friendly than strict neutrality should have allowed. The British and Irish co-operated in trying to avoid navigational errors by Allied aircrew. In 1942 the Irish authorities painted the word EIRE, along with the number of the associated Look Out Post, in giant, bold letters upon almost 90 prominent capes and headlands around the country. Many are still legible to this day, and some have even been renovated as a memorial. A list of numbers and positions was given out to RAF and USAAF aircrew likely to need the information. The first official flight along the Corridor took place on February 21, 1941, by a Stranraer of No. 240 Squadron.

Shore facilities at Lough Erne were minimal at first with the first flying boats arriving with No. 209 Squadron near the end of March 1941. The squadron was in the process of exchanging its troublesome Lerwicks for Catalinas and was still working up on the new type. On May 15, a U-Boat was depth-charged and claimed as a 'probable'. However, the squadron's great coup occurred on the 26th when a searching Catalina crew re-discovered and shadowed the *Bismarck* for four and half hours.

The airman who actually first sighted the ship through a chance gap in the clouds was Ensign Leonard B. Smith of the US Navy, flying as co-pilot to Flying Officer Dennis Briggs, but his involvement had to remain a secret until after the war. As Smith later remarked, 'it was the blind leading the blind. Briggs had had plenty of operational flying but knew little about Catalinas. I knew something about Catalinas but had no experience of operational flying.'

The sighting report led to an attack by Swordfish from HMS *Ark Royal* which damaged *Bismarck*'s rudder and rendered her uncontrollable. The Royal Navy sank her the following day after a desperate battle.

No. 209 Squadron moved to Iceland in August 1941. Concurrently operating Catalinas from Lough Erne between March and August had been No. 240 Squadron whose nominal base was at Killadeas. However, as shore facilities had yet to be established here, it was perhaps used only for satellite moorings. This proved to be the only time that this sister station of Castle Archdale was used by an operational unit. Thereafter it was employed by training units but its origins deserve recording.

Early in 1941, the Chiefs-of-Staff of Britain and the USA held secret talks in Washington to plan the co-ordination of strategy should America be drawn into the war, as seemed likely despite the strong lobby for non-involvement. Much attention was paid to the problem of Atlantic security and agreement was reached about possible US naval bases in the UK.

Although much has been lost of the wartime buildings, the Operations Block has been converted into a cafeteria for the use of visitors to the Castle Archdale Country Park.

Sunderlands of the Canadian No. 422 Squadron on the concrete hardstanding.

Two naval bases, Londonderry and Rosneath, were to be placed at the disposal of the USA, along with two flying boat bases on Lough Erne and Loch Ryan. These pairs of bases, in Northern Ireland and Scotland respectively, were selected in case German bombing forced a move from one of them. The US Government was to be responsible for the construction of the necessary installations by US contractors supervised by American engineers. If and when the USA became involved in the war, these bases were to pass completely under its control. Work did not begin until August 1941 but the whole programme, which included the main base at Ely Lodge, repair facilities at Killadeas, an ammunition depot and a hospital, was completed in five months. Much of the Nissen-hutted accommodation was sited on a wooded peninsula.

The work evidently displaced No. 240 Squadron to Castle Archdale which was only about four miles along the shore. The squadron had a detachment in Iceland, which saw the bulk of its action until the whole unit deployed to the Far East during the first half of 1942. No. 201 Squadron's Sunderlands had been operating from Lough Erne since September 1941 but bad winter weather severely curtailed activity and led to three fatal acci-

dents. The monotonous patrols continued, with few sightings and a single attack on a U-Boat in July 1942.

The RCAF's fifth coastal squadron — No. 422 — formed here from Canadian personnel on April 2, 1942. Saro Lerwicks were the initial equipment but these were only used for work-up and training and by August were being superseded by Catalinas. Having become operational with these, the squadron's first task was to transport Hawker Hurricane spares to the Soviet Union from Invergordon. This was interspersed with convoy patrols in and out of Russian ports. The unit moved to Oban in November 1942.

Another Canadian squadron, No. 423, took over at Lough Erne that month with Sunderlands and was destined to stay here for the rest of the war. Sorties were few at first but as more aircraft and crews became operational, its output increased so that by March 1943 it was flying 30 sorties a month and making several inconclusive attacks on U-Boats.

December 1942 saw another Sunderland unit arrive, No. 228 Squadron from Oban. Its

main duty was patrolling the North-West Approaches but there were few U-Boat actions and no confirmed results. A move was made to Pembroke Dock in May 1943. No. 201 Squadron was still operating from the Lough and made three attacks in March, the squadron sinking its first submarine, the *U-440*, on May 31, 1943. The end of the year was marked by an attack on the surface raider *Alsterufer*. It was then shadowed until other aircraft were homed onto it, one of which sank it. The squadron moved to Wales in March 1944.

Extracts from a report written by Flight Lieutenant H. J. King after he was attached to No. 201 Squadron in August-September 1943 give an insight to operational procedures at Castle Archdale:

'The squadron was working "on loan" to No. 19 Group and its chief and almost only duty during my stay was a patrol known as a *Sea Slug* in an area as far west as 12°W and down to latitude 42°N. This area fits in with other areas patrolled by aircraft under No. 19 Group. The areas are so fitted together and operated that the sea from

Today a quiet corner of the Castle Archdale Country Park.

The seat of the Archdale family became the station headquarters in 1942. The rudimentary flying control on the roof was later replaced by a purpose-built structure on stilts made out of oil drums, and situated on Gay Island in the centre of the lough.

The house was demolished after the war, this picture being taken in 1983 when the grounds were being used for an International Scout Jamboree.

Regarding operations on and off the Lough, Flight Lieutenant King had this to say: 'At present, the Flying Control is situated in the Operations Room, which is not convenient, but this is being changed and soon the control room will overlook the Lough. The control pinnace remains on the Lough for 24 hours and is in radio contact with the Flying Control Officer.' (A rudimentary glasshouse was later positioned on the roof of Castle Archdale House until replaced by a control tower on stilts on Gay Island. This was in the centre of the Lough with much better visibility.)

The report went on to say this about night flying: 'The take-off path is denoted by three lights on anchored floats which can be changed. After the elaborate layout of the Aerodrome Lighting Mk II, this appeared to be very scanty, and during take-off, once the third light is passed, there is nothing to keep straight on in the form of totem poles on the shores of the Lough and, as boats require a very large run, sometimes up to three minutes, quite a long part of the take-off is in darkness.

'The Lough is buoyed for day and night flying, but pilots are required to "know" the areas which are safe, as they are not defined as are runways. The take-off path is controlled by a sergeant airfield controller at night, who is also responsible for changing path lights on instructions from the flying control officer.'

latitude 45°N, longitude, 12°W eastwards and southwards across the Bay is constantly patrolled by aircraft, including searchlight Wellingtons at night. The enemy also patrols this area with long-range Ju 88s in formations varying up to 14 aircraft and is having some success in that they sometimes shoot down patrolling aircraft or damage them sufficiently to cause the patrol to be abandoned, but Coastal Command have Mosquitos and Beaufighters operating on interception.'

'The chief duty of a pilot is to keep watch on the automatic pilot and keep up a constant anti-aircraft search, and in the patrol area an anti-submarine search with binoculars. During a month, a pilot may fly as many as 100 to 150 hours. Navigation during flight is entirely by D.R. [usually referred to as Dead Reckoning but should be Deduced Reckoning — author]. Flights are often 12 hours out of sight of any feature on which to take a bearing. Wind is determined every hour by change of course and drift of white caps on drift sight, navigator operated, or flame-float and drift observed by tail gunner. When possible astro and solar sights are taken. The ASV (radar) is not used on every patrol. Instructions are received during briefing as to whether it is to be used on patrol or not. It is known that the German submarines have means of picking it

up, but it is regarded as invaluable during negative weather, especially along the very rugged and irregular coast of Eire, and is used to fix aircraft positions.'

In January 1945 the Lough froze with the risk of the hulls being crushed.

In flat calm conditions, it is difficult to get a flying boat to unstick from the water, so a motor boat would be used to make waves to help them to become airborne. Likewise, landing on a glassy surface is dangerous, especially at night, owing to the difficulty of judging height. On May 7, 1941 a Catalina of No. 240 Squadron returning from a patrol ploughed into the Lough and remains there as a war grave. A memorial to the crew is located on Rossmore Point overlooking the crash site. Across the water at the Navar Viewpoint are two more memorials to crash victims on the Lough; a Sunderland of No. 201 Squadron on November 18, 1943 and a Catalina of No. 202 Squadron on November 20, 1944.

No. 422 Squadron returned in April 1944 for a relatively uneventful stay before moving to Wales in November. No. 201 Squadron returned that month and also saw little action. It did however have the distinction of flying Coastal Command's last operational patrol of the Second World War which took place on June 3, 1945 as a precaution against stray U-Boats which might still prove dangerous. A move was made to Wales in August.

Meanwhile No. 423 Squadron's Sunderlands were still soldiering on from the Lough, flying 89 sorties in June 1944 alone. Many U-Boat attacks were mounted, the last one being on May 4, 1945, but no claims were made. In June the squadron transferred to Transport Command for re-equipment with Liberators.

In September 1944, No. 202 Squadron flew in from Gibraltar to train with Leigh Lights and began night coastal patrols looking for Schnorkel-equipped U-Boats. There were no successes and the squadron disbanded at Castle Archdale on June 27, 1945. The last unit here was No. 230 Squadron whose Sunderlands were based from April to September 1946.

The end of a long flight. Pilot Officer Ralph Tierney from No. 422 Canadian Squadron gives a helping hand to Pilot Officer D. W. Cooke as the crew leave their Catalina on Lough Erne for the shore.

Unfortunately the code '3J' is not sufficient to identify the squadron.

handed over as a satellite to Killadeas in August 1943. It served as a land aerodrome for various support functions. Killadeas closed in 1947 and became the home of the Lough Erne Yacht Club which still uses the slipway and aircraft hardstandings. Rings that once held Catalinas down in gales now secure boats, and a memorial to the OTU stands nearby.

Castle Archdale, which is now a country park, is dotted with wartime remains, a caravan site occupies the extensive concrete maintenance area. At the Archdale Centre, which is in a corner of the main courtyard to the long-demolished house, is a permanent exhibition of 'Castle Archdale at War' which highlights the flying-boat station's role in the Battle of the Atlantic. Behind the courtyard is a stone inscribed 'RAF Castle Archdale 1941-1957'. The Donegal Corridor is commemorated by a plaque on the bridge over the River Erne at Bally-shannon and one with slightly different wording on the bridge at Belleek, marking its eastern extremity.

A large dock was built in 1945 for the Short Shetland (a type which never reached production), although there is only circumstantial evidence to support this. The dock remains in use by small craft to this day. Minimally staffed, Castle Archdale was retained well into the 1950s for Sunderland weather diversions and exercises. USAF Grumman Albatross rescue amphibians were also frequent visitors from their base at Manston in Kent.

Although intended for the US Navy on completion in 1942, neighbouring Killadeas was never used by them, and in July 1942 it became the base of No. 131 Operational Training Unit. The OTU was equipped with Catalinas to which were added Sunderlands in 1944. Castle Archdale's flare path was used for night flying and a satellite was established at Boa Island/Rock Bay, also on the Lough. A target-towing detachment was based at St Angelo, near Enniskillen, built originally as a fighter sector station but

Mobile homes now occupy the former flying boat hardstanding.

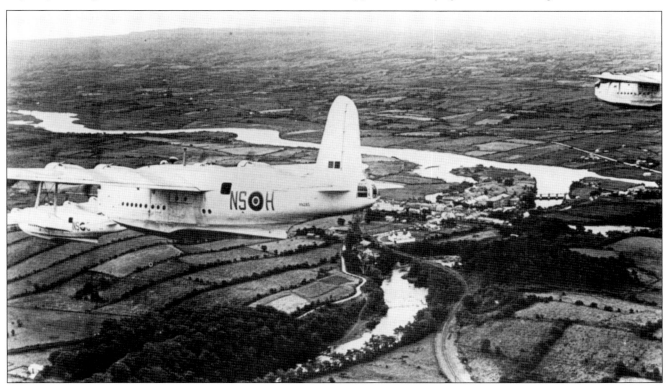
This rare shot was taken in August 1945 as No. 201 Squadron prepared to leave Castle Archdale. The picture shows the last flight down the Donegal Corridor — the Sunderlands are just about to leave Irish airspace and re-enter Northern Ireland. In the centre of the village, behind the tail of NS-H, is the world famous Belleek Pottery.

HOOTON PARK

Previously a race course, Hooton Park on the Wirral Peninsula in Cheshire dated from 1917. Three blocks of double General Service hangars were erected to house No. 4 Training Depot Station. Sopwith Dolphins and Avro 504s were the main types operated and the unit was redesignated No. 4 Training Squadron in March 1919, only to disband two months later.

Hooton briefly achieved licensed airport status in 1933 but continued to subsist on flying club acitivites, along with small factories established by Nick Comper to produce the Comper Swift and Douglas Pobjoy to build its engines. Both men played a very significant role in light aircraft development during the 1920s and 1930s. In 1936, No. 610 Squadron formed as a light bomber unit in the Auxiliary Air Force. It later became a Spitfire-equipped fighter squadron before moving south to its war station.

The airfield was taken over by the regular RAF in October 1939 and Ansons of 'A' Flight, No. 206 Squadron arrived for anti-submarine duties under the control of No. 15 Group. At that time, the station was in a rather chaotic state with some of the hangars and buildings let to private firms, including a canning factory. The RAF were only tenants of a few of the buildings and there was obvious difficulty in exercising control and discipline within the confines of the camp. The new Commanding Officer was determined to turn Hooton into a proper operational station as soon as possible and did this by requisitioning some of the buildings and establishing a compound around the RAF site. Almost surrounded by trees and not very large, the grass landing area was initially deemed unsafe for blind take-offs or night flying. After an Anson was written off after failing to clear the trees — fortunately without serious injuries to the crew — some of the tallest of them were cut down.

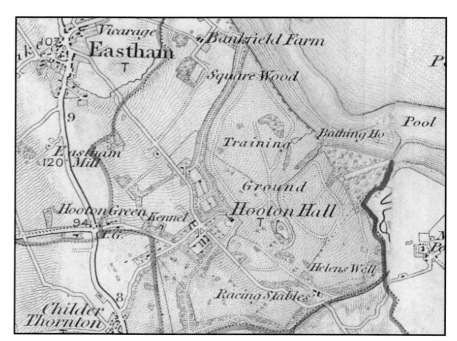

A mansion had stood in Hooton Park since the 15th century, Hooton Hall replacing it in 1778, being extended after 1854 with the addition of a chapel, tower and smoking room. By the early 1900s, a race course and polo ground had been created in the park but in 1914 all was requisitioned by the War Office for use as a military camp, the final race meeting taking place in April 1915.

As a warplane, the Tiger Moth would not be an obvious choice but in the winter of 1939-40 it found itself in the front-line of the U-Boat war. Coastal Command was unable to cover all of Britain's vulnerable coastline so Coastal Patrol Flights were formed to watch for submarines and signs of seaborne invasion. No. 3 CPF formed at Hooton at the beginning of December 1939 and flew its first two sorties the same day. It was joined by No. 4 CPF which flew over from Aldergrove a few days later. The two units now shared four daily patrols during the hours of daylight. No armament was carried of course, nor a radio, but a carrier pigeon was available in case the aircraft came down in the water! Late in January 1940 most of the Tigers were replaced by Hornet Moths, no more potent than the former but possessing the comfort of an enclosed cabin.

The hall itself was converted into a military hospital while one single and three double 'Belfast' hangars were constructed, the name being adopted due to the unique latticed timber roof originally designed for use in the Belfast shipyards.

CONTROL TOWER

The Royal Air Force (created from the Royal Flying Corps and Royal Naval Air Service in April 1918) relinquished the aerodrome at the end of the war. In 1927 it was purchased by a local aviation enthusiast to become the home of the Liverpool and District Aero Club and, even for a period, being used as the city's main airport. The RAF moved back on the outbreak of the Second World War and in 1941 runways were laid down, the longest being 1,500 yards, extended to 2,000 yards after the war.

The RAF departed in 1957 and three years later the site was sold to Vauxhall Motors for the construction of a manufacturing plant. The WW1 Belfast hangars had been granted Grade II preservation orders but in 1968 Vauxhalls applied for this to be set aside for them to be demolished. The Hooton Park Trust was set up to oppose the move and, in a magnanimous gesture, General Motors passed it freehold together with generous financial support. With Belfast hangars now very rare in the UK, English Heritage increased the classification to two star listing. This comparison photograph was taken by the Trust in 2007.

During February, two daily patrols were flown alternately, covering the north coast of Wales and the Isle of Anglesey and the west coast of England from Liverpool to St Bees Head in Cumberland. No enemy submarines were ever encountered and the only sighting of any note was a large oil patch with turbulent bubbles off the North Wales coast. The cause was never discovered. The deterrent effect of these so-called 'Scarecrow Patrols' is impossible to calculate but undoubtedly a U-Boat commander would crash-dive at the sight of *any* aircraft. The last sortie was flown on May 30, 1940 but the aircraft returned early because of very low cloud. On that day No. 15 Group disbanded the CPFs.

Refugees arriving from the south were the Ansons of the School of General Reconnaissance whose Guernsey base was soon to be under new management but the school was transferred to Squires Gate the following month. Meanwhile, a detachment of No. 502 Squadron had replaced the one from No. 206, until it, in turn, was displaced by No. 48 Squadron in July. Its task was to shepherd the convoys into and out of the Mersey. To do the same for the Clyde, and to cover the northern Irish Sea, detachments were maintained at Scottish and Northern Ireland bases. No. 48 Squadron's Ansons remained at Hooton until July 1941, by which time the station's bomb storage capacity had been increased to 288 tons.

To accommodate larger aircraft, contractors Monk & Co. Ltd began the construction of two runways in December 1941, the original grass landing ground having been extended considerably. The main strip was 1,500 yards and the subsidiary 1,100 yards in length. However, Coastal Command aircraft were not destined to use the new facilities operationally as Hooton was transferred to a training role in December 1942 and housed a Radio School until August 1944. Martin Hearn Ltd had performed aircraft repair mainly for Ansons and, later, Mosquitos, and also run an Aircraft Assembly Unit to handle aircraft from the USA. After the war the main use was for No. 610 Squadron but the disbandment of the Royal Auxiliary Air Force in March 1957 marked the end of flying at Hooton. The south-eastern section of the airfield was subsequently engulfed by a Vauxhall car factory but the Belfast hangars can still be seen in varying states of repair.

Back in 1935, Martin Hearn, an ex-pilot and ground engineer who had previously worked on Alan Cobham's Flying Circus, set up in business at Hooton Park servicing aircraft. When war came, Martin obtained a contract from the Ministry of Aircraft Production to repair large numbers of Avro Ansons and de Havilland Mosquitos. By the end of the war the airfield presented this incredible sight as hundreds of redundant Halifaxes and Wellingtons were sent to what was then No. 100 Storage Sub-Site to be scrapped.

The airfield was purchased by Vauxhall Motors in 1960 for a vehicle production plant at Ellesmere Port and the tower was demolished soon after.

The tower stood here in what is now part of Vauxhall's press shop where the company produce the body panels for the New Astra.

Today, the Vauxhall plant has expanded right across the former flying field, save for the area held by Hooton Park Trust.

In 2007 the Hooton Park Karting Circuit opened beside the remaining short section of the old runway.

LIMAVADY

The war is over — this is the view looking out over Limavady when the aerodrome closed in August 1945. In August 2015 Ernie Cromie of the Ulster Aviation Society went back to match the shot from the control tower.

With a range of hills topped by Binevenagh at 1,260ft only two miles north-northeast, this was a strange choice for an airfield site in Northern Ireland. The reason, perhaps, was that it was planned in 1938 as an Armament Training Station to serve the bombing range in Lough Foyle. Only daylight fair weather flying was envisaged from its coastal location to the east of Londonderry. However, despite its shortcomings, it seems that in any future emergency there was a back-up plan to use it for Coastal Command operations.

The contract for construction was given to Stewart and Partners and consisted of three runways, one of 1,600 yards and the others each of 1,100 yards. The two subsidiaries were later considerably extended. Two blister hangars and three Bellmans were erected, with four Bellmans and two T2s added as the war progressed. For administrative and residential purposes, a number of nearby premises were requisitioned and a temporary Station Headquarters was established at Red Pillar House on Main Street, Limavady. A 'Q' site decoy was laid out at Crindle, a few miles to the north-east.

Unfortunately, as the upper floor had collapsed, he had to be satisfied with this shot taken from the ground level.

The progressive deterioration of the building is evident from these two photographs taken in 2002 by John Pudney and today.

Since Limavady closed, industrial concerns now encroach upon the former flying field.

In the words of Aircraftman Frank Leighton who was there at the beginning, 'the thing which set the Limavady station apart from most postings was the social life. The warm citizens of Ulster welcomed us with open arms and more than compensated for the frustrating lack of amenities from which we all suffered in those early days of the new station. There was a certain sense of excitement in helping to start a whole new RAF station from scratch. We all pitched in, enjoying the sense of relaxed discipline which accompanied our pioneering efforts.'

The first recorded use was by the Whitleys of 'A' Flight, No. 502 Squadron from early December 1940, equipped with the new and very secret Air to Surface Vessel (ASV) Mk. 2 radar. The entire squadron moved in from Aldergrove towards the end of January 1941, followed by No. 224 Squadron's Hudsons which were resident from April to December. Other Northern Ireland-based units kept detachments at Limavady in 1941, including Blenheims of No. 272 Squadron and Hurricanes of No. 245 Squadron. In its first year, aircraft operating from the airfield accumulated a total of 25,600 flying hours on anti-submarine patrols over the North-West Approaches, a record achievement for a No. 15 Group station. Much of it was monotonous convoy escort work with occasional sightings and inconclusive attacks on U-Boats. No. 502 Squadron moved to St Eval in December 1941 and No. 224 returned in April 1942.

In April 1942, Limavady was handed over to No. 17 Group for training purposes and the operational squadrons were withdrawn, to be replaced by No. 7 OTU equipped with Wellingtons. This tenure lasted until January 1944 when a change of policy resulted in the OTU being moved to South Wales. Now the station once again became a base for operational Wellington squadrons. No. 612 arrived in January but operations were badly hampered by the lack of de-icing equipment on the aircraft and the fact that

In 1982, Ernie and author David Smith obtained permission to visit the Operations Block where they found the notice boards were still in situ, almost as if the war had just finished. Unfortunately the building has since been demolished.

Limavady had no Standard Beam Approach (SBA) or Beam Approach Beacon System (BABS) for landing in bad weather. One vital aid that had been installed was a system of lead-in lights to assist aircraft in keeping clear of the nearby high ground. Projector lights were sited on the coast with a series of guide lights along a path to the aerodrome and obstruction lights on each of two hills to the east of this path. This innovation was no doubt a result of several Wellington crashes on Binevenagh. Fittingly, to the post-war Shackleton crews based at nearby Ballykelly, this hill was known as 'Ben Twitch'.

One of No. 612 Squadron's sorties in February was highly successful when a radar contact turned out to be a surfaced U-Boat. A perfect attack was made without the need for the Leigh Light. The radar contact disappeared and debris and small orange lights were seen on the surface. Thus died the *U-545* but her crew were lucky to be picked up by a fellow submarine.

The squadron personnel were not impressed with Limavady. Its living sites were considered too far apart: 'dispersal gone mad' was one way it was described. From the flying point of view, it was recorded that 'the QGH procedure [code for instrument let-down through cloud] is complicated by the nearby hills and will probably not be used except under the most favourable conditions. Few pilots would have confidence in it in really poor weather on the admission of most aircrew and ground staff. It looks as if Limavady QGH has been worked out by a wingless wonder or else the baker has not tested his own bread!'

At the beginning of March 1944, No. 612 Squadron moved to Chivenor owing to enemy submarines having changed their area of operations. This left No. 407 Squadron that had been on station since

January 1944 with Leigh Light Wellingtons. They were engaged in concentrated training combined with operational patrols, one of which almost certainly claimed a U-Boat on February 18. At the end of April, No. 407 moved out for pre-invasion patrols whereupon Limavady was bereft of Coastal Command as the centre of activity swung to the south-west. As a result the Royal Navy seized the opportunity to base several squadrons there during the summer of 1944, flying such types as the Avenger, Wildcat, Swordfish and Sea Hurricane.

As the Allied forces moved eastwards across Europe, attention returned to the North Atlantic and the Wellingtons of Nos. 172 and 612 Squadrons were sent to Limavady in September 1944. In an attempt to combat the new Schnorkel breathing tube, by means of which U-Boats could remain submerged and undetected for several days at a time, a comprehensive anti-Schnorkel training programme was begun in November. Few crews, however, had any confidence in the ability of their existing radar to detect such tiny objects and there were no successes. So few were the U-Boat sightings that No. 612 Squadron was posted to Norfolk in December. No. 172's last attack on a U-Boat took place as late as May 11, 1945 but by then most of the patrols were tasked to round up surrendering submarines. The squadron disbanded at Limavady in June 1945 and the station closed in August 1945.

Although much of the airfield has been taken over by industrial units, a surprising number of wartime buildings survive, most of them in a derelict condition. Fortunately, the local council is aware of their historical value and is seeking to secure their preservation. The control tower still stands, as do several hangars. Also extant is Station Sick Quarters complete with ambulance garage and mortuary, but sadly the Operations Block with its ops boards has been demolished.

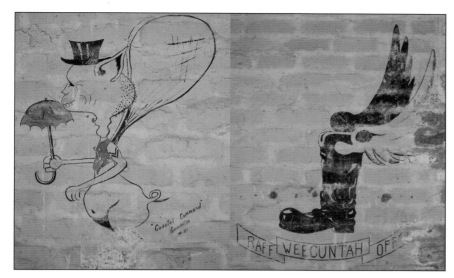

In August 2015, concerns were raised regarding the impending sale of the Aghanloo Industrial Estate which included several buildings from the former technical site. Some of these included wall drawings and other notices from the wartime period and, as the operations block had already been demolished, it was feared that even more or Northern Ireland's aviation history might be lost.

The Irish terrain could be very unforgiving to aircraft that became lost or were in distress, and one of the earliest crashes was that of Wellington W5653 of No. 221 Squadron on April 11, 1941. Having taken off from Limavady shortly before 6 a.m., the aircraft headed out over the Atlantic on a convoy escort patrol but on its return the crew found that the ground was invisible due to a heavy mist. The Wellington is believed to have overflown its base before crashing into the Urris Hills in the Irish Free State. Detachments of soldiers began a search and because the mist was so thick they were told to link hands on the way up the mountain. The wreckage was found at a height of 1,200 feet. The six bodies were retrieved the following day and handed over to personnel from the United Kingdom at Bridgend. *Right:* John Quinn (left) and his dedicated group of aviation wreckologists have investigated the loss of over 50 aircraft stationed at Limavady and began their search for the crash site of W5653 in October 1989.

The most prominent piece of wreckage was an undercarriage leg which was set upright, and a cross was erected to record the loss of this crew. John is pictured with colleague Robert Taylor and former Irish soldier John Ferguson who was a member of the search party in 1941. (The full story was published in 1995 in *Wings Over The Foyle* by John Quinn.)

NUTTS CORNER

The Air Ministry Aerodromes Board had selected this Northern Ireland site to the west of Belfast in the summer of 1940 and within months the War Cabinet had directed that the very highest priority should be given to aerodrome construction in the Province. In the face of mounting shipping losses, the primary aim was to have more bases as far west as possible from which Coastal Command could operate its anti-submarine aircraft.

Three runways were constructed of 1,600, 1,200 and 1,160 yards, later to be extended to 2,000, 1,600 and 1,200 yards, respectively. There were no hangars initially but four T2s were erected later in the war. Also at a later date 50 hardstandings were constructed, most of them of the loop type. A 'Q' site decoy known as Groganstown was established in the hills to the south-east.

No. 120 Squadron, a short-lived First World War unit, was re-formed at Nutts Corner on June 2, 1941 at the same time that the station was opened. Its specific purpose was to use the long range of the new Liberator bomber to close the gap of air cover in the North Atlantic where U-Boats were causing unacceptable shipping losses. The station was still under construction when personnel started to arrive to join the squadron and facilities were sparse. Former Sergeant Pilot Harry Wilson describes his first impressions: 'I was shaken rigid when we did get to Nutts Corner. The Nissen huts were dispersed and

none of them even had electric light at that time. There were no ablution facilities and we had to draw water from a well in order to wash and shave. We were taken, once a week, to Aldergrove for a bath. I could only compare it with Flying Training School in Rhodesia, where I was a member of the second course and — well — there was just no comparison! However, as time went by, things improved and there was a small farm nearby so we were able to buy eggs, milk, butter and bread and we used to settle down to scrambled eggs on toast, cooked on a stove in the hut.'

In the words of Flight Lieutenant David Evans: 'We all arrived early in June 1941 and within days decided that whoever called this new and only partly finished airfield "Nutts Corner" knew what they were about. Living conditions were initially liable to be fairly primitive, especially for those who, like ourselves, had been living in relative luxurious accommodation, superbly designed and built, as was that at Thorney Island in the heyday of the mid-1930s expansion of the Royal Air Force. '

Another newcomer was Sergeant Wireless Operator/Air Gunner Eddie Cheek: 'In June 1941, I was posted to No. 120 (General Reconnaissance) Squadron at Nutts Corner, In Northern Ireland; of course nobody had heard of the place. After crossing the Irish Sea on the Stranraer/Larne ferry, I eventually arrived at Nutts Corner. After reporting

to the Orderly Room I found I was to fly on Liberator aircraft, whatever they were. I asked for directions to the Mess, and was more than surprised to be told that it was one mile up the road, with another walk of half a mile to the accommodation site. My first impressions on Nutts Corner were, though it was not the end of the world, if the Good Lord decided to give the world an enema, here was the place. Living conditions could hardly be described as comfortable on this vast dispersed station. We were housed in those semi-circle monstrosities called Nissen huts, with just one eighth of an inch of corrugated metal separating us from the far from benign Irish elements.'

For the WAAFs stationed at Nutts Corner, matters were even worse. Mrs Jean Davis recalled: 'We were billeted in the local Orange Hall in Dundrod, which meant about fifty of us in this large cavern, lit by candles most of the time. We had to break the ice at the village pump to wash, and our idea of bliss was to hitchhike into Belfast and have a "Chance Bath" at the Grand Central Hotel for one shilling and sixpence. After which we treated ourselves to tea there, because luxury was being able to put the milk in last, if we wanted to, instead of having "cha" ladled out of buckets — one with and one without sugar, in the mess. My abiding memory is of the charming habit of those who delivered the food to the cooks, dumping first the paraffin and then the sack of potatoes on the

This aircraft carried out the first operation on September 20, 1941. It was parked here at the south-eastern end of the NW-SE runway.

The following year HM King George VI and Queen Elizabeth visited the Province, being escorted by General Harold Franklyn, the GOC Northern Ireland. On June 26 they first visited units of the 59th Division and 72nd Infantry Brigade before moving to inspect RAF Maghaberry where No. 231 Squadron were based.

The tour ended at Nutts Corner with lunch in the Mess. Ernie Cromie pinpointed where the picture was taken (see overleaf) — just north of the hangar (now demolished), looking south-west. A new two-storey dwelling has since been built close to where the most distant of the three Liberators was parked.

door-mat, so that everything in retrospect seems to have been flavoured with paraffin. I also seem to remember a stern lecture from our WAAF Admin Officer in reply to com-

plaints, which, in effect, informed us that there was, after all, A WAR ON.'

(I am grateful to Peter Clare for kindly permitting me to use the above reminis-

cences gained from his researches. Peter's focus of interest is the anti-U-Boat war, with particular emphasis on No. 120 Squadron's part in it.)

Nutts Corner took its name from that of the owner of a small farm near Straidhavern. According to local legend, his daughter

Molly became a popular performer, 'with the voice of feathered songster's charm' in the music halls of Paris in the 1780s.

53

PHOTO TAKEN HERE

Training began on the Liberators, with the first operational patrol taking place on September 20. The squadron's first action, and indeed that of the B-24 Liberator, occurred on October 4 during the escort of a convoy some 500 miles west of Ireland. A Focke-Wulf Condor was sighted, chased and slowly overhauled. At a range of 800 yards the front-firing 20mm cannon were fired but the Condor evaded into cloud. When it re-emerged soon afterwards, the Liberator's gunners fired at it but the fight had to be abandoned as their aircraft had received hits. Although one of the engines had to be shut down, the aircraft landed safely back at base.

Atlantic sweeps became the daily task and by December the duties were more varied to include convoy escorts, shipping searches (including one for the cruiser *Prinz Eugen*), and two strikes in the Bay of Biscay in which four ships were attacked. On October 22, a Liberator made a head-on attack at a Focke Wulf Condor, scoring hits but return fire damaged one of the Liberator's propellers. The Condor disappeared into cloud. An hour later a U-Boat was sighted and straddled with depth-charges to no apparent effect. It was January 1942 before another U-Boat came under fire but the result was again unconfirmed.

Flight Lieutenant A. F. Martindale on attachment to the squadron remarked in his report to the Royal Aircraft Establishment at Farnborough that the 1,600-yard runways available were marginal with a fully-loaded Liberator and aircraft were often pulled off the ground at 125 mph with just 50 yards to spare. To service a 110-foot wingspan aircraft in a 90-foot hangar meant that it had to be lifted on trolleys and dragged in sideways. He also commented that 'the aerodrome at Nutts Corner was built on what is partially a bog, and as the runways are of tarmac they give trouble. If an aircraft leaves the runway it gets bogged down at once. The dispersal parks have concrete taxi-tracks and these had been covered with tar and stone chippings for camouflage. The stones came loose and damage to propellers resulted. The hard standings were excellently arranged, being a series of circles round which an aircraft can easily be taxied and are far superior to a narrow track terminating in a concrete square on which it would be impossible to turn a big aircraft.'

Some 31 sorties were flown by No. 120 Squadron in April 1942, ranging from Iceland to the coasts of Portugal and Spain, St Eval being employed as an advanced base

for some of these. On the 25th a U-Boat was depth-charged but, as usual, the result was unknown. For a few weeks in May/June 1942 No. 160 Squadron's Liberators operated with No. 120 Squadron on Atlantic patrols. Early in June the former ceased operations before an overseas posting. No. 220 Squadron had arrived at Nutts Corner in January 1942 with Hudsons and Fortresses. The latter were the Mk I version which had proved sadly lacking over Europe but were now deemed suitable for maritime work. Uneventful anti-submarine patrols were flown by both types until the unit moved to Ballykelly in July 1942.

In June 1942, seven Lancasters of No. 44 Squadron from Waddington arrived for training in anti-submarine tactics and convoy escort. On June 14, a Lancaster on escort duties was forced to ditch, the crew being picked up by a destroyer and taken to Freetown in West Africa. The detachment returned to Lincolnshire in mid-July. This was one of the few 'loans' from a reluctant Bomber Command in response to pleas from Coastal to reinforce its anti-submarine efforts.

Now that more airfields were available in Northern Ireland for long-range patrol,

In the latter stages of the war, Nutts Corner was the preserve of the USAAF, this oblique shot *(left)* being taken by them in June 1943. *Above:* This photograph shows a Spitfire and a Halifax from No. 518 Squadron over-flying the airfield sometime in 1945. When the RAF quit Nutts Corner in 1946, civil air operations were transferred there from Belfast Harbour Airport to make use of its longer runways. It then became known as Belfast-Nutts Corner Airport, but unfortunately it became the location of Northern Ireland's worst air disaster. It was on the evening of January 5, 1953 that a British European Airways Vickers Viking, having flown from Northolt, approached the airfield too low. It hit the posts carrying the approach lights leading to the runway before hitting a mobile beam approach van. It then struck a brick building housing the instrument landing equipment some 200 yards from the threshold causing the aircraft to disintegrate. Of the 34 people aboard, 27 were killed.

Nutts Corner was selected for a new role — that of a transatlantic reception centre. The station, however, was not transferred to No. 44 Group, Ferry Command, until January 19, 1943 and there was limited flying activity while the runways were lengthened and loop hardstandings were built. No. 231 Squadron was a lodger from early January until March 1943 with Tomahawks, Mustangs and Lysanders for army co-operation duties and detachments returned in July. No. 104 (Transport) Operational Training Unit formed here on March 12, equipped with Wellingtons. Some of the crews were posted to British Overseas Airways Corporation on completion of their courses. The OTU disbanded at Nutts Corner in February 1944.

The first USAAF B-17s began to arrive from Gander in Newfoundland in July 1943, B-24s and C-47s following in August until a steady stream built up. Despite the demands of anti-submarine operations, it seems that Nutts Corner had been offered tentatively to the USAAF for an Air Support Command back in February 1942. Nothing came of this, however, and nor did allocation to the Eighth Air Force as a bomber training base in August of the same year. Now, from September 24, 1943, it became Station No. 2 of the European Wing, Air Transport Command. On July 18, 1944, it was re-designated the 1404th Army Air Forces Base Unit. July 1944 proved to be the record-breaking month with the arrival of 372 aircraft. They consisted of 246 B-17s, 90 B-24s, 12 B-26s and 24 C-47s.

With most USAAF North Atlantic deliveries now routeing via Prestwick, the Base Unit was disestablished on October 18, 1944. The same month, No. 1332 (Transport) Heavy Conversion Unit arrived from Longtown in Cumberland with Stirlings, Liberators and Yorks. Towards the end of May 1945 the HCU left for a Yorkshire base. An advance party of Royal Navy personnel arrived in June, preparatory to the station being taken over by that service on July 9. It was commissioned as HMS *Pintail* but did not see much use before being handed back to the RAF on April 1, 1946.

Soon afterwards civil air operations were transferred to Nutts Corner from Sydenham, whose cramped location next to Belfast Harbour precluded development. Ex-RAF buildings were cleverly converted into a rudimentary terminal and the new airport came into use on December 1, 1946. With much improvement it gave good service until the advent of higher performance airliners. The airport's location close to the Belfast hills made comparatively steep approaches necessary and only one of the three runways was suitable for modern aircraft. It was thus replaced by Aldergrove in September 1963.

A section of the A26 Moira Road, running south-west from Nutts Corner roundabout was constructed on the old 04-22 runway. The airfield was used from 1984 to 2004 for events such as the Irish Superbike Championships and Rallycross, but it was restricted due to noise complaints from local residents. A small section of the circuit continues to be used for go-carting. The airfield is still very much recognisable as such, with long stretches of runway and taxi-tracks still intact, as well as some of the dispersal hardstandings.

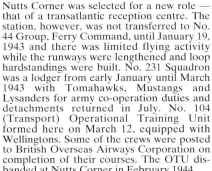

A wolf in sheep's clothing! BEA had ten tri-motor Ju 52s on their books, G-AHOJ being pictured at Nutts Corner in 1947 although the whole fleet appear not to have been used after August that year.

STORNOWAY

The 18-hole golf course at Stornoway on the Isle of Lewis extended for some three and a half miles and was described as having 'good sandy soil with seaside turf, pleasant to play on and pleasing to the eye'.

This station on the Isle of Lewis off the western coast of Scotland grew from a modest pre-war civil airport, itself established on part of a golf course. Pioneer of Scottish aviation, Captain E. E. Fresson of Highland Airways, had been using the beach adjacent to the course for ambulance flights to and from Inverness in the mid-1930s. It was soon obvious that a proper airfield should be established on the island and he was able to demonstrate that four 600-yard strips could be marked out if some bunkers were filled in and that it would still be possible to retain 18 holes. Predictably, the golf club did not want the ground altered and negotiations dragged on for four years until the site was finally approved. Unfortunately, completion coincided with the outbreak of war and it never came into use. The Air Ministry then obliterated the golf course and built a large four-runway airfield for Coastal Command instead. It was to be 1944 before the planned Inverness-Stornoway service began.

The new airfield had a main runway of 1,800 yards, later lengthened to 2,000 yards and three subsidiaries, two of them 1,350 yards and one of 880 yards. A number of frying-pan hardstandings were dispersed around the western perimeter track. Ten T2 hangars of the less weather-prone half-size were erected and the initial bomb storage total was 162 tons. It was also nominated for use by Fighter Command if this proved necessary.

The RAF Station Headquarters was established at Stornoway in April 1941 and a detachment of Ansons from No. 612 Squadron soon arrived but it was the end of July before a full operational squadron was based there. This was No. 48 Squadron from Hooton Park. Even then, some of its Ansons were detached to other aerodromes such as Aldergrove and Islay. The rather more potent Lockheed Hudson had almost entirely replaced the Ansons by the time the squadron moved to Skitten in October 1941.

Mention should also be made of shore station HMS *Mentor* at Stornoway Harbour, from which Walruses of 701 Squadron operated between November 1940 and June 1941. Other naval activity at the nearby airfield included 827 Squadron's Albacores, here from March to May 1941 and 842, a Wildcat squadron, here in August/September 1944.

CLUB HOUSE

The golf course had its formal opening on August 27, 1913. It had been developed over many years with crofters retaining grazing rights . . . that is until 1940 when the Air Ministry summarily requisitioned it for the construction of an airfield for Coastal Command.

At the beginning of April 1942, No. 500 Squadron arrived from Norfolk with more Hudsons, detaching some to Limavady to increase the radius of action for U-Boat patrols. Two submarines were attacked in April 1942 but in neither case was there a definite sinking. Success came to Flying Officer M. A. Ensor on August 24 when he blew the bows off a surfaced U-Boat. He was awarded the DFC for this exploit but on a later patrol he dropped his depth-charges only to see a very dead whale rise to the surface, a sad and all too common occurrence in this type of warfare.

Stornoway was not a popular posting because of local restrictions on drinking hours and the playing of football on Sundays. A story is told of a No. 48 Squadron pilot who, after returning from a patrol on a Sunday, was making his way to Station HQ, via a path which was a public right of way. He encountered an elderly lady who proceeded to hit him about the head with her umbrella for daring to fly on the Sabbath! Another incident also occurred on a Sunday, when dockers at the harbour refused to work on the Sabbath to unload a consignment of aviation spirit. As it was vital for the squadron to receive the fuel immediately, RAF personnel ended-up unloading the cargo themselves. One crew rebelled, it is said, and beat up the town in a Hudson at 3 a.m. on a Sunday

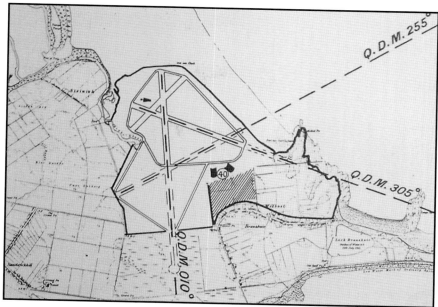

The wartime magnetic bearings (QDM) of the runway approaches have changed considerably with the shift in the magnetic variation.

In 1945 the Air Ministry decided to acquire the whole of the airfield so the golf club received compensation of £12,028. Now the lengthened main runway is 2,500 yards and the secondary 1,100 yards. The NE-SW runway has been withdrawn from use.

A crew from No. 502 Squadron approach their Handley Page Halifax Mk III for an anti-submarine sortie from Stornoway in February 1945.

morning. Unluckily for them, an admiral was on board a battleship moored in the bay, which probably contributed to their swift transfer to a mainland squadron!

No. 500 Squadron left for St Eval at the end of August 1942, its patrols being taken over by No. 58 Squadron with Whitleys, until this squadron moved to Hampshire in December. Stornoway was then occupied by No. 303 Ferry Training Unit, a lodger unit in No. 17 Group, forming here in December 1942. The unit was tasked with holding up to 20 Wellingtons and their crews at any one time and dispatching them to overseas stations.

During June 1943, about a hundred officers and men from the USAAF were brought in to handle the ever-increasing numbers of American aircraft using the airfield as a transatlantic staging post. There had been spasmodic visits since July 1942 when some of the first P-38 Lightnings to reach Britain had flown in via Greenland and Iceland with a B-17 to navigate for them. In June 1943 alone, 68 aircraft passed through on delivery. The unit involved was the 1405th Army Air Forces Base Unit. The Americans objected to the allocated call-sign 'Pigsty' but were over-ruled by the RAF! At the same time the airfield call-sign was 'Breadcrust'.

In July 1943, around the same time as the USAAF began a shuttle weather reconnaissance service between Iceland, Stornoway and Prestwick with three B-25 Mitchells, No. 518 Squadron formed at Stornoway for similar meteorological duties with Halifaxes. Perhaps because of the congestion caused by the FTU and ever-increasing American ferry flights, No. 518 Squadron moved to Tiree in September 1943.

Then, in December, the main runway which ran almost north-south was extended to 2,000 yards to better accommodate larger aircraft. As part of this expansion, Sandwick Hill to the west of the airfield was removed, as it presented a hazard to aircraft landing from the west. Meanwhile, the station had been transferred temporarily to Transport Command in November 1943. No. 303 FTU continued to operate but moved to Talbenny in South Wales in March 1944.

Stornoway's most active contribution to the war effort came when it was selected as the base for a pair of Halifax squadrons, which wreaked havoc on German shipping in Scandinavian waters during the closing months of the war. By August 1944, potential prey off the French coast was non-existent so Nos. 58 and 502 Squadrons were moved to the Outer Hebrides and commenced anti-submarine sorties. Again, there were no results so at the beginning of October they were ordered to switch their efforts to night anti-shipping patrols. Their general area of operation would be the Skagerrak and Kattegat, but they were to concentrate on the shipping lanes between Oslo, Kristiansund and the Danish ports.

During October, the two squadrons operating in conjunction made 27 attacks but as usual with night engagements results were difficult to assess, despite the use of parachute flares. One exception occurred on October 25 when a No. 58 Squadron Halifax set a motor vessel on fire with a stick of bombs. The occasional U-Boat was found lurking off the Norwegian coast and on October 27 two 502 aircraft shared in the sinking of the last of many submarines credited to the squadron.

At the end of April 1945 the Stornoway crews received a letter from the Air Officer Commanding, Coastal Command, saying in part 'Hearty congratulations on the fine

An early post-war shot of a BEA Douglas Pionair Dakota on the apron. G-AGJW was sold to Ghana Airways in December 1958, and British European Airways was merged with British Overseas Airways Corporation to form British Airways in March 1974.

operational achievement, particularly during the last two months. You have sunk more than 25,000 tons of shipping and damaged 50,000 tons since the beginning of the year.'

In the last month of the war, the Halifaxes reached a new peak of success and shipping movements between Norway and Denmark almost ceased. On the basis of tons sunk or damaged per sortie, for the three months ending April 10, 1945, the Halifax's effectiveness was claimed to be three or four times that of the average for all other types of Coastal Command aircraft, including Beaufighters and Mosquitos.

On May 10, 1945 the squadrons' work was rewarded when four aircraft flew over the western Baltic. Their crews estimated that they sighted over one hundred enemy craft from U-Boats to houseboats, all heavily laden with German troops heading towards the Kiel area and all flying white flags. Their job completed, the two squadrons disbanded at Stornoway on May 25.

The airfield passed into civil hands in 1946 and in 1948 it saw the start and finish of the first double-crossing of the Atlantic by jet aircraft — Vampires of RAF Fighter Command. In 1973 it was designated a Strike Command forward operating base which resulted in the main runway being lengthened to 7,500ft and other improvements, as well as the construction of an entirely new bomb store. This role ceased in the 1980s and the airfield is now operated by HIAL, a company controlled by the Scottish Government.

Most of the more recent military buildings, including the NATO bomb store and a large Gaydon hangar are in good condition. Wartime remains are sparse but the original bomb storage area remains substantially complete to the west of the airfield. The two short runways are disused, as is most of the western perimeter track. Near the small terminal is a memorial to RAF Stornoway and those who lost their lives flying from here.

No. 502's sister squadron, No. 58, was also operating from Stornoway against enemy shipping off Norway and Denmark. This crew were pictured with their Halifax Mk II.

With the disbanding of Coastal Command in 1969 — or rather its absorption into the new Strike Command — the air/sea rescue role around Britain's coastline was maintained by the Royal Air Force and Royal Navy. However, from 2015 the task has been privatised, now coming under the Maritime & Coastguard Agency. The ASR aircraft are based at ten locations around the United Kingdom including Stornoway where these Sikorsky S-92s were pictured by Steve Branley.

STRANRAER/WIG BAY

In the far south-west of Scotland, RAF flying boats had been using Loch Ryan as an 'advanced alighting area' for landings and take-offs since 1929. It was therefore an obvious choice for a more permanent base situated at the southern end of this 12-mile sea loch.

Contemporary official documents describe it thus: 'Loch Ryan provides good shelter from all directions except northerly, highest ground being on the east side. With north and north-west winds a rough sea may be expected. Stranraer Harbour, enclosed by the East and West piers, provides little further protection and is very shallow, although a flying boat could safely be beached in an emergency. In north-west gales there is a good anchorage in Wig Bay, situated about five cables [about 1,000 yards] from Kirkcolm Point and three miles from Stranraer. The harbour is used to an increasing extent by shipping which is anchored to the easterly side of the loch, whilst RAF marine craft may be at moorings on the west side.' The position and extent of the landing area at both high and low water was stated to be unlimited in the loch but landings should not be attempted in the harbour and while 'there are no obstructions in approach to the mooring buoys, it is inadvisable to taxi further than 50 yards beyond the second trot towards Stranraer town'.

An emergency slipway for beaching all types of flying boats was constructed at Rock McGibbon on the south-east side of the loch and equipped with all the necessary tackle for hoisting and securing. Lead-in guidance marks consisted of a white triangle and vertical white bar marked out on the hillside. The North West Castle Hotel in Stranraer was taken over as the Officers' Mess, and the Masonic Hall served as the Airmen's Mess.

Appropriately, the first aircraft to be based there were the obsolete Supermarine Stranraers of No. 240 Squadron which

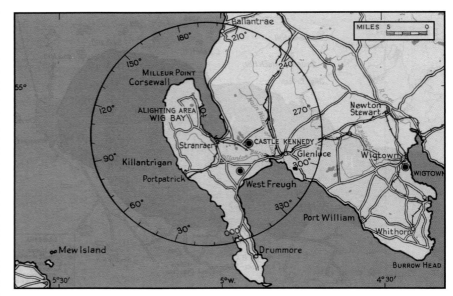

Wig Bay flying boat base, 3¾ miles north of Stranraer. This 1945 plan marked 'Confidential', notes that Lough Erne is 57 miles away and Pembroke Dock 224.5 miles. the call-sign for the watch office on the west side of the bay on 6440kcs was 'Figtree'.

arrived in July 1940. Anti-submarine patrols were flown without any sightings but four aircraft were lost, sunk at their moorings in gales. For reinforcement, some Short Lerwick twin-engined flying boats arrived from No. 209 Squadron's main base at Pembroke Dock. In December, the entire squadron moved to Stranraer and began operational patrols with this aircraft, a short-lived type that had already proved unsuitable. One Lerwick suffered a fatal accident in January 1941 and the Commanding Officer failed to return from patrol in February. The squadron moved to Lough Erne in March, soon to be re-equipped with Catalinas. No. 240 Squadron soon followed, also for Catalina conversion.

At this point, RAF Stranraer reverted to a training role when the Flying Boat Training Squadron which had moved north from vulnerable Calshot the previous summer took over the station. Now redesignated No. 4 (Coastal) Operational Training Unit, its equipment was a mixture of out-dated Singapores, Londons, Stranraers and Lerwicks, but one of the first of the newly-delivered Catalinas had just been allocated. The stay was short, however, and the OTU moved to Invergordon in June 1941, although from March 1942 its initial flying boat training was detached to Stranraer. Part of the reason was that it was thought a good idea to disperse some of the aircraft away from the vulnerable east coast.

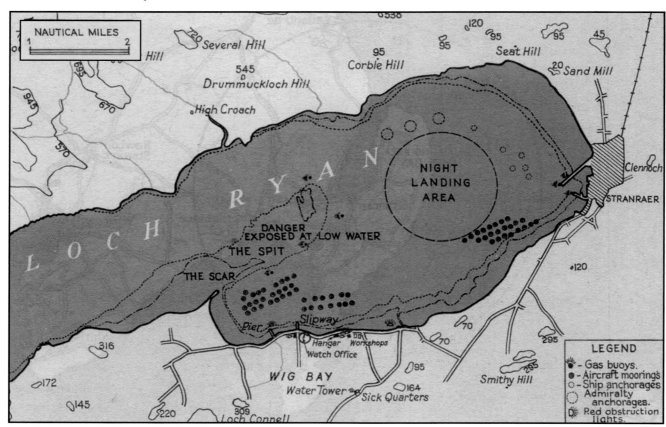

What appears to be a Supermarine Stranraer of No. 240 Squadron and a visiting Sunderland ride at anchor in the bay in November 1940.

The flying boat moorings in sheltered Wig Bay eventually formed the basis of a new RAF station on the nearby shoreline, known as Wig Bay. Opening in March 1942, it housed No. 1 Flying Boat Servicing Unit which was absorbed into No. 57 Maintenance Unit in October 1943. Although RAF Stranraer remained a separate entity until it closed in February 1944, the two stations were inevitably interlinked. The MU's task was the preparation, modification, repair and storage of Sunderlands, Catalinas and the new — and soon proven unsuitable — Martin Mariner. This work went on until war's end, followed by the mass scrapping of surplus flying boats. The MU disbanded in October 1951 with its duties mostly taken over by Short Brothers under contract until the base finally closed in November 1955.

One J Type and two Shetland Hangars were erected at Wig Bay, along with seven large and ten small flying boat pens. These were designated Type 'W' and Type 'A' Pens, respectively. Concrete hardstandings for up to 150 flying boats were constructed and several slipways were provided. All of the hangars and pens are long gone, although their floors and the grooves for the door runners are still in situ. Some of the extensive hardstandings now serve as a ready-made caravan park and a few buildings are dotted around the area in various states of disrepair.

Standing instructions advised pilots that although Loch Ryan provided good shelter from all directions, a rough sea should be expected if the wind came from a northerly or north-westerly direction. Here, a Stranraer comes to grief — possibly K7301 of No. 240 Squadron — which sank in a gale in August 1940.

In March 1941, Wig Bay became solely a training base, these Catalina Mk Is belonging to the newly-formed No. 4 (Coastal) Operational Training Unit.

Ken Pearson matched the photograph from the old slipway, looking north-west.

In March 2015 an investigation was mounted by Scotland's Coastal Heritage At Risk group to see what still existed of the wartime structures at Wig Bay which had been abandoned by the RAF in 1957. Armed with plans and aerial photos of the site, a diverse survey team comprising engineers, archaeologists, electricians, together with two ex-RAF personnel who served there, explored the remains, right down to establishing that the bricks used in the buildings came from Dunaskin Brickworks, part of Dalmellington Iron Works in East Ayrshire. *Above:* Derek Fitzgerald had this photo of a Sunderland sitting on the compass base, vital yet often forgotten. The tractor in the background would have towed the machine around 360 degrees while its compass was checked and adjusted. *Right:* Here members of the team inspect the boiler house which heated the whole base from eight coal-fired boilers via a network of undergound pipes. The coal was delivered through the large openings in the wall. *Below:* Bill Sandiford, one of the volunteers in the group, even traced the location of a childhood photo as he lived on the RAF site where his father worked as a flight engineer. The family home is on the left with the rear wall of one of the maintenance hangars on the right. In the background is the boiler house.

TIREE

Tiree, pictured on August 11, 1941, in the early stages of construction. The view is looking north. This was one of the island bases off the western coast of Scotland (the others being Benbecula and Stornoway) which gave Coastal Command vital extended range.

As with several outlying Scottish RAF stations, Tiree in the Outer Hebrides owed its location to a pre-war landing strip, in this case one known as The Reef. It had been selected by Midland and Scottish Airways in 1934 as an intermediate stop on a new Glasgow to Skye service but a rental dispute delayed the start of a daily summer service until 1937. This continued with some breaks during the Second World War when a civilian grass strip remained open alongside the sprawling RAF aerodrome. In 1940 when Atlantic convoys were forced to re-route to the north of Ireland to avoid Occupied France, new airfields in the Western Isles became an urgent priority. The civil site was requisitioned and contractors imported hordes of unruly labourers, including, it is said, borrowed convicts from the mainland.

Tiree was planned for a double role in supporting one general reconnaissance squadron along with a fighter squadron. The defence of the Western Isles was seen as a priority now that Norway was under German occupation. Thus two separate operations

blocks were built, one close to the road on the west side of the airfield, and another for the fighters about 1,100 yards beyond the eastern perimeter. The fighter role was supported by dispersed sleeping shelters, some of them close to the half-size T2 hangars off the southern perimeter track. No dispersal pens were provided, so presumably the fighter aircraft would have been hangared for weather protection. Eventually, Tiree had a total of ten half T2s and the main runway had been extended to 2,000 yards, with two others of 1,840 and 1,400 yards.

The station was first occupied in November 1941 but electricity and water had yet to be laid on. The first Christmas was a miserable affair, the only highlight — if can be called that — was an officer playing in the New Year on his saxophone! Life improved when Tiree became operational and a roster was kept by the station adjutant of all personnel who wished to travel on leave to the mainland. When possible they were given seats on the Station Communications Flight aircraft or any other available service machine.

The Hudsons of No. 224 Squadron arrived from Limavady in April 1942 and were dispersed on the adjacent civilian landing ground, and Wellingtons of No. 304 Squadron flew in during May. However, Wellingtons and Hudsons lacked the range to venture very far out over the Atlantic where they were desperately needed for convoy protection. Thus, No. 304 Squadron was transferred to south-west Wales and No. 224 Squadron converted to Liberators at Tiree during July 1942. The extremely long range of this aircraft compared to its contemporaries successfully plugged the gap in air cover over the middle of the Atlantic. In September 1942 No. 224 Squadron was sent to Hampshire, its task at Tiree being taken over by Northern Ireland-based aircraft.

The proximity of the seashore to the base resulted in an incident when windows in the Officers' Mess were broken by a mine exploding on the beach. On another occasion in 1942 the RAF helped rescue the crew of a fishing trawler that had been driven aground and was threatening to break

The runways were extended later to permit the employment of the heavy long-range aircraft.

taken. Shipping observations were an important secondary role and during briefing the expected positions of the convoys would be pointed out. The convoys had hitherto been adhering to radio silence so their positions had to be estimated, unless confirmed visually.

The code-name for the second flight pattern was 'Bismuth', ranging 700 miles towards Iceland and then turning on a northern leg before returning to base. Each pattern would be flown about midday and the other around midnight. The Halifaxes were fitted with radio-altimeters, essential for flight down to 50ft and sometimes even lower. The altimeters were commonly calibrated by using the known height of the 138-foot Skerryvore lighthouse when skimming a wingtip over the lighthouse would confirm the instrument's accuracy.

Weather squadrons did not fly at set altitudes but followed certain pressure readings in millibars in order to provide a consistent reading for weather reports. Outward bound, the aircraft would be climbed to 850 millibars which could be anywhere between 800 and 2,000 feet. The climb was regulated to level out every 15 millibars and the met observer would take readings which were then radioed back by number code every 50 miles. At the extremity of the sortie the aircraft would be climbed to the 500-millibar level, an altitude of between 17,000 and 20,000 feet. The navigator would ensure that the final climb was done in an orbit, keeping as near as possible to the same point on the surface. The return journey was maintained at the maximum height until the halfway stage was reached, then a regulated descent leveling off temporarily at each 50 millibars would be commenced. This was continued right down to sea level to ascertain ground level temperature and pressures. The aircraft would then be climbed back to 950 millibars — approximately 1,500 feet — for a normal approach to Tiree.

up on the rocks. Another notable event was when a tanker ran aground and the RAF helped evacuate the crew with the aid of a Breeches Buoy. It appears that they also rescued some of the ship's liquor supply at the same time!

Tiree was downgraded to Care and Maintenance in October 1942, not being reactivated until September 1943 when No. 518 Squadron's Halifaxes moved in from Stornoway. They were a Meteorological Reconnaissance unit, with the apt motto in Gaelic 'We Hold the Key' and were to remain in occupation until September 1945. The squadron was associated with the Met Conversion Unit which trained Halifax crews between October 1943 until it was disbanded in February 1944. Another specialist unit appeared in February 1944: No. 281 Squadron from Thornaby equipped with lifeboat-carrying Warwicks for air-sea rescue. It remained active until September 1945, although the HQ had moved to Northern Ireland in February that year, leaving just a detachment at Tiree.

Tiree's war was relatively low-key but the Met Squadron played a vital role in conjunction with sister squadron, No. 517 in Wales. The raw information regarding weather systems approaching Europe was sent direct to the Meteorological Office. It was then used in the production of weather forecasts on which Bomber Command and USAAF planners based their operations. There were four daily met flights out over the Atlantic, two of them code-named 'Mercer', which tracked due west for 700 nautical miles, climbing to an altitude of between 18 and 20,000 feet. The aircraft would be leveled off every 2,000 feet to take a complete set of weather observations. On the route back, near to the halfway stage and descending over a specific point, more weather observations would be

Today all take-offs and landings are carried out on the NE-SW runway.

The squadron lost several aircraft in accidents, the worst occuring on August 16, 1944 when two Halifaxes collided in low cloud in the airfield circuit. One was returning from an operational sortie with radio failure and the other was on a local flight. A total of 16 aircrew of four nationalities lost their lives, one of them being the grandson of the Czech Foreign Minister, Jan Masaryk. Initially all 16 were laid to rest at the island's Soroby Burial Ground, but after the war nine were reinterred in other cemeteries at the request of their families. On the 70th anniversary, a memorial to the victims was unveiled and dedicated at Tiree Airport. Attending the ceremony was Antonín Hradilek, Deputy Ambassador of the Embassy of the Czech Republic, families of the fallen airmen, local dignitaries, representatives of the air forces of Australia, Canada and the UK, the memorials project team and many Tiree residents.

From January 1945, No. 518 Squadron began carrying depth-charges in case an enemy submarine should be sighted. There were, however, no encounters and the squadron moved to Aldergrove in September. No. 281 Squadron — by now reduced to a detachment — also left for Northern Ireland.

Graham Sharpe photographed the pre-war civilian club house which became the RAF control tower during the war.

It was replaced by a modern air traffic control tower alongside the new terminal building, photographed in 2005 by Jim Murdoch.

At the beginning of July 1946, Tiree was handed over to the Ministry of Civil Aviation for air links to the mainland, a service that continues to the present day. As is customary with wartime aerodromes adapted as airports to support remote communities, maintenance costs have been reduced to a minimum by closing sections of the three runways not needed, and almost the entire perimeter track apart from a short section joining the modern parking apron to the threshold of the N-S runway. Access to and from other directions has to be done by back-tracking.

Despite demolitions and tidying up, Tiree shows much evidence of its wartime role in the number and variety of still extant buildings. Crofters were allowed to relocate some of the Nissen huts at no cost. They benefitted from the fact that early in 1944, the Air Ministry Works Directorate had finally responded to endless requests to provide thicker gauge steel sheeting to cover the station's huts, which were not standing up to the climatic conditions. The station diesel-electric generator sheds now house a more powerful development of that system capable of taking over in the event of a power failure in the cable to the mainland. Many buildings, including the former NAAFI/Airmen's dining hall, are in use today.

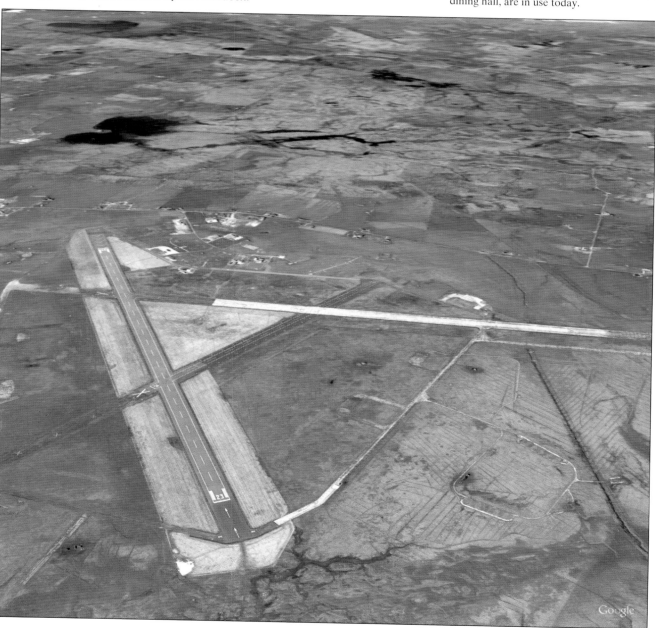

WARMWELL

Known when it opened on May 1, 1937 as Woodsford, this station was built as No. 6 Armament Practice Camp to accommodate squadron detachments using the gunnery and bombing ranges located in the bay west of Portland. These consisted of floating targets in the sea and static ones constructed on the Chesil Bank. Drogue towing aircraft accommodated aerial gunnery target practice. Soon it was hosting a steady stream of operational aircraft and, from January 1938, regular attachments from Flying Training Schools. In April 1938 it became No. 6 Armament Training School and a few months later probably because of confusion with Avro's factory airfield at Woodford, near Manchester, it was renamed Warmwell after an adjacent village. The grass surface had a longest run of 1,900

yards and a 12ft wide vehicle track surrounded it. Two Bellman hangars were constructed early in 1940 and were later supplemented by eight blisters.

After war was declared, Warmwell remained a training station and the Central Gunnery School formed here on November 6, 1939 with the aim of improving the standard of RAF gunnery. The latest in a succession of Warmwell unit redesignations was No. 10 Bombing & Gunnery School which formed out of No. 10 Air Observers School on January 1, 1940. When the naval base at Portland came under threat once the Luftwaffe were using French bases, fighter squadrons were detached to the station from Middle Wallop on a rotational basis. No. 13 Squadron kept a section of Lysanders at the

airfield during 1940 flying anti-invasion patrols. The personnel eventually formed the Warmwell detachment of No. 276 Air-Sea Rescue Squadron.

On August 25, 1940, the station was bombed by seven Ju 88s, causing damage to the hangars and sick quarters and leaving a scattering of unexploded bombs over the airfield. It was extremely fortunate that there were no casualties. When the Luftwaffe resumed their attacks, it was with small numbers of low-flying aircraft. On April 1, 1941, three He 111s appeared over the airfield with no prior warning. The main hangar, which had been constructed in 1937, was destroyed, the station workshops were hit and ten men were killed and 18 injured. Four nights' later, the 'Q' site decoy at Knighton, three miles to

The road which bisected the camp can be seen crossing left to right from the memorial. Three local roads have been named Spitfire Close, Hurricane Close and Airfield Close in what is now Crossways village. The airfield memorial was unveiled in 1989.

So what still remains? The former station gymnasium/church is still in use as Crossways Village Hall.

the east, was bombed. In May there were two night raids which destroyed two aircraft and left the grass runways heavily cratered. These proved to be the last attacks on Warmwell.

No. 10 B&GS moved to Scotland in July 1940, as did Central Gunnery School in June 1941. Shortly after the departure of CGS, No. 10 Group opened its own Armament Practice Camp at Warmwell, forming No. 1487 (Target Towing) Flight to service squadrons operating within the Group, including Fleet Air Arm units.

Other units used the airfield to convert to new types of aircraft and the Canadian No. 402 Squadron worked up on bomb-carrying Hurricanes. On November 1, 1941 it flew its first sorties when eight Hurricanes dropped pairs of 250lb bombs on Berck-sur-Mer airfield. The so-called Hurribombers made further forays throughout the winter until March 1942, when the squadron moved to Colerne. Another Hurribomber squadron at Warmwell in 1942-43 was No. 175 which attacked enemy shipping and coastal targets which included airfields.

The Westland Whirlwinds of No. 263 Squadron were here between September 1942 and December 1943. They were fitted out as fighter-bombers for attacks on shipping and airfields and continued the work initiated by the Hurricanes. Typhoons of No. 266 also operated from Warmwell from September 1942 until the beginning of January 1943. Their duties included the interception of low-level fighter-bomber attacks and escort for raids on the French coast. They were replaced by the Typhoons of No. 257 Squadron on similar operations until January 1944. These heavy aircraft often had to operate from Ibsley because of the limitations of Warmwell's grass surface.

Although in poor condition, two Bellman hangars remain on the southern side of the airfield and are now used by a local farmer.

When the US Ninth Air Force began to build up its strength in England for tactical operations preparatory to invasion, Warmwell was allocated to the Americans becoming Station 454. It had been earmarked for Eighth Air Force fighter use in August 1942 but the offer was not taken up. Its new occupants were the three squadrons of P-38 Lightnings which comprised the 474th Fighter Group. The USAAF sometimes referred to Warmwell as Moreton, after another local village. The P-38s ranged across northern France on bombing and strafing missions and on one occasion went as far as Orly airfield, south of Paris. On occasion they also flew fighter escort to USAAF bomber raids. The unit moved to the Continent early in August 1944.

Warmwell's other function was air-sea rescue and this served as most of its Coastal Command presence from October 1941, when a detachment of No. 276 Squadron arrived. It was destined to be here until April 1944 operating at various times Lysanders, Walrus, Defiants, Spitfires and Hurricanes. They were replaced by a detachment of No. 275 Squadron, to cover ever-increasing Channel operations. The Ansons, Spitfires and Walrus moved to Bolt Head, Devon in August 1944.

No. 17 Armament Practice Camp meanwhile had assumed the responsibilities for fighter gunnery and bombing training and were joined in November by No. 14 APC. Both APCs were exceptionally busy with squadrons flying in from the Continent for

Best of all is the control tower. In 1938 it would have cost a few pounds to build . . . now in 2015 it is up for sale for £650,000!

Remains of a structure in West Knighton Wood, most probably a sleeping shelter for night duty crews. Aldon Ferguson who explored Warmwell found that the trees in the area are covered with inscriptions, carved by long-forgotten airmen.

This group of pilots are surveying the aerodrome from one of the revetments on the edge of the wood.

Looking north from the southernmost dispersal on the western side.

gunnery practice. They included a series of Typhoon and Tempest units. This activity went on until September 1945 with the station closing in November 1945.

On the east side of the airfield the small hamlet of Crossways has expanded and now occupies the former domestic site. Two of the roads in the development are named Spitfire Close and Hurricane Close and a third is Airfield Close. The old gymnasium is now the village hall and the watch office has been converted into a dwelling called Egdon House. It has been extensively modified, however, and is not easily recognisable as such. A small plaque on the front explains its origins. The house is located on the north-east corner of what is left of the airfield, to the west of Crossways. Both Bellman hangars survive for farm use and other buildings exist in the local woodland areas, including some fighter dispersal pens but sand and gravel quarrying has obliterated most of the grass runway area.

In Crossways is an information board about the station history, alongside a stone with the inscription: '1937-1946 A memorial dedicated to those men and women who whilst serving with the Royal Air Force, United States Army Air Force, Military and Allied forces at RAF Warmwell made the supreme sacrifice in defence of freedom. Lest we forget. 11th June 1989.'

Immediately to the north of the airfield site was a World War I airship station known as Moreton. It was still under construction when the war ended so was never used. There are some areas of concrete still remaining, including a hangar base.

Workings to extract gravel have slowly wiped out the aerodrome . . . probably one of the saddest of those used by Coastal Command.

BEAULIEU

The airfield at Beaulieu photographed by the US 30th Photographic Reconnaissance Squadron on March 4, 1944 — three days after the Ninth Air Force took it over in readiness for operations leading up to D-Day. Note the wiggly anti-glider trenches.

Although there had been a World War I aerodrome of the same name, the later one was built on an entirely different site on the opposite side of the Lymington to Beaulieu road. For those unfamiliar with the name, it is pronounced 'Bewlee' and located quite close to Southampton but on the opposite side of Southampton Water. Contractors J. Mowlem & Co Ltd began construction on Hatchet Moor in September 1941. There were to be three runways: one of 2,000 yards and two of 1,400 yards, and 50 frying-pan hardstandings were distributed round the perimeter track. The original intention was for it to be a satellite of Thorney Island but plans changed as it now became necessary to increase the accommodation to cater for two, rather than the single general reconnaissance squadron which had been originally envisaged. The dispersed living and communal quarters were distributed in the New Forest to the north-west, while bomb storage was concentrated at a safe distance to the north. Two T2 hangars were erected but two others never got further than the concrete floors. One of these was utilised for the foundation of a blister hangar later in the war.

The station opened in August 1942, although it was still unfinished and initially some personnel had to live in tents. The following month, No. 224 Squadron's Liberators arrived from Scotland to reinforce

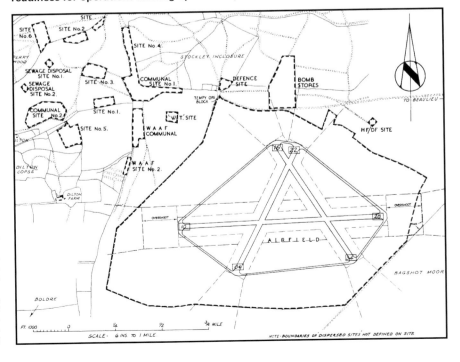

LADYCROSS LODGE

Site No. 1 comprised officers', sergeants' and airmen's quarters, latrines, ablutions and drying rooms and the contractor's canteen. Site No. 2: Sergeants' and airmen's ablutions, WAAFs Mess and quarters, plus further airmen's and Sergeants' barracks. Site No. 3: More huts for officers, sergeants and airmen with the fuel compound behind a chain-link fence. There was also a disused hut left by Mowlems, the contractors. Site No. 4: More quarters for all ranks plus the Operations Block and transformer sub-station. Site No. 5: More barrack hutting for officers, sergeants and airmen with another fuel compound. Site No. 6: Additional quarters for all ranks. Communal Site No. 1 including the post office, ration store, institute, tailors, barber and shoemaker shop, gymnasium, dining hall, sewage pump house and fire tender building. Communal Site No. 2 contained the catering office, Sergeants' Mess and dining room, stores for grocery and local produce, squash court and showers and baths.

No. 19 Group's operations against a renewed U-Boat offensive from the bases in Brittany. On October 20, a U-Boat was attacked but the exploding depth-charges damaged the aircraft's elevators and rendered it almost uncontrollable. A successful crash-landing was made at Predannack. The patrols continued with no confirmed results until a move was made to St Eval in April 1943.

The then Wing Commander A. E. Clouston, who was posted to Beaulieu to take command of No. 224 Squadron, summed up

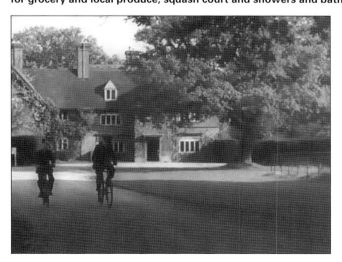

The Czechoslovakian Film Unit produced a documentary called *Night and Day* featuring the activities of No. 311 Squadron. Initially in RAF Bomber Command, it was transferred to Coastal in April 1942, moving to Beaulieu in May 1943. This still shows officers relaxing at their Mess located in Ladycross Lodge.

A Liberator Mark III of No. 224 Squadron undergoing a daily inspection by ground staff at Beaulieu in December 1942. The American-built Consolidated Liberator was Coastal Command's most effective anti-submarine aircraft. Very long range variants, flying from Northern Ireland and Iceland, were able to reach the mid-Atlantic 'Gap' — the area of ocean where previously U-Boats had been able to operate unchallenged from the air. Numbers were limited at first, but Liberators eventually became the most successful U-Boat killers in Coastal Command.

the strain of patrol duties in his book *The Dangerous Skies* (Cassell & Co Ltd 1954): 'Our days were long and tiring. We spent from 14 to 16 hours in the air hunting for submarines, and there was no let-up or relaxation. A perpetual lookout had to be maintained. Binoculars ceaselessly searched the sea and sky. Eyes never left the radar screen that scanned the ocean for submarines. The eight members of the crew worked hard as a team all the time they were on patrol.'

No. 224's replacement in May 1943 was No. 311 Squadron which converted from Wellingtons onto the Liberator at Beaulieu and recommenced operations in August. The first days proved disastrous, with the loss of the Commanding Officer on the first anti-submarine patrol, followed a few days later by two separate Liberator crashes in the vicinity of the airfield. On the 30th an attacking Ju 88 was shot down but the aircraft returned to base with a dead gunner. During September, No. 53 Squadron was transferred from Thorney Island and both squadrons were soon engaged in operations over the Bay. With the aid of a Leigh Light, No. 53 claimed Beaulieu's first confirmed U-Boat kill on December 13, 1943. The captain, Squadron Leader G. Crawford, AFC, was awarded an immediate DFC for this action.

Aldon Ferguson who visited the airfield explains that this is the only remaining dispersal (No. 19) in the south-eastern corner.

No. 311 Squadron's Liberators were attacked by anything up to eight Ju 88s on a number of occasions but survived by skilled evasive action. Several U-Boats were depth-charged with unknown results, apart from one which was credited jointly to No. 311 Squadron and a US Navy Liberator unit. The squadron's most successful operation occurred on December 27, 1943 when a German blockade runner, the MV *Alsterufer* was sunk in the Bay of Biscay. She had sailed from Japan with a cargo which included 344 tons of wolfram (raw tungsten), vital for Germany's war effort. A barrage of bombs and rockets left her a blazing wreck, despite heavy return fire.

Another still from *Night and Day*. Aldon says that this is where the dispersal joins the perimeter track.

No. 53 Squadron left for St Eval in January 1944 and No. 311 went to Predannack in February. After a temporary occupation by several Typhoon squadrons, the airfield was transferred to No. 10 Group, Air Defence of Great Britain, in readiness for the arrival of American units. A Ninth Air Force Thunderbolt group was then based for bomber escort and dive bombing in the build-up to D-Day. When they moved to France at the end of June, a B-26 Marauder unit replaced them in a general move closer to northern France, as the fighter bombers vacated the English forward airfields.

After the Marauders left for a French base at the end of August, Beaulieu remained empty until the Airborne Forces Experimental Establishment started arriving from Yorkshire during December 1944. Their activities took in a very wide range, ranging from gliders and early helicopters to paratroop and freight transports. The old airfield site across the road served as a convenient drop zone. With new aircraft types, equipment and techniques coming along, work carried on right up to September 1950 when AFEE was absorbed by the Aeroplane and Armament Experimental Establishment at Boscombe Down, Wiltshire. Beaulieu then reverted to Care and Maintenance but was allotted to the US Third Air Force as a standby base in April 1953. Interesting, as it had been considered for upgrade to a Very Heavy Bomber base in the later stages of the war. No flying took place, however, and the station was returned to Air Ministry control in 1955 and was finally restored to the Forestry Commission in November 1959.

Eventually, the runways were torn up, leaving only a small section near the road which is used as a model aircraft flying area. Despite this, the imprint of the entire airfield is plainly visible from the air, as are the uncovered 'BL' airfield identification letters in concrete in front of the long-gone watch tower.

A mass take-off by the 365th Fighter Group before they moved to France in June.

The same location at the threshold of the E-W runway. The patch of light concrete marks the spot where a plaque was fixed in memory of Squadron Leader David Sleep (see page 232) who died on June 29, 1989.

A significant relic of Beaulieu's past lives on in the area. The blister hangar was dismantled after the war and taken to New Milton. Here it was re-erected on a site on the corner of the junction between Ashley Lane and Ashley Common Road and became part of a garage. Another survivor, the tall water tower, remains in good condtion close to Roundhill campsite. Just across the Beaulieu road are a few hut bases, but these date from the adjacent World War I site.

The East Boldre Village Hall is the sole remaining building from the First World War and the identification letters in front of the demolished control tower have now been uncovered from World War II.

BENSON

Unique among Coastal Command bases, Benson's position in south Oxfordshire was very remote from the sea for reasons which shall be explained.

It started life as a typical RAF 'expansion' station and opened officially on April 1, 1939. Four C Type hangars dominated the south-eastern perimeter and the administration and accommodation buildings were concentrated nearby. With scant regard for future requirements, the airfield was grass surfaced.

Early in April 1939, Nos. 103 and 150 Squadrons moved in with Fairey Battles, taking them to France in September. The intention was to form a Group Pool here with Whitleys, a forerunner of the soon-to-be-introduced Operational Training Units (OTU). However, test landings soon proved the grass surface to be inadequate so the Whitleys went to Abingdon instead. They were replaced by two Battle squadrons that formed another Group Pool. Reinforced by a third Battle unit, they amalgamated to form No. 12 OTU in April 1940 and began training replacements for the Battle crews lost in France. Re-equipment with Wellingtons was now in the offing but, although a perimeter track had just been completed, there were still no hard runways. The problem was solved by the new satellite at Mount Farm whose three concrete runways could provide for Wellington day and night flying, leaving Benson then available for maintenance and limited day flying.

The birth of an aerodrome. This is Hangar C under construction at Benson in 1939, Hangar D to the right has not yet been started. The hangars were built by specialists who set them out and erected them . . .

. . . before moving on to another airfield, letting the main contractor follow up and construct the rest of the station.

Towards the end of December 1940, No. 1 Photographic Reconnaissance Unit (PRU) moved in from Heston with Spitfires, Blenheims and a few Hudsons. PR was destined to be Benson's main role for the remainder of the war years and the reason why the station was soon to come under the control of Coastal Command. In the summer of 1940 the status of the existing Photographic Development Unit was under intense discussion. A high-level, inter-service meeting in London revealed major conflicts of interest. The Admiralty demanded that all the photographic efforts should be devoted to watching enemy ports, but Bomber Command would not accept this. They considered the bombing programme an integral part of anti-invasion measures, and had urgent need of sorties for damage assessment. The suggestion that Bomber Command should control the photographic unit was bitterly opposed. If the unit went to Bomber Command, the Admiralty might be driven to setting up its own organisation.

There are four C Type hangars at Benson. This is Hangar A with B beyond. The doors have since been replaced and the side

offices extended. Station Headquarters in the centre background is today obscured by trees.

The former WAAF photographic interpreter, Constance Babington Smith, in her book *Evidence in Camera* (Chatto and Windus, 1958) wrote: 'Within a few days the Air Staff found a solution. Coastal Command was already in charge of the RAF's visual reconnaissance of enemy shipping; its ties with the Admiralty were close; and its Commander-in-Chief, Air Chief Marshal Sir Frederick Bowhill, was much interested in nautical matters. What could be more appropriate than to give the photographic unit to Coastal, when its prime responsibility was to be a watch on the invasion ports? Besides, the whole scope of its work was to be expanded; forward bases were to be started up in northern Scotland and in Cornwall so as to bring a vast stretch of enemy coastline within range. The moment had evidently come to establish the unit on a regular Air Force footing.'

As No. 1 PRU's activities increased, No. 12 OTU moved elsewhere in July 1941. The PRU was beginning to receive Mosquitos, the first operational sortie taking place on September 17. Early in 1942, two concrete runways were built at Benson, with lengths of 1,990 and 1,420 yards, operations temporarily transferring to the satellite at Mount Farm. Flights of aircraft were being detached to bases all over Britain and the unit's strength was becoming such that it was decided to amalgamate flights and create new squadrons. Consequently, on October 19, 1942, Nos. 540, 541, 542, 543, 544 Squadrons were formed. Their nominal base was Benson but in practice aircraft were still detached to stations much closer to particular areas of interest such as the Norwegian fjords and Brittany ports.

In May 1943, Benson despatched a Spitfire to photograph the results of the Dams Raid. The iconic photos of the breached Möhne Dam were the first ever published from the PR units in order to bolster morale in those very dark times. During their ever deeper flights into Germany, Mosquitos of No. 540

Benson started out as an all-grass airfield, but plans were drawn up *(below left)* **for the addition of two concrete runways.** *Below right:* **The main N-S runway was later extended to 2,000 yards.**

Squadron returned with photographs of the Peenemünde experimental establishment which, when interpreted, confirmed the existence of the V1 flying bomb.

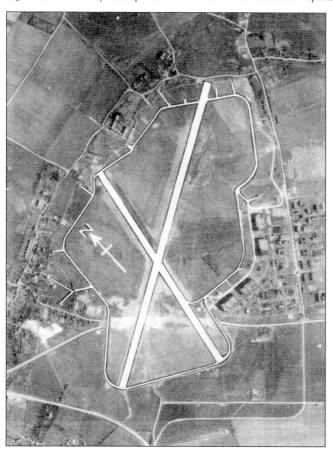

An unusual visitor to Benson in 1944 was this Focke-Wulf 190 (now in RAF markings) of the No. 1426 Enemy Aircraft Flight at Farnborough. It is parked on the taxiway in front of hangars C and D. There were two taxiways, one inner close to the hangars and one outer one.

Both have been subsequently widened, the outer one now being reserved for the servicing of large types of aircraft. It is also now being used by the resident helicopter squadrons. The houses of Benson village can just be seen in the background.

Deputy Prime Minister Clement Attlee and wife (second and third from the left) at Benson in 1945. Hangar B is in the background with A to its left.

it was exactly 32,000ft. I therefore decided to do the photography at 31,000ft, so that I was just below the vapour trail area and would have the advantage that any aircraft attempting to dive on me would have to pass through the vapour trail area and would thus be much easier to see.'

He went on to summarise: 'Programme of work: The required photographs are compiled by Air Ministry according to the requirements of the Command, and are sent down on a pro-forma to Benson, where the planning of the various reconnaissance trips is arranged, so as to cover as many targets as possible in each sortie. During periods of bad weather this programme is inclined to become somewhat congested, but given two or three clear days it can be very largely cleared off by working at full pressure. In periods of uncertain weather a very considerable amount of unproductive flying has to be done to photograph targets where small breaks in the clouds may permit it.

'The work is largely divided up into two categories — routine jobs and special jobs. Instances of routine jobs may be given as harbours, marshalling yards and constructional or repair work in progress. Special jobs are usually those recording the result of bombing, such as blitzed towns, the Möhne and Eder Dams, damaged factories etc.'

A few weeks before D-Day, Benson became the hub of a finely co-ordinated organisation. There, a joint committee that was responsible directly to the Combined Chiefs-of-Staff, co-ordinated the priorities of the flying programme. It was connected to the American PR Headquarters at High Wycombe, the RAF and USAAF PR squadrons, and the interpretation unit at Danesfield House, Medmenham. With the USAAF having taken over the Mount Farm satellite as long ago as February 1943, plus another Oxfordshire base at Chalgrove, all the Allied photographic and interpretive assets were now within a few miles of each other.

Group Captain A. H. Wheeler, test pilot at the Royal Aircraft Establishment at Farnborough, made a typical operational Spitfire sortie over northern France with No. 541 Squadron in September 1943. Extracts from his subsequent report read as follows:

'The main target was constructional work of a special character in a large wood near Watten. An alternative target was given close to St Omer, and on the way out they required photographs of wireless masts and any aerodrome which might lie on the route, also the harbour at Boulogne. In order to find the height of the vapour trails before crossing the coast, I had to do one circuit over the south of London, and found out that

The building on the right has been demolished, being replaced by a car park, and the paving covering the heating duct has been moved to the left. The central heating plant for the station is on the left of the access road.

Now in the post-war era, the year is 1954 with a Venom visitor. Hangar D in the background was used by the Queen's Flight **when it was based at Benson, and the re-clad Bellman on the right, currently used by Oxford University Air Squadron.**

With the end of the war in Europe, the PR squadrons were soon disbanded, but not before a comprehensive aerial survey of the UK was flown. Nos. 540 and 541 Squadrons were re-formed at Benson on December 1, 1947, both units converting to jet types in the early 1950s. When the PR squadrons moved to East Anglia in 1953, Benson became a Transport Command station and in the early 'sixties the home of three squadrons of Armstrong Whitworth Agosies. It also hosted the Queen's Flight and in more recent years support helicopter squadrons.

Today, the station remains much as it was built, with the four C Type hangars still in situ. The wartime blister hangars are long gone, as are some of the dispersal hardstandings. A public road separates the airfield from the main administrative and accommodation area. Benson continues to represent a particularly pleasant station of the pre-war era when the RAF was being expanded. A replica gate guardian Spitfire PR XIX bears the markings of that flown by Flight Lieutenant Duncan McCuaig, DFC, who failed to return to Benson from a sortie to Bremen on September 28, 1944.

Before No. 540 and 541 Squadrons were stood down in the autumn of 1946, they carried out a complete survey of the United Kingdom. The photographs were enlarged to a scale of 1:1250 (50 inches to one mile) and annotated with street names before being offered for sale by Ordnance Survey. In this example, the damage from a V1 can be seen at the eastern end of Empress Avenue, South Woodford. One person was killed at No. 3; two at No. 7; one at No. 9 and one at No. 11.

BIRCHAM NEWTON

Situated in the north of the county of Norfolk, Bircham started life in May 1918 when it housed a School of Aerial Fighting and Gunnery, operating such types as the SE5a and Sopwith Camel. Soon afterwards, it was destined to become a base for the long-range Handley Page V/1500s which were capable of bombing Berlin. However, the war ended before the squadron was fully equipped and used in anger. Eventually, two V/1500 squadrons were based here but were disbanded in 1919. More modern heavy bomber types subsequently arrived such as the Vickers Vimy and Virginia, and in 1928 the Boulton Paul Sidestrand. A succession of light bomber squadrons also occupied the station.

In 1936 the station was transferred to Coastal Command and a major re-building programme was begun, with the intention of providing accommodation for three general reconnaissance squadrons. The original General Service hangars were replaced by three C Types. Three Bellmans were added later and, during wartime, nine blisters. The grass surface was retained, with a longest run of 1,200 yards, and a narrow perimeter track was constructed. In April 1936, 'B' Flight of the Anti-Aircraft Co-operation Unit formed at Bircham to serve the new AA ranges at Weybourne on the Norfolk coast.

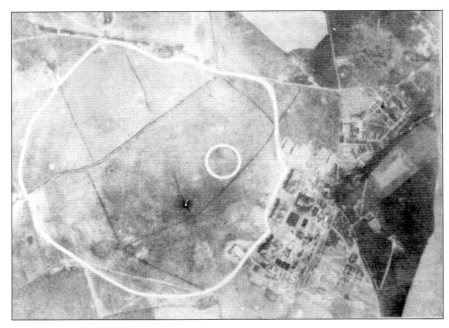

Bircham Newton, situated close to the Wash at 230 feet above sea level, was a grass airfield surrounded by a perimeter track.

On the formation of Coastal Command in 1936, the station was earmarked as a major airfield in No. 16 Group, the first squadron to be posted in being No. 206, initially equipped with the Avro Anson but replaced by the American-made Hudson in March 1940. This aircraft had been specifically designed to meet British requirements for an aircraft for coastal reconnaissance and an order for 250 had been placed with Lockheeds in 1938. No. 224 Squadron were already operational with the Hudson on the outbreak of hostilities and shot down their first German aircraft of the war off Aberdeen on October 8, 1939.

With the invention of radar, Coastal Command was particularly interested to test the ASV (Air to Surface Vessel) version and

No. 221 Squadron was specifically re-formed at Bircham with Welllingtons, under Wing Commander T. R. Vickers.

The first Coastal Command unit to arrive was No. 206 Squadron at the end of July with the first of the Ansons coming into service. Two weeks later the second Anson squadron, No. 220, formed here and in August 1939 moved to its war station at Thornaby. The outbreak of war saw No. 42 Squadron at Bircham equipped with the totally obsolete Vickers Vildebeest biplane. More potent aircraft were in short supply, however, so it was deemed suitable for convoy escort along the East Coast. This activity continued until the summer of 1940 when the squadron began converting to Beauforts and left for Thorney Island, leaving only a detachment in Norfolk.

No. 206 Squadron, meanwhile still in residence, had re-equipped with Hudsons and was roaming the north German coast attacking shipping, but by the time of the Dunkirk evacuation, attention had switched to patrols of the Dutch and Belgian coasts. Anti-invasion patrols followed but there was still time for offensive duties such as an attack on Den Helder by nine aircraft, which sank a coastal defence ship. Aircraft were detached all over Britain until the whole squadron moved first to Cornwall and then to Northern Ireland to join the anti-submarine war.

On November 21, 1940, No. 221 Squadron formed here with the main objective of test-

ing the new Air to Surface Vessel radar (ASV) fitted to its Wellingtons. It moved to Northern Ireland in May 1942. No. 254 Squadron was at Bircham from January to April 1940, using Blenheims for convoy escort duties and protecting the North Sea fishing fleet from marauding German bombers. No. 235 Squadron's Blenheims took over and extended operations to escorting MTBs and minelayers and then providing cover for Dunkirk. On August 15, the squadron was on a Danish coast sweep when it encountered 40 bombers returning from a raid on England and was able to account for two He 111s. In September, 323 sorties were

Surplus to requirements, the Ministry of Defence closed the airfield in 1962. Two years later it was acquired by the Construction Industry Training Board which needed a base to

set up a training centre. Bircham Newton was deemed an ideal venue and the site is now the location of the National Construction College.

Although much of the former aerodrome has been lost, a nice link with the past is that the original RAF Operations Room has been retained by the college.

flown and on the 11th, although two Blenheims failed to return, two Bf 109s were shot down. Into 1941, the escorts, shipping reconnaissance and other duties continued with many detachments around the country. The entire squadron moved to Scotland in June 1941, whereupon No. 248 Squadron took over its duties. Its Blenheims were being replaced by Beaufighters and, after working up on convoy patrols and mine searches, the first shipping strike was directed against armed trawlers and R-Boats (minesweepers) on August 22, 1941.

No. 248 Squadron was spread very thinly over several detachments and finally left for Dyce in March 1942. While at Bircham, a fellow squadron, No. 500, had been making night intruder sorties over Holland and bombing French ports. During a strike on November 9, 1941, a 3,000-ton motor vessel was sunk in a convoy off Holland. The same month, the Blenheims began to be replaced by Hudsons and the unit moved north for Atlantic anti-submarine patrols in March 1942.

Unfortunately one of the casualties was the fairly unique Type 1959/34 control tower, unfortunately since demolished.

No. 407 Squadron's Hudsons then arrived for attacks along the Dutch, north German and Danish coasts, which cost four crews during April. On May 15, 11 aircraft took part in a convoy attack, setting three ships on fire but four of the aircraft were missing and two crashed on landing. September 1942 saw a move to Cornwall.

The Dutch-manned No. 320 Squadron served at Bircham after it moved in from Scotland in April 1942, its main area of operations being the Dutch coastline but the defences were now much stronger and the cost in lost Hudsons and crews proved high. Nevertheless, they soldiered on until March 1943 when the squadron was transferred to Bomber Command.

It should be noted that at least seven Fleet Air Arm squadrons, granted lodger facilities by the RAF, operated from Bircham Newton for various periods under Coastal Command's control. Their duties included minelaying and anti-shipping strikes, often at night, using such types as the Swordfish and Avenger. They frequently operated from the satellite aerodrome at Docking, as did all or most of the RAF units at Bircham. (More details can be found in the Docking entry.)

Throughout much of the war, Bircham housed air-sea rescue squadrons, including No. 279 which formed here in November 1941 with Hudsons, and No. 280 with Ansons. The station's other subsidiary function was weather reconnaissance with No. 401 Meteorological Flight here from October 1941 until it was formed into No. 521 Squadron — the earliest of the met squadrons — on August 1, 1942. The North Sea was covered, along with flights over enemy-held territory using Spitfires and Mosquitos. Most of the work was carried out from the Docking satellite.

Operational in 1944 were Wellingtons of Nos. 524 and 415 Squadrons for anti-shipping attacks. No. 415 Squadron very unusually also operated Fairey Albacores. Its tactics were for the Leigh Light Wellington to illuminate an E-Boat and an accompanying

The Royal visit to the station on January 26, 1941, was the first of a group of visits made by the King and Queen to RAF stations in East Anglia. The following day they visited Waddington, Swinderby and Syerston (the King inspecting four Polish squadrons at the latter two stations), and on the 28th Stradishall and Debden.

Albacore to attack it. The final wartime operational unit at Bircham, although most of its sorties were mounted from advanced bases such as Manston in Kent, was No. 119 Squadron. It was equipped with Albacores for anti-shipping patrols in the southern North Sea and off the Dutch coast. Disbandment came at Bircham in May 1945.

The lack of concrete runways meant that Bircham had little or no future as a post-war flying station, but some limited radio aids training took place with Airspeed Oxfords until 1948 when Technical Training Command took over. RAF ground training

schools were based here until the station finally closed in 1962, Chipmunk aircraft having been used for flying experience. In late 1964, the site was acquired by the Construction Industry Training Board (CITB) to house its Head Office. In September 1966, CITB opened a training centre on the site, which has become the National Construction College (East). Flying briefly returned to Bircham in 1965, when the Tripartite Evaluation Squadron of the Central Fighter Establishment at West Raynham used the former airfield as a landing ground while evaluating the Hawker Siddeley Kestrel V/STOL aircraft.

The tower can just be seen in the left background of this rather poor quality shot of the Royal visit. The King and Queen and the two young princesses were escorted by Air Vice-Marshal J. H. S. Tyssen (on the extreme left), the AOC-in-C of No. 16 Group.

Various personnel were decorated by the King including Squadron Leader Stanford-Tuck (not seen in this photograph) who had driven over from Coltishall where he was CO of No. 257 Squadron, to receive the DSO and a bar to his DFC.

Apart from the station's main role of coastal patrols over the North Sea, it also had secondary duties for air-sea rescue and weather patrols. No. 401 Meteorological Flight was based at the station from October 1941 with a Gladiator. Later the flight was enlarged into a full squadron — No. 521 — equipped with Spitfires and Mosquitos.

Peter Gunn, who kindly took our comparison photographs at Bircham, Docking and Langham, could not resist in mocking up this shot with Jon Plumb, the Health and Safety Advisor, standing in for the long-forgotten airman.

Bircham Newton closed its gates on December 18, 1962 in a ceremony which accompanied a parade of 43 graduates from the Administrative Apprentice Training School. Two Marshals of the Royal Air Force were in attendance: Lord Tedder, who had been at the station from 1920-22, and Lord Portal there in 1927. Here we see the changing face of a wartime aerodrome. Ten years separates these two views.

Although the entire flying field has been torn up during ongoing construction training and demonstrations, many of the original buildings on the main site are still intact and well maintained, as are the three C Type hangars. An unfortunate loss was the watch office, demolished in 2010, but the CITB very generously provides the accommodation for the RAF Bircham Newton Heritage Centre.

Located within the former Commanding Officer's house, the centre opened in 2005 with a single room of exhibits. Since then the discovery of more photographs, documents and memorabilia has expanded the exhibition to three rooms. Regular open days are held and for interested parties viewings can be arranged at other times. A memorial to those who served at Bircham is situated outside the centre. It was unveiled and dedicated on September 2, 2006.

DETLING

Grass-surfaced throughout its life, Detling, located two and a half miles north-east of Maidstone in Kent, dated back to 1915 when it was prepared as an air defence landing ground to cover the south-eastern approaches to London. Plans changed however, and it was allocated first to the Royal Naval Air Service and then to the Royal Flying Corps. In 1919 the site reverted to farmland but during the 1930s it was chosen for an Expansion Scheme station, although not on the grand scale of most of the other aerodromes earmarked for enlargement.

As was customary with the armament training stations and other training establishments built at that time, the buildings were mostly of hutted construction. The longest take-off run on the grass was 1,250 yards, later extended to 1,400. The domestic and technical sites were concentrated on the northern perimeter of the airfield, a Bellman hangar followed by 14 blisters being erected during wartime. An extensive dispersal area spread out into the fields nearby, and in the early war period a 'Q/K' decoy site was laid out at Lenham, about five miles to the southeast, the double designation denoting both day and night capability.

The station opened in September 1938 in No. 6 (Auxiliary) Group, of Bomber Command and was then occupied by the Hawker Hinds of No. 500 (County of Kent) Squadron, but at the beginning of November that year it was transferred to No. 16 Group, Coastal Command, as was No. 500 Squadron which now became a general reconnaissance unit. Re-equipped with Ansons, the crews soon learned to cope with the mysteries of twin-engined monoplanes and retractable undercarriages. They started patrols over the North Sea on the first day of the war and were soon escorting convoys, but saw little or no action throughout the winter of 1939-40.

In May 1940, No. 500 Squadron became involved in covering the Dunkirk evacuation and during this period, WAAF Corporal Daphne Pearson was awarded the Empire Gallantry Medal for her courage, also being promoted to commissioned rank. After the revocation of the EGM and its replacement by the George Cross, she was invested by King George VI in January 1941, the first woman to receive the new award. Her citation reads: 'On 31 May 1940, an hour after

Opening the show in Kent were the Ansons of No. 500 Squadron from Detling, transferred to Coastal Command in November 1938. Here a formation is pictured passing Dover harbour before heading out over the English Channel.

Members of the squadron line up for a photo taken on the eve of war being declared.

Very badly bombed in August 1940, save for the Bellman hangar, few wartime buildings now remain standing. Today the former technical site is occupied by a variety of commercial concerns.

But not all has been lost. Today a forlorn pillbox guards the entrance and the roundabout still marks the eastern end of the site.

Another vertical photo from the files of No. 540 Squadron at Benson: Detling under the lens on May 1, 1946.

midnight, an aircraft crashed near the Women's Auxiliary Air Force quarters at Detling in Kent, the pilot being seriously injured, another officer killed outright and two airmen slightly injured. Upon hearing the crash Corporal Pearson rushed out and although she knew there were bombs on board she stood on the wreckage, roused the pilot who was stunned, released his parachute harness and helped him to get clear. When she got him about 30 yards from the wreckage a 120lb bomb went off and Corporal Pearson threw herself on top of the pilot to protect him from the blast and splinters. She remained with him until a stretcher party arrived and then returned to the burning aircraft to look for the fourth member of the crew. She found him — the wireless operator — dead in the bomber. Her prompt and courageous action undoubtedly helped to save the pilot's life.'

In August 1940 Luftwaffe Intelligence wrongly identified Detling as a major fighter base even though it was only used for ad hoc refuelling. Photo-reconnaissance showed fighters on the ground so a decision was made to attack it. The raid took place on August 13 during which 67 civilian and service personnel were killed and 94 injured. The station had no warning that it was about to be attacked because the force of 40 Ju 87s with an escort of Bf 109s reported by the Observer Corps over Kent, was assumed by AA Command to be heading for Short's aircraft factory at Rochester. The damage to Detling was so extensive that any bus that passed near to the aerodrome is said to have had police on board who made passengers look away. Hangars had been wrecked, all three messes badly damaged and 22 aircraft, mostly Ansons and Blenheims, were destroyed. Two WAAFS subsequently received the Military Medal for bravery, both remaining on duty throughout the bombing.

The one benefit that came from the raid was a comprehensive review of how the Observer Corps operated. The local observer post had the information Detling needed but no direct telephone line with which to convey it. Whilst damage to the base could not have been prevented, casualties could have been much reduced had an early warning been received. After this débâcle, Observer Corps posts were thereafter allowed to contact their local RAF station directly rather than going through the convoluted process that had existed previously. Another attack on Detling took place on September 2, 1940, a high-level raid by Do 17s which inflicted yet more damage.

Also here in 1940 was No. 53 Squadron whose Blenheims were mainly used for attacks on French ports until moving to Thorney Island in November. On June 1 one of the pilots of No. 500 Squadron took advantage of the slow speed of the Anson and managed to shoot down a Bf 109 which had overshot its target with his single forward firing gun. The squadron continued in residence until May 1941 when it re-equipped with Blenheims and moved away. No. 59 Squadron's Blenheims were based at Detling from June to August 1941 but thereafter the aerodrome became something of a backwater, being occupied mainly by second line units such as an Anti-Aircraft Co-operation Unit and an air-sea rescue squadron.

It was transferred to Army Co-operation Command in January 1943 but this organisation was soon absorbed into Fighter Command, the station hosting many Second Tactical Air Force Spitfire squadrons until becoming non-operational in December 1944 being put on Care and Maintenance.

After the war, gliding was the main activity, both civil and military, until the site was de-requisitioned in October 1959. The Kent County Agricultural Ground was established on part of the site and there was some consternation when pipe-mines were discovered under the turf and had to be deactivated. These devices had been laid at a number of aerodromes in southern England in 1940 as an airfield denial weapon in the event of invasion. An original Bellman hangar and one of the blisters are still in situ, along with other smaller buildings, including the armoury. The aviation connection is maintained by the presence of an VOR/DME radio beacon for air navigation.

At the end of the war No. 1336 Wing of the RAF Regiment was at the base running an Air Disarmament School, No. 5 Signals Wing of No. 60 Group replacing them in October 1945. Then for over eight years Detling was the base for the Home Command Gliding School, two gliders can be seen in this shot. The aerodrome was finally de-requisitioned on October 1, 1959.

Geoffrey Hall circled the site at low level — the livestock market is in the foreground.

The southern end of the aerodrome has now become the Kent County Showground.

DOCKING

This aerodrome was laid out as an operational satellite of Bircham Newton in the early months of the Second World War, both airfields being located in Norfolk to the north-east of King's Lynn. It remained grass-surfaced for its relatively brief existence, with a longest run of 1,730 yards and was described as having a well-drained surface. A 'Q' site decoy was established at North Creake, later to be adapted as an airfield in its own right.

Docking was a large, flat site, much more suitable for night flying than its parent station. Consequently, after Drem lighting had been installed, Docking was utilised for Bircham's night operations. Aircraft would be flown to Docking in the late afternoon in preparation for ops and flown back to Bircham in the early morning for maintenance.

By mid-1940 Bircham Newton was making full use of Docking as an operational satellite. The first squadrons to use it included No. 206 with Hudsons, No. 235 with Blenheims and No. 500 with Blenheims and Hudsons. Their presence tended to be brief

Unfortunately captions to Canadian wartime photographs do not give locations, simply stating: 'July 14, 1942, No. 407 Canadian Squadron. This is a welcome moment for the boys of the Demon squadron'. The existence of the Spitfire coded TE identifies it as being from the No. 401 Met Flight which was based at Bircham Newton on that date along with Gladiators (see page 86), but as the flight also used Docking on occasion, it gives us the excuse to include this lovely evocative shot here.

and often just detachments rather than the full squadron, for example, No. 502 Squadron's Whitleys in January/February 1942 with a detachment in Cornwall.

From November 1942 to February 1943, No. 407 Squadron used its Hudsons mainly for anti-E-Boat patrols over the Channel and Dutch coast. It also carried out operations at night against enemy convoys transporting iron ore from Sweden into ports such as Rotterdam. The Dutch No. 320 Squadron flew alongside it on similar duties. These anti-shipping operations were extremely dangerous because the convoys were protected by air cover and flak ships. Losses in aircraft and crews reached a peak in 1942, when at least three aircraft were being lost for every ship sunk or seriously damaged. No. 524 Squadron's Wellingtons were here in the second half of 1944, mainly operating off the Dutch coast and finding and bombing enemy shipping of all descriptions.

Docking closed as a flying station at the end of the war, but was used as part of an Aircrew Holding Unit to accommodate airmen who were awaiting demobilisation. These included many cadets who had undergone flying training in Canada and other Commonwealth countries. Coincidentally, the future well-known actors Richard Burton, Warren Mitchell and Robert Hardy found themselves at Docking during this period, idling away the time waiting to be released from the service.

But for the presence of a derelict watch office in the corner of a field, it would be hard to know that there has ever been an airfield here. Sections of the concrete perimeter track survive as farm tracks and a public road on the eastern boundary. Small copses break up the flying field, making it difficult to imagine that large aircraft like the Wellington and Whitley ever flew from here.

Seventy years have passed and even the instruction, once visible on the derelict control tower, has now virtually faded into history.

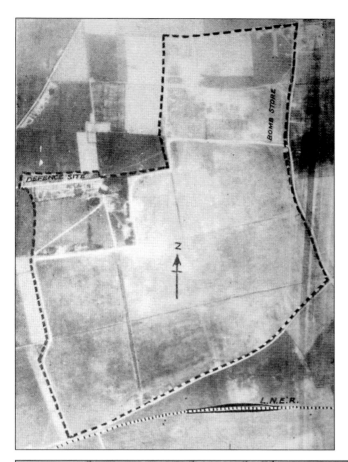

Today, little is left of the airfield, which has returned to farmland. One mile north of Docking, at a fork on the B1153 road, Peter Gunn photographed this small memorial that commemorates all who served there. It is close to the former Communal Site, on which stood the Airmen's Dining Room, the Officers' and Sergeants' Messes and a NAAFI. Most of the buildings are long gone save only their floors, but the sturdy Gas Decontamination Centre is still standing.

Even the LNER railway line disappeared in the Beeching cuts of the 1960s, its course only barely visible from the air today.

EASTCHURCH

Flying at this site just to the south of the Thames Estuary began as early as July 1909 when the Hon C. S. Rolls started using Standford Hill for testing a Short-built glider. The level grassland nearby proved ideal for development as an aerodrome so the land was purchased by the Royal Aero Club. Many pioneers of British aviation flew from here and some of them are reflected in the names of local roads.

Eastchurch became a station for the Royal Naval Air Service which, in April 1918 combined with the Royal Flying Corps to form the RAF. By this time there were no less than 29 aeroplane sheds, including six 200ft by 100ft hangars on the 600-acre site. Many ancillary buildings had also been constructed to a point where so much money had been spent that the aerodrome's post-war future was assured.

Flying activity was much reduced by 1919 so the accent was on ground instructional units, especially an Armament School. In April 1922, it became the Armament and Gunnery School, the airfield being used by aircraft on courses or firing practice over the Leysdown Ranges. In January 1932 the unit was renamed the Air Armament School. In September 1938, No. 48 Squadron's Ansons moved in from Manston to join No. 21 Squadron's Blenheims which had arrived two weeks earlier. This was part of the RAF's move towards a war footing during the Munich Crisis. Eastchurch was transferred to No. 16 Group, Coastal Command, in November, but No. 21 Squadron and the AAS remained as lodger units.

In March 1939, No. 21 Squadron moved to Norfolk and with mobilisation in August

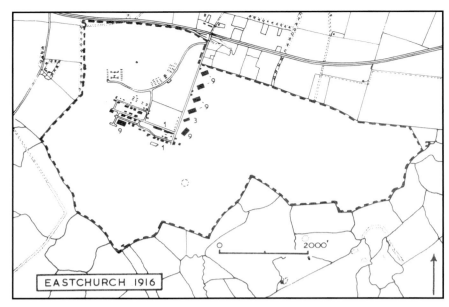

Although this plan is pre-Coastal Command, it sets the scene for the aviation connection with Eastchurch on the Isle of Sheppey. The River Thames lies just two miles to the north.

No. 48 Squadron went to its war station at Thorney Island. The Air Armament School relocated to South Wales and Eastchurch became a Polish Training Centre for ground crew displaced when their country was invaded. As the Battle of France proceeded, the Poles were sent to north-west England in May 1940. The airfield was then occupied by a detachment of Blenheims from No. 59 Squadron which, joined by No. 53 Squadron

in June, flew tactical reconnaissance over the last of the fighting in France before being recalled to regroup and be transferred to Coastal Command at other bases.

Eastchurch was now utilised as a forward airfield from which to carry out attacks on invasion barges massing in the Channel ports. Detachments were used at first but from early August the whole of Nos. 12 and 42 Squadrons brought in their Fairey Battles.

Careful comparison with the First World War plan shows the extent of the grass surfaced flying field during the Second World War.

A series of photographs of a Blenheim being salvaged which had come a cropper at Eastchurch in undisclosed circumstances.

The occasional presence of Spitfires on the ground at Eastchurch, as well as the Battles, prompted German intelligence to assume that this was a fighter base. The result was a heavy air raid on August 13 by 30 Dornier 17s, which caused severe damage to the hangars and destroyed a Spitfire and five Blenheims. Sixteen personnel were killed and 48 injured.

A further raid on September 2 hit the bomb storage area and 350 250lb bombs exploded, wrecking many buildings. A hangar was also hit, destroying six aircraft, killing four men and wounding 12 more. The station was effectively put out of action so the two Battle squadrons were withdrawn to Binbrook in Lincolnshire. Little use was then made of Eastchurch until it was transferred to Technical Training Command in June 1941. Flying was limited to spasmodic employment as a forward operating base by fighter squadrons. Particularly notable was

use by Spitfires of Nos 65 and 165 Squadrons to escort bombers during the Dieppe Raid on August 19, 1942. On their second mission that morning, three Dornier 17s were claimed as destroyed for no fighter losses.

During March 1943, the airfield was used for the large scale Army co-operation Exercise 'Spartan', after which it reverted to its usual second-line activities. No. 18 Armament Practice Camp was formed during October 1943 and the bomb-blasted hangars were replaced by three Bellmans. From January 1944 onwards the APC provided rocket-firing courses for Typhoon squadrons,

six of them being passed out before D-Day. The station was put on Care and Maintenance on September 1, 1946 and then abandoned in April 1947.

The unusual L-shaped landing ground is now the site of a large prison complex. In Eastchurch village, at the junction by the church, stands the British Aviation Memorial dedicated to the pioneers who once flew from here, and there is also a stained glass window in the church commemorating C. S. Rolls and Cecil Grace, who were killed in flying accidents in July and December 1910, respectively.

After Eastchurch was abandoned in 1947 the Home Office earmarked the isolated airfield as being an ideal location for a prison and Standford Hill was opened in 1950, being largely rebuilt in 1986. It has the lowest security classification, Category D. HM Prison Swaleside, a Category B, is for prisoners who do not require the highest security. Finally, HM Prison Elmley was added to what is now called the Sheppey Prisons Cluster. Opened in 1992 as a Category B, it now also has had a lower Category C unit added making it the largest of the three prisons.

LANGHAM

Ground crew re-arm a 'Torbeau' (the semi-official name for Beaufighters modified to carry a torpedo) of No. 489 Squadron when it was carrying out patrols with No. 455 as the Langham (or ANZAC) Strike Wing in June-July to protect the invasion area.

The airfield started its career in 1940 to serve the firing ranges on the nearby north Norfolk coast and housed an Anti-Aircraft Co-Operation Unit for target-towing duties. Grass runways were adequate for its purposes, which also included use as a dispersal airfield for RAF Bircham Newton. Its first operational aircraft were six Swordfish of the Navy's 819 Squadron for night anti-shipping patrols under Coastal Command during July and August 1942. Further support for Bircham Newton's busy squadrons was provided by No. 280 Squadron from July to October 1942, using Ansons and Warwicks to search for aircrew who had ditched in the North Sea. In November, Langham was reduced to Care and Maintenance while expansion and runway construction took place.

The main runway was 2,000 yards in length and the two others were both 1,400 yards. Thirty-six loop hardstandings led off the perimeter track and three T2s and four blister hangars were erected. The bomb storage area was to the north-east. The station reopened in No. 16 Group, Coastal Command, on February 22, 1944 and in April two Beaufighter squadrons arrived from Leuchars to form the Langham Strike Wing. They were the Australian-crewed No. 455 and the New Zealand No. 489. Typical tactical procedure was for a reconnaissance aircraft to make a sweep along the enemy coastline and report by wireless code any convoy at sea. If it was a particularly large one, the North Coates Strike Wing would join forces with Langham and some 80 Beaufighters would attack in several waves.

With continental roads and railways under continual onslaught from the air, coastal convoys had become increasingly vital for maintaining the flow of fuel and arms for the German forces. Many more flak ships were allocated to guard the merchantmen and Coastal Command losses rose accordingly. On one occasion four of Langham's Beaufighters were shot down when they flew inadvertently over a convoy obscured by haze. A fifth aircraft returned to base flown by its badly wounded pilot. After a landing assisted by his navigator, he was so weak that he had to be lifted out of the cockpit and rushed to hospital.

The Strike Wing's other major task was to render the eastern end of the Channel impassable for E-Boats during the prelude to the invasion. First 250lb and, later, 500lb bombs were carried and No. 455 Squadron was detached to Manston in Kent around D-Day for so-called 'Channel-bottling' operations. In August, the squadron began operating at night under the direction of a Langham-based detachment of No. 524 Squadron's Wellingtons, which located enemy shipping and dropped flame-float markers near them. Wing attacks saw the squadron in an anti-flak role, using rockets. In September, RAF Intelligence calculated that the Langham Strike Wing had sunk 36 ships, damaged a further 61 and sunk four U-Boats. The following month, both squadrons moved to Scotland to deal with enemy shipping in Norwegian waters.

All of No. 524 Squadron's Wellingtons were based at Langham from November 1944 until the unit disbanded here in June 1945. With the departure of the Beaufighters, the Wellingtons now operated on their own account, searching for shipping and attacking anything they found, but losing about one crew per month. Tactics were refined so that by April 1945, Royal Navy motor torpedo boats were being directed onto enemy vessels by radio. The squadron disbanded at Langham on July 7, 1945, another Wellington squadron disbanding here on the same date. This was No. 612 that had been based at the airfield since December 1944 operating at night along the Dutch coast, hunting for E-Boats. Two of these were destroyed in the first six sorties, and the score mounted steadily right up to the end of the war.

Today it is turkeys and light aircraft which have taken over at Langham. Henry Labouchere is restoring there this 1940-vintage Miles Magister, formally part of the Strathallan Collection.

On the other hand, No. 455 Squadron was equipped with 'Rockbeaus' — rocket-armed Beaufighters. This unit was the first Australian bomber squadron in Britain, originally flying Hampdens until it transferred to Coastal Command in April 1942. Beaufighters came in in December 1943. When it was posted to Norfolk in April 1944, its job was to help seal off the eastern end of the Channel.

A rather less aggressive but still important role was played by No. 521 Squadron which arrived in October 1944. Its Fortresses and Venturas flew meteorological sorties over the North Sea which continued until November 1945 when the unit moved to Chivenor. No. 254 Squadron arrived from there that same month and was the only Torbeau unit in the peacetime RAF. When it left for Thornaby in November 1946, the station was closed to flying and reduced to Care and Maintenance in September 1947. It was reactivated when the RAF expanded rapidly at the time of the Korean War, the runways being resurfaced so that they could be used by the Mosquito and Beaufighter target tugs of No. 2 Civilian Anti-Aircraft Co-operation Unit. By the time the unit disbanded in November 1958 it was operating Vampires and Meteors.

Langham finally closed in 1961. The site later became a turkey farm, which ensured the preservation of the whole of one of the short runways and half of the other because they formed convenient bases for turkey sheds. More sheds were built on some of the loop dispersals but most of the rest were torn up for road-building aggregate. Surviving buildings are few but include the control tower and a Dome Trainer building

These words by Andrew Hendrie, a wireless operator/air gunner with No. 524 Squadron, end with a telling statement about the realities of wartime flying: 'Operations were against E-Boats, which would attempt at night time, and at an estimated 50 knots, to come over from the Dutch coast to the Humber estuary or off Harwich to attack our shipping. Our patrols were off Den Helder, IJmuiden, Rotterdam and the Friesians. At briefings, therefore, areas of flak concentrations were usually stressed. We lost a lot of crews through aircraft going in too close to the coast. The first comment made to me by the squadron adjutant on joining 524 was, "Have you a car? There are so many here, and the former owners are now unknown".'

This camera gun sequence, taken by No. 455 Squadron, shows enemy shipping under attack at Wangerooge off the German coast in August 1944. The vessel, which had eight aircraft 'kills' painted on its superstructure, was believed to have been heavily damaged before being sent to the bottom.

The squadron left Langham in October 1944 for Coastal Command's No. 18 Group in Scotland where four Beaufighter squadrons — Nos. 144, 404 (RCAF) 455 (RAAF), 489 (RNZAF), formed the Dallachy Strike Wing (see page 122). It operated against German shipping along the Norwegian and Dutch coasts. Between April 1942 and the end of the war, No. 455 Squadron was credited with sinking 18 vessels, 10 merchantmen, four minesweepers, three escorts and one U-Boat. To set against this record, the squadron's losses in personnel during the war amounted to 91 Australians killed.

used for the instruction of anti-aircraft gunnery. The Dome has Listed Building status and is also recognised officially as Britain's youngest Ancient Monument. At the time of writing it was being restored with the intention of housing displays of Langham's history and interpretative audio visuals. Nearby stands a stone memorial unveiled in February 2011 by the Airfields of Britain Conservation Trust.

The station had two 'Q' site decoys, one at Warham St Mary, about four miles to the west, and Salthouse, three miles to the east, where the control bunker is still virtually intact.

Fortunately the control tower, pictured by Peter Gunn, has survived the passing of the years.

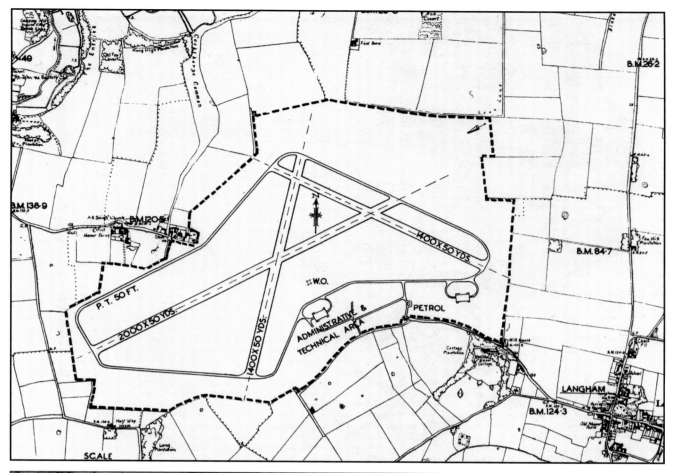

MEMORIAL

Access to Langham is restricted to avoid the risk of infection to the turkeys in the sheds erected by Bernard Matthews on the runways.

NORTH COATES

Bordering the North Sea, North Coates was established in 1916 as a forward landing ground for No. 33 Home Night Defence Squadron of the Royal Flying Corps so it was apt that David Porter brought in his replica SE5a to visit the North Coates Flying Club.

Located on the Lincolnshire coast five miles south-east of Grimsby, this airfield started life in 1916 as a Night Landing Ground for Home Defence aircraft. At that time it was known as North Coates Fitties. By 1918 it had achieved full flight station status and was sending out anti-submarine patrols. The site was abandoned in 1920 but reinstated in 1927 for squadron armament practice, and much later as an Air Armament School using the nearby ranges established at Donna Nook. Further expansion followed in the 1930s with the canvas Bessonneau hangars replaced by Bellmans and so-called North Coates hangars with side-opening doors. The 'Fitties' part of the station's name had been dropped by February 1940 when it was transferred to Coastal Command. (It should be noted that the local version 'Cotes' applied to the village is a fairly recent re-adoption of an archaic spelling.)

The first operational squadrons based at North Coates were Nos. 235, 236 and 248, all equipped with Blenheims. Offensive patrols were carried out over the North Sea until the three squadrons moved elsewhere in April 1940. They were replaced by No. 22 Squadron's Beauforts which made attacks on invasion barges massing in enemy-occupied ports. The squadron dropped torpedoes for the first time in anger in September 1940 when five aircraft attacked a convoy between Calais and Ostend and claimed one ship sunk. Fleet Air Arm Swordfish were also operating from North Coates around the same time for mine-laying and convoy escort, and that summer Spitfires from fighter squadrons based at RAF Digby used North Coates as a forward landing ground.

In May 1941, shortly before No. 22 Squadron moved to Thorney Island, No. 86 Squadron arrived with Blenheims and began to re-equip with Beauforts. After flying reconnaissance and air-sea rescue missions for three months, the crews attended a torpedo training course and began anti-shipping strikes in November. A move was made to Cornwall in January 1942 and Hudsons of No. 53 and 59 Squadrons were the replacement. Both units mounted shipping strikes until posted out in May and August 1942 respectively.

Although two narrow and very short paved strips (50ft wide and barely 700 yards in length) had been in existence since 1938, the intensity of operations now demanded a proper paved runway. By 1942, a partial

In the Second World War, one of the first Coastal Command squadrons to be based there was No. 22, another unit whose ancestry dated back to the First World War.

The two landing areas are indicated on this Air Ministry schematic. Today the club uses a 700-yard grass strip in front of the hangars.

perimeter track had been laid, together with a limited number of frying-pan hardstandings and bomb stores. The perimeter track was now extended right round the airfield, a new 1,400-yard runway was laid down but the 1,460-yard north-west/south-east strip remained grass-surfaced. There were 22 loop-type dispersals and a total of 15 pairs of torpedo stores were situated on the extended south-western part of the airfield. There were already four pre-war hangars of local design, and these were backed up by four Bellmans.

During the reconstruction, North Coates' Relief Landing Ground (RLG) at nearby Donna Nook was used for operations — the quaint name said to have arisen from the wrecking of a Spanish Armada galleon just off the coast. The RLG was laid out in 1936 and in 1940 became a 'Q/K' site, i.e. a decoy airfield with dummy Blenheim aircraft to attract attention by day, and lighting to do the same at night. In 1942 the decoy was dismantled and the site reverted to its RLG role. During operations from Donna Nook, a Hudson of No. 407 Squadron was involved in

very serious accident on January 22, 1942. Returning with a full bomb-load because no ships could be found, it crashed on landing, killing the five crew members and 13 ground personnel in the ensuing explosions. The RLG closed for flying in 1945 and most of the land was returned to agriculture, although some of the perimeter track and buildings still exist. Just offshore is the Donna Nook Air Weapons Range.

On November 20, 1942, the recently-formed North Coates Strike Wing, consisting of Nos. 143, 236 and the torpedo-carrying

A stunning photograph of the Beauforts of No. 86 Squadron at North Coates in September 1941, soon after they converted to the type from the Blenheim. The Beaufort was Coastal Command's standard torpedo-bomber from 1940 to 1943.

101

against shipping. It was intended to replace the machine guns and bombs on the anti-flak squadrons with a mix of RPs and cannon.

During April and May, the Beaufighters of Nos. 143 and 236 Squadrons were fitted with rocket rails and practice began against an old destroyer moored offshore near North Coates using inert concrete warheads to minimise damage to the target. Normal operations continued during the work up, including a sweep on May 1 to intercept the cruiser *Nürnberg* which was out of range of single-engined fighter escorts. Enemy fighters shot down five of the Beaufighters, the remaining aircraft landing at Wick. On June 22, the first full strike operation with rockets was not a success as only two of the 176 RPs fired hit their targets, nor did any of the torpedos.

A much improved performance on August 2 resulted in the torpedoing of an ore carrier and much damage to the rest of the convoy. Although five Wing strikes per month had been planned, poor weather and a lack of fighter escorts meant that only five had been flown since April. Few ships had been sunk although aircraft losses were considerable.

Squadron line-up of Beauforts in front of the technical site . . . then . . .

. . . and now! This is a Zenair Zodiac owned and built by Arthur Worrall of Preston.

254 Squadron, mounted its first operation. It was not a success: the Spitfire escort missed the rendezvous in the bad weather and three Beaufighters were shot down by fighters or flak. Another four aircraft were badly damaged and only one ship in the target convoy was damaged. As a result, the Strike Wing was withdrawn from operations for a period of intensive training. Those in command judged — rightly as it turned out — that the Strike Wing plan would ultimately prove of great effect if it could be developed to a high standard by training and co-operation in the air.

This was put to the test on April 18, 1943 when a convoy was reported heading north from the Hook of Holland. A force of 29 Beaufighters was despatched consisting of nine so-called Torbeaus carrying torpedoes, along with 12 aircraft for flak suppression. The remainder of the formation carried a pair of 250lb bombs, as well as their formidable cannon and machine gun armament. The attack was highly successful, resulting in only slight damage to two aircraft, and proved the effectiveness of the Strike Wing concept. A new and potentially devastating weapon now came on the scene; the 3-inch rocket projectile (RP) which was to prove so effective

In July 1941, the Hudsons of No. 59 Squadron were posted in from Bircham Newton to carry out anti-shipping patrols off the Dutch coast. On August 6 the following year, one of their aircraft (FH424), piloted by Squadron Leader Phillip Evans, received a direct hit from anti-aircraft fire and returned to the airfield with severe damage to its starboard wing.

In November 1942, North Coates came into its own with the formation of a special three-squadron Strike Wing. The aircraft were now Bristol Beaufighters, armed with .303 machine guns, 20mm cannon and 3-inch rockets, plus the 'Torbeau' versions with torpedoes. HM King George VI visited the North Coates Strike Wing on May 27, 1943. In the background are the Beaufighter XIs of No. 143 Squadron.

Coastal Command's strike squadrons were re-organised during October 1944 and No. 143 Squadron moved to Banff, leaving the Wing with just two squadrons, Nos. 236 and 254. For the remainder of the war, they ranged the enemy coastlines, with frequent detachments to other bases in response to tactical requirements. The Wing's final operations took place during the first few days of May 1945 when attacks on shipping in the Kattegat sank a number of U-Boats and other vessels. No. 236 Squadron disbanded on May 25 and No. 254 Squadron moved to Chivenor in June. Apart from a rescue helicopter detachment in the mid-1950s that marked the end of military flying at the station. From 1958 until 1990 it served as a launch site for a battery of 48 Bloodhound surface-to-air missiles after which it closed at the end of November 1990. The North Coates Flying Club — formed in 1995 — maintains a memorial room in their clubhouse which contains a collection of photographs paintings, models and artefacts relating to RAF North Coates, including the original station sign.

The wartime runway and most of the taxiways and dispersals have been removed. Two of the Bellmans and one of the pre-war hangars remain, all having been reclad. A number of memorials exist in the district.

Concern about Allied shipping losses in the Bay of Biscay resulted in squadron detachments to Cornwall from August 1943 onwards. By early 1944, despite reductions in strength, the North Coates Wing had honed its skills and was achieving excellent co-ordination with its attacks. This reached a point where Rotterdam, the gateway to the Ruhr — and up to the summer of 1943, the terminal of the North Sea shipping route — was now virtually denied to the enemy by day.

This was due to the joint efforts of the Strike Wing, Bomber Command mine-laying and the light surface craft of the Royal Navy's Nore Flotilla. The great Dutch port had handled most of the iron ore of Swedish origin and the ships were now forced to use Bremen and Emden, which lacked the necessary unloading gear. This was no doubt of even more concern to the enemy than the sinking in 1943 by the North Coates Wing of 13 ships of a total tonnage of 34,076 gross tons. The losses inflicted by other anti-shipping aircraft of Coastal Command were 19 ships of a total tonnage of 50,683.

Former pilot with No. 143 Squadron, Norman Carr recalls his first experience of a Wing strike from North Coates on February 21, 1944: 'I was flying Beau 'J' and we attacked a convoy off the Dutch coast. My own target turned out to be an R-Boat. I remember the coloured flak curling up slowly then whipping past and smoke around the target (with a

The contrast today — Peter Willmont's Gyroplane Tandem Trainer.

slight feeling of amazement that I was causing it), then a brief kaleidoscope of ships, wave tops, smoke, aircraft everywhere, and then streaking towards home at sea level. Settling down again on the homeward run, there came a feeling of disbelief, then relief that we were unscathed and going home. There was a peculiar mark on my windscreen that turned out to be a hit by an incendiary bullet.'

St Nicholas Church in North Cotes village has a memorial window, copies of the Roll of Honour boards and a war grave plot. The original boards are kept in the entrance corridor of the old Cleethorpes Town Hall. On the resort's sea front at Alexandra Road Gardens stands the North Coates Strike Wing memorial, surmounted by the statue of an aircrew member gazing out to sea.

And reliving history. A Hawker Hurricane built in 1942, and restored in 1985, and a Hawker Nimrod (single-seat Fury) from the 1930s.

THORNEY ISLAND

What was then RAF Thorney Island is now Baker Barracks named after Field Marshal Sir Geoffrey Harding Baker (1912-1980). Current residents are the 12th and 16th Regiments of the Royal Artillery and 63 (SAS) Signals Squadron D Troop of the Army Reserve.

Despite its name, this station is located on a peninsula rather than an island, roughly halfway between Chichester and Portsmouth on the coast of southern England. How it came to be built there is described on a memorial thus: 'In September 1933 the pilot of a Fury aircraft of No. 1 Fighter Squadron, crashed on this spot. Representatives of the RAF who came to investigate the crash observed the unique suitability of the adjoining land as an airfield. Their recommendations subsequently resulted in the building of the aerodrome. He died not in battle yet not in vain.' For the record, the pilot was Sergeant William Hodge and the memorial is sited in a small wood between the Officers' Mess and the church.

The 1,249-acre Thorney Manor estate was purchased in its entirety for the new airfield as part of the RAF expansion plan. As a result, a village of 300 inhabitants and a large manor house had to be demolished to make way for it as it was impractical to retain the village as it was effectively locked in by the

In 1938, No. 42 Squadron's Vickers Vildebeeste IVs were used on convoy patrols over the English Channel and off the East Coast until the squadron was re-equipped with Bristol Beauforts in 1940. Note the loss of the 'Fort' control tower in the background.

Two replacement towers have also been demolished. *Left:* First a non-standard watch office which was located on the east side of the airfield and *(right)* the final one built in the mid-1950s which had gone by 2012.

At the time, Vildebeeste biplanes of Nos. 22 and 42 Squadrons comprised the entire UK-based strike force of the Royal Air Force!

England in July 1940. In June a detachment of the Blenheim fighter version arrived from Detling. It was part of No. 235 Squadron and was joined soon after by more from No. 236 Squadron. They went on to shoot down several enemy aircraft while covering convoys and bombing attacks on French ports. The latter were the focus of attention of the Thorney-based No. 59 Squadron. Its Blenheims began to focus on trying to destroy the massed invasion barges in day and night raids.

The Luftwaffe paid little attention to the station until August 1940 when, on the 16th, a Ju 88 bombed a hangar and destroyed four aircraft. A deliberate mass attack came on the 18th in the shape of 28 Ju 87s escorted by a strong force of Bf 109s. Despite losing three of their number to defending Hurricanes, the Stuka pilots badly damaged two of the hangars and wrecked three aircraft. It was very fortunate that the only casualties were five civilian workmen who received slight injuries. Three Blenheims took off and pursued the raiders, accounting for two of them before Spitfires shot down more off the Isle of Wight. Altogether ten Ju 87s were destroyed and five more damaged, one beyond repair.

Another first at Thorney was when No. 48 Squadron received the first Ansons off the production line at Avros. The Anson was the RAF's first low-wing monoplane with retractable landing gear which entered service in March 1936, being operational with Coastal Command between 1936 to 1939 and for air-sea rescue duties until 1942.

aerodrome. With a few exceptions, the only building spared was the medieval parish church of St Nicholas. Six C Type hangars were constructed following the curve of the western perimeter, and the various technical and domestic buildings stretched behind them to the west. As was customary, the flying field was grass-surfaced with a longest run of 1,900 yards.

The airfield opened officially in No. 16 Group, Coastal Command, on February 3, 1938, with the arrival of the antiquated Vickers Vildebeeste biplanes of No. 22 Squadron. They were followed the next day by those of No. 42 Squadron, the two units forming the whole of the RAF's home-based strike force! No. 42 Squadron, still with Vildebeestes, moved to Norfolk in August 1939. No. 22 Squadron stayed at Thorney and anticipated re-equipping with the radically different Beaufort. For the moment, Vildebeeste anti-submarine patrols continued in the Channel, the first Beaufort arriving in November. By April 1940 when it moved to North Coates, the squadron had fully converted to the type.

No. 48 Squadron with Ansons was based at Thorney from August 1939 flying Channel patrols and sweeps, as well as escorting convoys from and to France. Detachments were sent to a number of Coastal Command bases until the squadron moved to north-west

Aldon Ferguson took the comparisons at Thorney and although the angle of the sun made photography difficult, he was pleased to see that the farm building still stood in the background.

Sandwiched on a spit of land between the Emsworth and Thorney Channels, there was little room for expansion.

By September 1940, only the Blenheims of Nos. 59 and 235 remained at Thorney but they were soon joined by 816 Squadron whose Swordfish spent six weeks here on very successful shipping strikes and anti-submarine patrols. In November 1940, No. 53 Squadron joined No. 59 in a continued effort aimed at the barge concentrations still posing an invasion threat. Further raids by single bombers during the winter of 1940-41 caused relatively little damage at Thorney. In an attempt to draw attention away from the airfield, a 'K/Q' site day and night decoy had been sited at West Wittering, three miles to the south-east. It featured dummy Blenheims and an electric flare path but whether it attracted any bombs is not known.

During 1941, three concrete runways were laid down along with a perimeter track. The two bomb-damaged C Type hangars were not rebuilt but 17 blisters were dispersed around the airfield. Limited flying took place during the reconstruction, a short grass runway being prepared well away from the main work area. The Canadian No. 404 Squadron formed at Thorney on May 1, 1941 under Coastal Command, but its Blenheims soon left to become operational in Scotland. Two more Canadian squadrons formed here during 1941. The first was No. 407 on May 8 with Blenheims which were soon replaced by Hudsons. The second was No. 415 Squadron, a torpedo-bomber unit, on August 20. It started off with a mixture of Blenheims and Beauforts but re-equipped with Hampdens in January 1942.

From October 1941, No. 217 Squadron was based, operating Beauforts in the torpedo-dropping role. Operations took them as far as the Hook of Holland, often using Manston in Kent as a forward operating base. On February 16, 1942, aircraft from the squadron made a brave but fruitless attack on the battle-cruisers *Scharnhorst* and

Gneisenau, losing one crew in the process. This was the so-called 'Channel Dash' when the ships left Brest to make a run through the English Channel for the relative safety of a German port. The weather was bad; there were delays in detecting that they had left harbour, and also problems in co-ordinating a meaningful response from three Commands of the RAF and the Royal Navy. In the subsequent analysis, a major cause of the failure was deemed to be the lack of a sufficient number of trained torpedo-bomber squadrons in Coastal Command.

On June 12, 1942, a Beaufighter from a detachment of No. 236 Squadron at Thorney was used for a special operation designed to create a heartening effect among the Parisians and expose the occupying Germans to ridicule. A routine daily parade down the Champs-Elysées was to be attacked but it was out of Spitfire range. Since all Fighter Command's Beaufighters were fitted with highly secret radar equipment, it was decided by Air Ministry that a Coastal Command Beaufighter should be employed. Unfortunately on the day in question there was no sign of a

The two hangars hit in the Luftwaffe raids in August 1940 were dismantled and never rebuilt.

The raid on August 18 effectively saw the end of offensive operations by the Ju 87 as eight were shot down, four of which crashed in as many minutes between the airfield and Chichester. Unfortunately this photograph of a funeral cortege for three Luftwaffe airmen buried at St Nicholas' Church in West Thorney is undated and as there are three sets of three graves with the same date of death, it makes it difficult to identify this particular burial.

parade, but a tricolour flag was dropped over the Arc de Triomphe and a German HQ was raked with cannon fire. The Beaufighter returned to Thorney unscathed, the pilot, Flight Lieutenant A. K. Gatward, being awarded the DFC. His navigator, Sergeant G. F. Fern, was granted an officer commission.

No. 415 Squadron continued working-up on torpedo-equipped Hampdens, moving to St Eval when they became operational in April 1942. That month No. 489 Squadron commenced conversion to the Hampden, moving to Scotland in August. A succession of Hudson, Blenheim and Hampden squadrons spent short periods at Thorney during the spring and summer of 1942. During August 1942, two Spitfire squadrons, Nos. 129 and 130, were based in support of Operation 'Jubilee', the Dieppe Raid. The same month, No. 59 Squadron arrived in order to convert from Hudsons to Liberators, moving to Chivenor in February 1943.

For much of 1942-43, Thorney was virtually a Liberator operational training unit, also hosting No. 86 Squadron until March 1943 and No. 53 Squadron from April to September. It began operations in May with a patrol over the Bay of Biscay. No. 415 had returned to Thorney as long ago as September 1942 for anti-shipping work. In September 1943 it ceased operations and began converting to Wellingtons and Fairey Albacores. When operational in November, the squadron specialised in anti-E-Boat patrols known as Operation 'Deadly'. The tactic was for the Leigh Light Wellingtons to find and illuminate the E-Boats and the Albacores to attack them. The squadron prowled along the Dutch and Channel coasts with some success, attacking any shipping it could find if no E-Boats were in evidence. Also of note was that

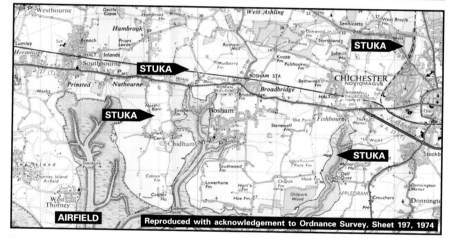

Reproduced with acknowledgement to Ordnance Survey, Sheet 197, 1974

The Officers' Mess is in the top right of the comparison but the accommodation blocks to the right and left have been demolished.

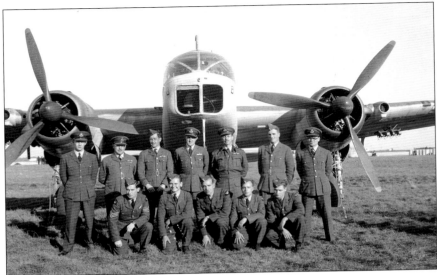

On August 20, 1941, No. 415 Squadron of the Royal Canadian Air Force was formed up at Thorney Island as a torpedo-bomber unit equipped with the Bristol Beauforts. These pictures were taken on November 21 that year. The commanding officer was 28-year-old

Wing Commander E. L. 'Wally' Wurtele of Montreal. He had joined the RAF in 1935 and had already had a varied career, serving on the *Furious* and *Glorious* in the Mediterranean followed by a stint as a catapult pilot on board the battleship *Malaya*.

in 1942-43 there were a series of detachments by Fleet Air Arm Swordfish squadrons to reinforce Channel cover.

In November 1943, No. 415 Squadron moved to Norfolk to leave room for No. 547 Squadron which began converting to Liberators and left for operations from St Eval in January 1944. The only Coastal Command presence was now a detachment of Warwicks from the Air-Sea Rescue Training Unit at Thornaby. These departed in March 1944 leaving Thorney to join the many airfields allotted to Second Tactical Air Force. It was soon to become the base for two wings of Typhoon squadrons which in the prelude to the invasion concentrated on destroying coastal radar stations. So effective were these operations that by D-Day all were out of action except one at Calais, deliberately spared so it could track the spoof radar returns made by Bomber Command to simulate an invasion convoy.

The Typhoons now turned their attention to attacking German armour but flak and fighters caused many losses. When the Typhoons left for the Continent in the middle of June, they were immediately replaced by No. 140 Wing, consisting of three squadrons of Mosquito fighter-bombers — Nos. 21, 464 and 487. They operated under Second TAF and mounted both day and night operations to deny the enemy supplies and reinforcements. The railway system was the chief target, as well as barracks and headquarters. Similar work continued as the battlefront moved across France.

One of No. 140 Wing's most celebrated efforts was the precision attack on the Gestapo's Jutland HQ housed in two buildings of Aarhus University. A total of 24 Mosquitos escorted by eight Mustangs, took part. It was one of the longest trips made by the wing, the round trip of 1,235 miles taking five and a half hours, and the HQ was completely

In February 1944, three Mosquito squadrons, No. 21, No. 464 (RAAF) and No. 487 (RNZAF) carried out a daring low-level raid on the prison at Amiens with the purpose of aiding the escape of Resistance prisoners (see *After the Battle* No. 218). Flying as No. 140 Wing, although part of Bomber Command No. 2 Group, the next operation took place from the Coastal Command base at Thorney Island on October 31 when the same three squadrons attacked the Gestapo headquarters in Denmark at the request of the Danish Resistance which wanted the Gestapo archive destroyed (see *After the Battle* No. 54). *Above:* The HQ was located in the University of Aarhus on the Jutland peninsula, a hundred miles west of Copenhagen. (In March 1945, the same squadron returned to Denmark to knock out the Gestapo headquarters in Copenhagen itself — see *After the Battle* No. 113.)

January 1942 and ground crews bring up their hot air van to warm the engines and de-ice the cockpit windscreen of this Hudson belonging to No. 233 Squadron.

With the snowy background, not much chance of taking a meaningful comparison as all the blister hangars have been demolished.

This is the C Type hangar which was blitzed in August 1940, since demolished. The Spitfire F16 has just been flown in on April 4, 1949 by the AOC of Fighter Command, Air Vice-Marshal Sir William Elliott.

1947 the station was transferred to Fighter Command. Spitfires were followed by Meteor-equipped squadrons.

In May 1950 the fighter units left and the station was switched to Flying Training Command for use by No. 2 Air Navigation School. It used a number of types beginning with Ansons and Wellingtons, then some Miles Marathons and finally Valettas and Varsities, along with some Vampires to provide jet experience. In January 1962, the school moved elsewhere and Thorney was transferred to Transport Command for No. 242 Operational Conversion Unit. Its aircraft were Hastings and Beverleys, which were joined by Argosies in 1963 and then Hercules from 1967. Thorney finally closed for flying on March 31, 1976.

After considerable refurbishment it was reallocated as an Army base for the Royal Artillery during 1984 becoming Baker Barracks. The three runways are still intact, as is the perimeter track and four of the C Type hangars. St. Nicholas Church has a stained glass window commemorating the Air Navigation School. In the churchyard are 52 Commonwealth burials of the 1939-45 War, as well as the graves of 21 Luftwaffe aircrew. Since the church is on a military base, access is obviously restricted but is possible by prior arrangement.

destroyed. Later, the Mosquitos harried von Rundstedt's supply line during the Battle of the Bulge. Early in February 1945, with accommodation at last available, the Mosquitos moved to a French base.

No. 16 Group had retained a presence at Thorney throughout almost all of the Tactical Air Force's occupation of the airfield, mainly in the form of FAA squadrons operating under Coastal Command directives. Examples included 848 Squadron with Avengers, 838 and 842 Squadrons with Swordfish and by January 1945 the Barracudas of 810 and 822 Squadrons for anti-submarine patrols. The final months of the war saw No. 278 Squadron on air-sea rescue duties until disbandment on October 14, 1945.

The post-war plan for Coastal Command included a reduction to only one Strike Wing, this being based at Thorney. Mosquito and Beaufighter squadrons arrived with the aim of conversion to the Bristol Brigand torpedo fighter. Abruptly, the Strike Wing concept was abandoned and on December 15,

The churchyard at St Nicholas contains graves of both Allied and German servicemen.

T4712

No. 18 GROUP

BANFF

The main entrance to the airfield. The building is the Airmen's Dining Room (138 on the plan opposite). Today the airfield is occupied by several different farmers, some industry and a small wind farm, seen in the distance of Aldon Ferguson's comparison (below).

Known locally as Boyndie, this airfield was planned from the start for Coastal Command, specifically to house two general reconnaissance squadrons and with a satellite at Dallachy. The location on a ridge and a slightly sloping hillside near the Moray Firth in north-east Scotland was not ideal. Construction by George Wimpey & Co Ltd began in early 1942 and was to have an unintended but lasting effect on the nearby town of Banff itself. Hardcore was needed in vast quantities for runways, taxiways and building bases, so a convenient area of the River Deveron estuary was stripped of its pebble barrier. As a result, the river changed its course and Banff Harbour became permanently silted up.

By the spring of 1943, work was nearing completion on the standard 'A'-shaped three runway pattern. The lengths were a main of 2,000 yards and two subsidiaries, both of 1,400 yards. A total of 40 frying-pan hardstandings led off the perimeter track and three T2 hangars were dispersed at intervals. Later, 13 blisters were erected. The majority of the accommodation and other buildings consisted of a very large number of Nissen huts, the majority of them on the south-eastern side of the airfield. Only key buildings such as the Watch Office and Operations Block were made from brick and concrete. The bomb dump was sited well to the north-east of the airfield, shielded within Whyntie Wood.

By this time, the need for advanced Bomber Command bases in north-east Scotland led to lodger facilities for Banff being offered for up to 24 aircraft. At the same time, it was noted that a Coastal Operational Training Unit was likely to be based here as soon as the station opened and that the resulting congestion was likely to be unacceptable. As so often happens in wartime, plans changed abruptly and the OTU moved to south Wales instead. Banff was then taken over by No. 21 Group, Flying Training Command and the airfield opened on April 21, 1943. Towards the end of May, No. 14 (Pilots) Advanced Flying Unit's Oxfords moved in from Nottinghamshire

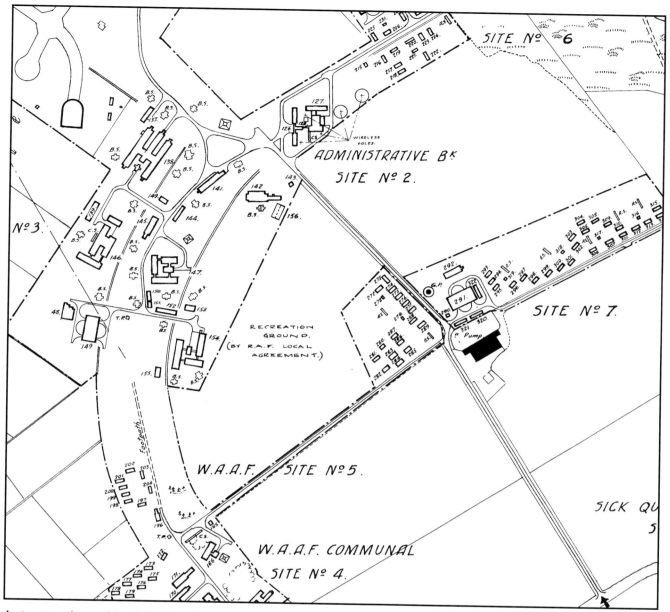

Just across the road lay Administrative Site No. 2 where the all-important Operations Block (Building 127) was located. With so many of the facilities having now been demolished, including the hangars, Aldon was thrilled to find that the Ops Block was still standing as we had photos we wanted to match up inside.

It is not often that one finds a photograph of an actual briefing, let alone taken in a building that has survived. Although the censor appears to have tried to obliterate the detail on the wall boards, we were fortunate to find this unadulterated version in squadron files showing the wall maps *(below)* in all their glory.

An enormous amount of flying took place as the AFU got into its stride again, despite difficulties with incomplete accommodation. The unit's establishment of over 150 Oxfords used Dallachy and Fraserburgh as satellites. In July 1944, the U-Boats were withdrawing from western French ports to Scandinavia and it was decided to transfer the bulk of No. 19 Group's squadrons from south-west England to Scotland in order to counter the threat from this new direction. Banff and Dallachy were expected to accommodate up to four Wellington squadrons and No. 14 (P) AFU was given notice to move. Instead it was disbanded at the end of August but its achievements had been considerable, having turned out over 2,000 multi-engined pilots and run up more than 150,000 flying hours.

The operational aircraft that replaced the trainers were not Wellingtons, however, but a mixed Strike Wing consisting of the Beaufighters of Nos 144 and 404 Squadrons and Mosquitos of Nos. 235 and 248 Squadrons. Also on hand, although not strictly part of the Wing, was 'P' Flight of No. 333 Squadron whose Norwegian-crewed Mosquitos would act as outriders due to their knowledge of Norway's coastline. Group Captain Max Aitken, son of Lord Beaverbrook, the newspaper magnate, was appointed to lead the

Banff Strike Wing and at one time his squadron commanders comprised an Englishman, an Australian, a New Zealander, a Norwegian, a Frenchman and an Irishman. Such was the severity of the losses that four of these commanding officers were killed on operations.

The weak link between Germany's main source of high grade iron ore in the far north of Sweden was the sea route between the Norwegian port of Narvik, to which it was conveyed by rail, and the ports of northern Germany. Deprived of this resource, the steel mills of the Ruhr valley would be unable to turn out the vast quantities of steel required to build all the weapons of modern warfare. Coastal Command had been gnawing away at this trade for years and lost many aircraft and crews so doing. Now, the Scottish-based Strike Wings would attempt to overwhelm it by sheer fire-power. In a mere nine months, they did so and brought seaborne traffic in western Scandinavia almost to a complete standstill. Over 100,000 tons of merchant shipping was sunk by the Banff and Dallachy squadrons, and almost as much again was damaged.

The Wing's first *Rover* (an armed reconnaissance against chance targets, usually shipping) took place on September 14 with 44 aircraft involved. There were 29 Mosqui-

And here is the bonus — part of the left-hand board still extant!

tos, including four of the Mk XVIII version (the Tsetse) fitted with an adapted 57mm six-pounder Molins quick-firing anti-tank gun. They were accompanied by 19 Beaufighters. Four ships with two escorts were spotted off Kristiansund and hits were scored on all of them, with one of the flak ships being sunk. The flak barrage was intense, forcing one Beaufighter to ditch, and another returned to Banff on a single engine. Four days later, Mosquitos came across a U-Boat on the surface, and attacked it with cannon and machine gun fire. Hits were observed with the U-Boat left listing and smoking. Later, 12 Mosquitos searched for the submarine but there was no sign of it.

In the autumn of 1943, de Havillands had studied the possibility of fitting rocket rails to the Mosquito. This proved to be feasible and the installation of four racks under each wing capable of carrying four 60lb rockets was approved. Flight tests determined that the ideal dive angle was 20 degrees and that there was no recoil stress on the airframe. The type of rocket used by the Banff Wing was normally the 25lb solid armour-piercing type, a salvo of which was said — perhaps optimistically — to be equivalent to a broadside from a cruiser. The 60lb high explosive version was tried initially but proved far less effective than the smaller missile which was able to punch through four inches of steel.

Towards the end of September, Banff's Mosquitos began to be retrofitted with eight rocket rails, but much firing practice was required so, in the meantime, a number of ships were sunk by conventional methods. It was not until October 26 that rockets were used for the first time in anger. Although the enemy was suffering from the repeated attacks that were beginning to strike directly at his harbours and anchorages, there was a steady toll of missing aircraft and crews. Surviving a ditching for very long this far north was virtually impossible, especially with winter looming. It was therefore of some comfort to know that an air-sea rescue detachment of No. 279 Squadron would fly out to meet the returning aircraft and escort any cripples. They were equipped with Warwicks, each carrying an airborne lifeboat and other survival gear.

Close up of the panel and other surviving stencilled inscriptions in the building.

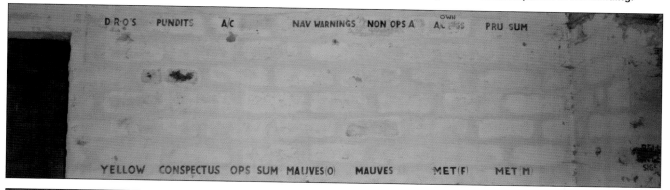

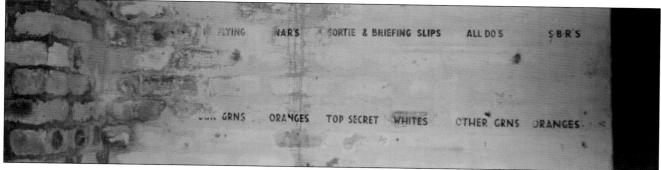

The view from the opposite direction with the wall boards behind the camera.

Probably one of the most dramatic photographs of a Coastal Command base is this shot, but, as Banff historian Les Taylor explains, there seems to be no record of who took it, nor where the original negative or even a print may reside today. However, beyond all doubt, is the sheer atmosphere of that now-famous picture of the multi-squadron Banff Strike Wing in March 1945.

One of the Warwicks was used to try a tactic which had not proved very successful in the southern part of the North Sea. It took off from Banff with a load of marine floats, drift lights and flame floats and dropped them to form a six-mile diameter ring about 100 miles west of Stavanger. Eight Mosquitos and 14 Beaufighters circled these lights and waited for the ships that usually used these shipping lanes at night. This ploy proved successful with a freighter and submarine hunter sunk and another ship damaged. All the aircraft returned safely but it seems that the tactic was not used again.

Now that the Banff Mosquitos had rocket capability, the Beaufighters of Nos.144 and 404 Squadrons, long since able to carry rockets, moved to nearby Dallachy to join its Strike Wing. They were partially replaced by No. 143 Squadron whose Beaufighters arrived on October 23 with the intention of converting to Mosquitos. By November 7 they were operational and flew an uneventful patrol off Norway. Bad weather hindered operations during the remainder of November; nevertheless three ships were sunk without any aircraft losses.

On December 5, a large-scale attack on shipping in a fjord resulted in damage to four German vessels but at the cost of one

The photograph was taken from the roof of the control tower but it has deteriorated badly since the Banff Flying Club used it and the outer staircase has now been removed. To match the classic shot we brought in a vehicle with a high lift.

Mosquito. Intense and accurate light flak damaged at least six aircraft, with one crash-landing at Sumburgh, killing its pilot.

December 7, 1944 saw a mixed strike wing effort by 25 Mosquitos from Banff and 40 Beaufighters from Dallachy, escorted by 12 Mustangs of the Polish No. 315 Squadron from RAF Peterhead. The target was Gossen fighter airfield in Norway from where the formation came under attack by Me 109s and FW 190s. In the ensuing combat the Mustangs claimed four Me 109s shot down, while two FW 190s collided in mid-air. Four aircraft were lost from the strike force — a Mustang, Beaufighter and two Mosquitos. Another major attack occurred on the 16th, two ships being sunk for the loss of a pair of Mosquitos. With so many combat aircraft — at one point totalling 138 Mosquitos — there were simply not enough hardstandings for all of them. The answer was to take the south-western end of a little-used runway out of service and turn it into a big aircraft park.

January 1945 was a month of bad weather and heavy snow that was reflected in the reduced number of operational strikes carried out. A strike against shipping in Leirvik harbour on January 15, 1945 destroyed two large merchant ships and an armed trawler but resulted in the loss of six Mosquitos which were met by a pack of nine FW 190s as they turned for home. This was the heaviest loss

A similar shot was taken of the Mosquitos about to set off on an operation to Norway at Christmas Time in 1944, possibly the Boxing Day sortie to Leirvik harbour. It became an infamous target in the annals of the Wing as one Mosquito was lost on December 26 and five aircraft failed to return from an abortive raid on a merchant ship in the harbour on January 15 with the loss of nine airmen. All told, by May 1945 over 100 crewmen had lost their lives serving with the Banff Strike Wing.

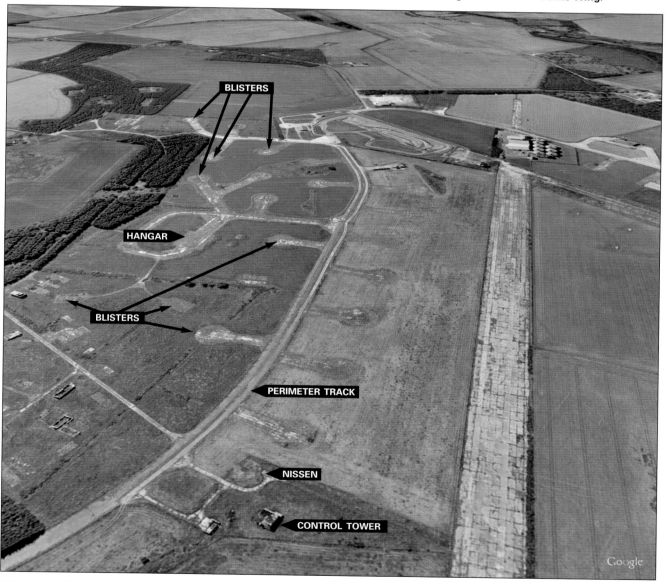

This low-level oblique view looking south-west, probably gives a better idea of the airfield dispersals as they appeared in 2004.

117

Each Mosquito could carry four 3-inch rockets under each wing but these had to be loaded carefully as there were instances of the rockets self-launching when the electrical connection was made. These armourers are seen working on loading a Mosquito of No. 143 Squadron on one of the frying pan dispersals which lay south of the tower.

The firepower of a Mosquito: the four .303 Brownings in the nose and four 20mm Hispano cannons below are tested on the firing butt which lay off the northern perimeter track.

sustained by the Banff Wing in any one action and a Tsetse Mosquito is said to have frightened off the fighters by firing its Molins gun at them. This attack also proved to be No. 248 Squadron's last Tsetse sortie from Banff before they were withdrawn, leaving the squadron to operate Mosquito Mk VIs only.

February saw no major strikes and only a few sinkings but on March 7 40 Mosquitos attacked self-propelled barges in the Kattegat with gun-fire and rockets. Twelve Mustangs provided fighter cover, with two Warwicks on hand to drop lifeboats to any ditched crews. Four aircraft of No. 333 Squadron led the way with the flak suppression Mosquitos following behind. Four barges were sunk, as well as a flak ship but two Mosquitos were lost in the attack, appar-

ently from a collision. There were further successful shipping attacks that month and on the 24th part of No. 404 squadron arrived from Dallachy to begin conversion from Beaufighters to Mosquitos. The remainder of the squadron moved to Banff in early April.

An anti-shipping sweep through the Skagerrak and Kattegat by the Wing on April 9 came upon three U-Boats on the surface heading towards Norway. All three were attacked and sunk but the accompanying RAF Film Production Unit Mosquito was lost having been caught in the explosion of one of the submarines. It spun into the sea. Damage was so severe to three other aircraft that they had to make emergency landings in *Brighton*, the code-name for neutral Sweden. Two days later four merchant vessels were sunk and on the 19th another U-Boat. On April 21, 45 Mosquitos failed to find any ships but encountered a mixed formation of 18 Ju 88s and Ju 188s intent upon attacking a

Fortunately it has survived — a photo by Colin Jeffries.

There were three T2 hangars but all have gone leaving just the overgrown concrete bases.

convoy off the Scottish coast. Nine of them were swiftly shot down but an investigation of German records post-war revealed that no less than 14 had been reported missing.

The Banff Strike Wing's final attack on shipping in the Kiel and Kattegat areas took place on May 4. The force consisted of 41 Mosquitos and 18 escorting Mustangs, with three Warwicks on hand to drop lifeboats to any ditched crews. A convoy of three cargo ships plus escorts was spotted and attacked, resulting in the sinking of one of the merchantmen and damage to the other two. The flak barrage was intense which resulted in four Mustangs failing to return. Two Mosquitos suffered battle damage and landed in neutral Sweden and another landed back at Banff with the German ensign and part of a ship's mast embedded in the nose of the aircraft!

Whereas VE-Day brought an end to operations for most Allied air units, Coastal Command continued its work. There was fear of enemy submarines ignoring or being unaware that hostilities had ended. Thus the Mosquitos flew convoy escort sorties until May 21, 1945 as well as searching for survivors from ditched aircraft. Typically, Max Aitken who had flown on the very first day of the war in Europe, made sure that he also flew on the last. The final hours before the cease-fire had seen him patrolling out as far as northern Denmark.

On June 1, No. 143 Squadron was renumbered No. 14 Squadron, retaining its Mosquitos until disbandment at Banff on March 31, 1946. No. 333 Squadron departed to Norway in June and No. 235 Squadron disbanded in mid-July 1945, with No. 248 Squadron moving to Devon in the same month. No. 404

Squadron, which had come from Dallachy to convert to the Mosquito in March 1945, disbanded at Banff on May 25. No. 489 Squadron repositioned from Dallachy on June 16, 1945 but disbanded at the beginning of August.

The airfield closed in the middle of 1946 and later became a target for simulated bombing by Fleet Air Arm aircraft based at Lossiemouth. It was reopened in 1976 by the Banff Flying Club who refurbished the watch tower and cleared one of the runways. The by-now Sir Max Aitken formally reopened his old airfield on June 2, 1976 but sadly the club folded a few years later. The site largely reverted to agricultural use although a go-kart track occupies the southern end of the north-south runway and a small industrial estate lies on the western perimeter. The Boyndie Wind Farm has also been erected on another part of the airfield.

With over 150 Mosquitos in residence, Banff ended the war as the largest Coastal Command station.

A Mosquito of No. 404 Squadron taxies from its dispersal off the perimeter track . . . then and now.

A memorial was unveiled on September 28, 1989 on A98 adjacent to the road to the aerodrome, the inscription reading: 'This memorial commemorates the men and women who served with the six multinational squadrons which formed the Banff Strike Wing at R.A.F. Banff between September 1944 and May 1945. Under the command of group captain the Hon. Max Aitken the mixed Mosquito and Beaufighter units mounted concentrated attacks on German surface vessels and U-boats in the North Sea and along the Norwegian coast. Their success in the closing months of World War II was important in the defeat of Germany and strike wing aircraft operating from the airfield near here inflicted heavy damage on enemy shipping and supply routes. Many thousands of tons of vital iron ore and other supplies were lost to the German forces as a result of rocket and cannon attacks carried out by this gallant strike wing. Losses amongst R.A.F. commonwealth and Norwegian squadrons were high. More than 80 aircrew gave their lives flying with the R.A.F. Banff Strike Wing.'

Les Taylor has written up the history of the airfield in his magnificent *Banff Strike Wing at War* (Halsgrove, 2010), which is, in my opinion, one of the finest tributes to a wartime airfield and its flyers I have ever read. This is one evocative passage: 'Another aspect vividly remembered by people all across northern Aberdeenshire was the awesome sight and sound of Banff Strike Wing in the air. With often as many as 50 or 60 Mosquitos forming-up over Banff, joined by perhaps 30 or 40 Beaufighters from Dallachy, this huge formation would roar over Buchan, rattling window frames with their massed throbbing drone. At the rallying point of Rattray Head lighthouse between Peterhead and Fraserburgh, they would be joined by a dozen or more P-51 Mustang fighters from Peterhead, before setting course out across the North Sea. On their return, often scattered, they would celebrate survival by 'beating up' towns, villages, pubs and even individual houses of friends and girl-friends at very low level. They were a highly visible and audible presence in the north-east Scottish skies, making victory seem all the more inevitable to those who witnessed them'.

The charismatic leader of the Banff Strike Wing was Group Captain Max Aitken. Technically he was the station commander and not a member of any of the squadrons and also not officially allowed to take part in operations. Nevertheless, in spite of repeated orders from No. 18 Group headquarters, he ignored all that and still did so, leading his men from the front. On the very last day of the war in Europe, he made a point of joining the Wing on a sortie to Aalborg, Denmark. Here, three months earlier, he performs a low-level beat-up of the 'drome for the benefit of aviation photographer Charles E. Brown.

DALLACHY

Planned as a Coastal Command station, Dallachy on the north-east Scottish coast, was constructed by George Wimpey & Co Ltd in 1942-43. The local terrain dictated two runways rather than the customary three, their lengths being 1,600 yards and 1,400 yards. Two T2 hangars and three blisters were erected and the dispersals consisted of 35 loop hardstandings and a solitary frying-pan. The accommodation sites, designed for 1,530 airmen and 408 WAAFs, were built to the south and south-west of the airfield, and an extensive bomb storage area was laid out well to the south-east of these.

Long before it was finished, the airfield was the subject of much discussion. First, Bomber Command showed interest in it as an advanced base, but was warned by Coastal Command that it was intended to move one of its Operational Training Units here from South Wales and the resultant congestion might prove unacceptable. The runways were, in any case, too short for heavy bombers so the plan was dropped.

In 1942, the Navy had an urgent requirement for an aerodrome at which to establish an observer school. As existing naval aerodromes were already overcrowded, the Air Ministry was approached and Dallachy was offered as a temporary solution for three months after its scheduled completion date of March 31, 1943. In the meantime, the Admiralty was told that it would have to build its own new base and move there, or alternatively build a new station for the RAF using its own funds, and retain Dallachy permanently. It was decided that this was not a good idea with only two runways and various other problems, so they made do with expanding the training programme at Arbroath.

Three stages in the life of an aerodrome. The Luftwaffe pictured what they called 'Portgordon Flugplatz — Target GB 10 450' on September 26, 1942, naming the airfield after the town two miles to the east.

Left: **This cover by No. 540 Squadron recorded the progress of the construction as at February 21, 1943.** *Right:* **End of war photo taken on August 31, 1945 shows the extensive loop** dispersals which were an essential addition to cater for the three squadrons which were brought together to create the Dallachy Strike Wing in the autumn of 1944.

Striking shot of a 'Torbeau' of No. 489 Squadron, showing off with a torpedo loaded under the port wing and starboard engine feathered. The caption on the original print stated: 'Not recommended for combat operations'.

When No. 14 (Pilots) Advanced Flying Unit moved into Banff in May 1943 with over 150 Airspeed Oxfords, Dallachy was taken over as a satellite. In July, the unit's Night Flying Flight was established here, as well as an associated Beam Approach Training Flight. The purpose of AFUs was to bridge the gap between initial flying training and operational training, conversion being made onto higher performance aircraft types. At Dallachy and Banff, pilots were taught how to handle a twin-engine aircraft. Since many of them had done their basic flying training overseas, the secondary purpose of an AFU was to get them accustomed to British weather, as well as wartime flying conditions and procedures.

In July 1944, with the U-Boats withdrawing from the threatened Brittany ports, Coastal Command prepared to transfer much of its force to north-east Scotland. Dallachy and Banff were earmarked for Wellington squadrons, so Flying Training Command was informed that it must vacate both stations at two weeks' notice. Since there was now a surplus of trained pilots, it was decided that No. 14 (P) AFU would be disbanded, which duly took place on August 31, 1944. However it was not Wellingtons that arrived but Beau-

fighters. A Royal New Zealand Air Force Squadron, No. 489, had been in Norfolk attacking shipping from the Dutch and Belgian ports. By October, it became obvious that Norwegian coastal traffic was far more worthy of attention, so the squadron switched to Dallachy at the same time as the other units that were to form a Strike Wing.

They consisted of Nos. 144, 404 and 455 Squadrons, all with Beaufighters that roamed off the rugged coast of Norway, searching for prey. The tactical sequence was a cannon and rocket attack on the escort to suppress the flak before the torpedo launch at the main targets: the ships carrying iron ore. Losses from these actions were high, with a steady drain on crews from accurate flak and the German fighters that sometimes made an appearance. The Dallachy Wing was to remember February 9, 1945 as 'Black Friday' because on this date no less than nine Beaufighters — six of them from No. 404 Squadron — and an escorting Mustang were lost. The target was reported by reconnaissance as a destroyer with escort vessels. A force of 31 Beaufighters took off from Dallachy and rendezvoused with a dozen Mustangs, with two Warwicks following to locate any ditched aircrew.

The Banff Wing also took part in the strike as a separate formation, losing one Mosquito to fighter attack. Braving heavy flak from the ships and shore batteries, the Beaufighters blew up the destroyer and badly damaged a minesweeper and other craft. One aircraft returned to base with a two-foot-square hole in its tailplane and most of its companions had lesser damage. The next morning, 17 Beaufighters flew out in line abreast along the return track looking for survivors, but found nothing.

A detachment of No. 524 Squadron's Wellingtons from Langham, Norfolk, joined the Wing for a time for a trial known as Operation 'Ashfield'. The radar-equipped aircraft were supposed to locate enemy shipping at night and lay a wide circular pattern of flame floats on the sea so the strike aircraft could assemble for an attack. The experiment proved unsuccessful, however and the Wellingtons soon returned to Norfolk.

Both Nos. 144 and 455 Squadrons disbanded towards the end of May 1945, but No. 489 moved to Banff to convert to the Mosquito. No. 404 Squadron having already gone to Banff in March 1945. By VE-Day, the Dallachy Strike Wing had flown 2,230 sorties, sunk 15 ships and damaged 55 others.

In the Operations Record Book of No. 489 Squadron at war's end, the Commanding Officer wrote a fitting epitaph: 'Already some of our crews who were prisoners of war are returning to this country. It is good to know that they are safe and well. In the midst of the celebrations, those who have not and will not return are not forgotten. Most of us knew at least one or two of these grand fellows who gave all they had in the service of their country for the cause of free men everywhere. They were cheerful, generous and brave. We shall remember them with gratitude and affection.'

The strike photographs in the Dallachy Squadrons' Operations Record Books show many scenes of Norwegian tranquillity — fir trees, neat little houses, patches of snow, still water in tiny harbours — but the brutal contrast is a ship in the foreground smothered in cannon and rocket fire. Today, the airfield from which this destruction took place, is a peaceful sight itself and it is hard to imagine all the frantic activity that was carried out here in that last bitter winter of the war.

The late Squadron Leader William (Bill) Mullen, Senior Operations Officer at RAF Dallachy from September 1944 to May 1945, wrote a memoir of his time here. Some extracts are quoted with the kind permission of his family and Russell Boyd who published the account on his web-blog in 2007.

Aldon Ferguson explored Dallachy in August 2015. He reported that 'most buildings have been removed but the runways and taxyways remain together with dispersals and hangar bases. The tower still stands but all adjacent buildings on the technical site are gone and their bases removed. The airfield itself is now open fields with no trace of its former use. A Moray Council recycling centre, with several new buildings and piles of scrap, occupies the north-east end of the NE-SW runway. The other runway is used as a dump by the farmer but both are fully recognisable.'

The Dallachy Strike Wing comprised Nos. 144, 404 and 455 Squadrons equipped with Bristol Beaufighter TF MkXs, which operated in conjunction with the Mosquitos of the Banff Strike Wing on their airfield, 15 miles away to the east.

The Norwegian-crewed tanker *Inger Johanne* was attacked by a combined force of 21 Beaufighters and 17 Mosquitos off Lillesand on October 15, 1944. Two Beaufighters can be seen overflying the ship as it explodes.

In this sequence of photos, Flight Lieutenant B. J. Daventry pictured the armourers loading 25lb armour-piercing rockets in preparation for a raid. Meanwhile fitters stand by the trolley acs ready for the pilots to start their engines.

The escorting flak ship *Mosel* comes in for a hammering from No. 404 Squadron, one of their machines on the right still wearing invasion stripes. All the aircraft safely returned to Scotland while the ship was consigned to Davy Jones.

The aircraft return, a signal flare indicating that they are cleared to land.

For many years the tower was left open to the elements but now the local farmer has sealed the windows and doors.

'Life on an RAF Station in wartime tends to become rather small town. One is thrown into close contact with those people with whom one works, and it is essential that those companions be friendly and congenial. This is necessary for smooth and efficient working and also for pleasant relaxation in off duty hours. We were fortunate at Dallachy in this respect.

'We were suddenly notified that three squadrons of Beaufighters were to be stationed at Dallachy and in fact they arrived within 48 hours and stretched our resources almost to breaking point. The sudden addition of about 200 officers meant that our small staff of women cooks were terribly overworked and we urgently needed further help. We now settled down with four squadrons: one British — No. 144, one Australian — No. 455, one Canadian — No. 404 and one New Zealand — No. 489. A real mixture if ever there was one. We were also to co-operate with the Banff Wing of Mosquitos for major efforts.

'A typical day at Dallachy started three or four hours before dawn. The operations officer on night duty would see that the three crews already warned the night before were called in good time for operational breakfast, after which they would

report to the Ops Room for briefing. Their job would be to carry out a reconnaissance of the whole Norwegian coast from Trondheim to Oslo. For this purpose it was divided into three sectors and each crew took one sector. These flights were usually trouble-free and we would expect all three to return more or less on time. Occasionally we would receive a sighting report which would bring all squadrons to readiness. The report was evaluated at Command and a decision would then be made as to which squadrons would take part in the strike and what armament would be used in the attack.

However, the mission to Fordefjord on February 9, 1945 to attack the German destroyer *Z-33* and its supporting vessels ended up with nine of the 31 Beaufighters from Dallachy failing to return. Flight Sergeant S. Butler, pilot of PL-0 of No. 144 Squadron, and Flight Sergeant Nicholls, his navigator, were the last to go in to attack. Flak from the *Z-33* and fire from a Focke Wulf 190 severed the hydraulics and, although they managed to get back to Scotland, the undercarriage could not be lowered. The damage was too severe and the Beaufighter had to be scrapped.

The aptly-named Beaufighter Lane runs from the village of Nether Dallachy and utilises part of the old perimeter track, passing the loop dispersals which still exist on the northern and eastern sides.

'If a strike was to be initiated as a result of an early morning recce, it would be ready to take off about midday and would not return till about 4 p.m. After seeing the aircraft take off, there would be a let down and lunch would be taken. No word would be received from the aircraft and we would wait anxiously for the first one to land and then start counting them in. It would be unusual to get a full count and we had to wait for details till the crews returned to the Ops Room for debriefing. Hot coffee and rum were available to help the men relax after their ordeal but it would be some time before a clear picture of what had happened could be seen.'

In November 1945 the airfield was placed on Care and Maintenance before it became a Territorial Army training centre until 1958. Fleet Air Arm aircraft from Lossiemouth also used it for simulated bombing. In later years, part of the east side of the airfield was in use as a gliding site. A waste recycling plant has now been built on the north-eastern end of one of the runways. The taxi-track north of the 11/29 runway was converted into a local road, known as Beaufighter Road. The derelict watch tower lies in a field approximately 400 metres northeast of the Strike Wing monument. This is sited near the entrance to the former camp, on the road from Fochabers to Spey Bay. The concrete runways, taxiways and perimeter road are still clearly visible, but are heavily overgrown in places. A major survivor is

the Operations Block, adjacent to a modern bungalow close to the southern perimeter. Apart from roadways, the dispersed accommodation sites have been cleared and at least one — the former Communal Site — has smart bungalows built over it. The bomb store in woodland to the south-east still shows some signs of earth traverses and brickwork.

Next to the impressive Strike Wing memorial at the airfield entrance is a stone commemorating the site's training role. The inscription reads: 'To all who served and gave their lives while with the 14 (Pilot) Advanced Flying Unit Royal Air Force at RAF Stations Banff, Dallachy and Fraserburgh May 1943 — August 1944'

Maßstab etwa 1: 11 800

500   0   500   1000   m

(1cm = 118 m)

Aberdeen (Dyce)
Fliegerhorst

GB 10 2 bc
(2. Ang.)

Bild:
F 29/40/09 (Lfl5)

vom
21. 9. 40.

Karte GB/Sc
1:100 000
Blatt 15

Länge
(westl. Greenw.):
2° 11' 50"
Nördl. Breite:
57° 12' 10"

Mißweisung:
— 12° 56'
(Mitte 1940)

Zielhöhe
überNN 61 m

November 1940

Ⓐ GB 10 2 (2.Ang.) <u>Fliegerhorst</u> (Aberdeen)(Dyce)

Rollfeld etwa 1150 x 830 m, mit 3 Startbahnen in NS,NO/SW - u.NW/SO Richtung.

<u>Westteil:</u> 1) 4 Flugzeughallen,massiv,flache Satteldächer,mit Tarnanstrich,etwa 6700 qm. 2) Flugleitungsgebäude,einstöckig, Satteldach, in U-Form gebaut. 3) Kesselhaus mit 1 Schornstein,massiv,einstöckig,Satteldach. 4) Fahrzeughalle,massiv, Satteldach. 5) ummalltes Gebäude, wahrsch. Bombenlager. 6) Kommandantur-u.Verwaltungsgebäude,massiv,Satteldächer. 7) Unterkunftsbaracken, Satteldächer, 8) Baustellen mit ostw. anschließendem Zeltlager.

<u>Ostteil:</u> 9) 3 Flugzeughallen, massiv, Sattel- u. Lamellendach, etwa 2 300 qm. 10) Flughafen-u.Nebengebäude.

DYCE

Originally Dyce was a grass landing ground but by the time the Luftwaffe photographed what they called Aberdeen Target GB 10 2 in September 1940 it had been given three intersecting concrete runways.

Located to the north-west of the city, the site was used first by Captain E. E. Fresson of Highland Airways in 1933 for a business charter flight. It was merely an improvised 400-yard strip of grass in an area which had already been suggested for an airport. However, another Scottish aviation pioneer, Eric Gandar Dower, very soon purchased the land for use by his firm, Aberdeen Airways.

The new airport opened officially on July 4, 1934 and in June 1937 No. 612 Squadron formed here as an army co-operation unit of the Auxiliary Air Force. A hutted camp was constructed but plans for the opening of an Elementary and Reserve Flying Training School were cancelled immediately before the war.

No. 612 Squadron transferred to a general reconnaissance role with Ansons in July 1939 and began coastal patrols in September. Dyce became an RAF station the following month and began life with four grass strips, the longest being 1,400 yards.

In December 1939, No 1 Coastal Patrol Flight formed here with Tiger Moths and Hornet Moths to cover the waters between Kinnaird Head and Montrose. These so-called 'Scarecrow' patrols carried a signal pistol and the only survival gear in the event of a ditching was an inflated car inner tube and two carrier pigeons. On January 25, 1940, two of the Flight's Tigers were instrumental in the destruction of a submarine. They sighted a moving line of oil and attracted the attention of a passing destroyer. Depth-charges were dropped and the U-Boat was confirmed as sunk.

Three much-needed runways were built in 1940, intersecting in the middle of the airfield because the terrain precluded the usual triangular layout. Other improvements included the erection of four Bellman hangars, to which were added later in the war 14 Blisters and two 'twin T3s'. Three Pickett-Hamilton retractable forts were installed out on the airfield and a 'Q' site decoy was laid out at Harestone Moss about four miles to

the NNE. This attracted bombs on at least four nights in 1940/41. When incoming air raids were plotted, aircraft were flown to a dispersal satellite — little more than prepared fields — at East Fingask, about ten miles to the north-west. Aircrews waited for the 'All Clear' before returning to Dyce airfield. Today, the sole remnant is a single RAF building.

By June 1940, No. 612 Squadron was flying over 280 sorties a month and made four attacks on suspected U-Boats in June and July. In November the first Whitleys arrived, but the conversion to the new type and the first patrols of the Faroes and Shetland resulted in five bad crashes before the squadron moved to Wick in March 1941. From May to July 1940, No. 248 Squadron had been operating Blenheims on anti-invasion patrols around the Scottish coast as well as convoy protection. After a period when No. 254 Squadron's Blenheims took over these duties, No. 248 returned to Dyce and resumed this task between January and June 1941.

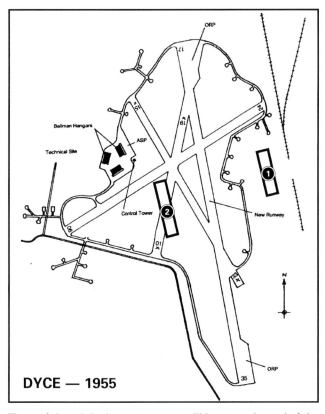

DYCE — 1955

Three of the original runways were still in use at the end of the war but the longest was only 4,000ft long and inadequate for jet operations. As Dyce was to remain a fighter base for No. 612 Squadron, a new main runway, 6,000ft long, was constructed between July 1951 and November 1952 on a new alignment ready for the squadron's Vampires. Operational readiness platforms were provided at either end. The first civil terminal building [1] was located on the eastern side of the airfield but relocated to the western side [2] in 1977. (Drawing by Peter Howarth.)

Blenheims and Beaufighters of No. 143 Squadron were present from July to September 1941. Although formed as a coastal strike unit, the duties at Dyce were the training of crews for overseas posting. From June 1941 to March 1942, No. 235 Squadron flew Blenheims from here, replaced in December by Beaufighters. They covered the North Sea and the Norwegian coast and also flew night intruder missions over Norway, shooting down a Ju 88 in December. Arriving in September 1942, No. 404 Squadron converted from Blenheims to Beaufighters for North Sea patrols before moving to Chivenor in January 1943.

Although nominally a Coastal Command station, Dyce had a Sector Operations Room within No. 13 Group, Fighter Command. Various fighter squadrons had spent brief periods at Dyce during 1940 for rest and/or re-equipment, but No. 603 Squadron was a longer resident from January to August 1940, whereupon it moved south for the Battle of Britain. Action around Aberdeen had already resulted in at least 12 victories for the squadron. In 1941. No. 310's Hurricanes were here from July to December on defensive duties, while at the same time re-equipping with Spitfires. No. 603 Squadron took over from them in December but consistent bad weather hampered defensive operations and little had happened by the time they left Dyce in April 1942.

At the beginning of March 1943, No. 8 Operational Training Unit moved in with a fleet of Spitfires and Mosquitos for photographic reconnaissance training.

They ranged all over Britain taking photographs from high level and a limited number of operational sorties were made over Norway by instructors and advanced pupils during the last quarter of 1944. The OTU moved to South Wales in January 1945.

Aldon Ferguson explored the airfield with the Operations Manager John Donald and Communications Director Kellie Heath and was thrilled to discover evidence of former years.

This is the site of the original control tower, the remains (left) of the concrete circle which surrounded the windsock, and (right) even the cut-off steel pole which carried it.

During the war, 'Pundit Beacons' flashed the airfield code — in the case of Dyce it was 'DY' — in morse, but this post-war aerodrome beacon flashed green and white.

Another abandoned relic of earlier years — a cloud height searchlight device, since replaced by recorders that scan the sky overhead with a laser beam.

A significant event occurred in May 1943 when a Ju 88 night fighter landed at Dyce, having been flown to Scotland by a crew who wanted to defect to the Allied side. The capture of this aircraft was of great intelligence value at the time, as it was fitted with the latest FuG 202 Liechtenstein BC A.I radar. The aircraft is now displayed in the RAF Museum. In a similar incident on December 26, 1944, an Me 109G, signalling intentions to surrender, crash-landed at the airfield.

The end of the war in Europe brought a series of fighter squadrons for short periods, No. 122 being the last between July and October 1945, when its Spitfires left for Wick. Then followed a gradual transition

This is the one remaining Bellman hangar from the original three. The unusually-shaped control tower was built in 1977 to cater for the increasing traffic movements, particularly by helicopters servicing the needs of the North Sea oil rigs. The very first oil-support helicopter flight by BEA to Shell rig 'Staflo' took place on August 1, 1967.

back to civil use, military interest being sustained by the Spitfires of No. 612 Squadron which re-formed in May 1946 and moved to Edzell in July 1951 to re-equip with Vampires. For many years the airport was a quiet backwater, but North Sea oil changed that almost overnight.

Helicopter operations began in 1967, linking the growing number of oil rigs to the mainland. As Aberdeen became the largest oil-related centre in Europe, the airport

became the world's largest commercial heliport. At the time of writing, the airport handles more than 37,000 rotary wing movements, carrying around 468,000 passengers annually. Helicopters account for almost half of all aircraft movements at the airport. In January 2013, it was renamed Aberdeen International, with the intention of extending the runway further still to allow bigger aircraft to fly from Aberdeen to inter-continental destinations.

Left: On May 17, 1942, No. 404 Squadron of the Royal Canadian Air Force were detailed to take part in a raid to cripple the German heavy cruiser *Prinz Eugen* then off Norway. Six Blenheims assigned to make dummy torpedo attacks to confuse the enemy gunners and provide fighter cover accompa-

nied the strike force of Bristol Beauforts. The operation turned out to be a disaster as eight of the aircraft sent to Norway failed to return. *Right:* Original World War II dispersal off the northern perimeter track and used until recently. The 'X' has been added to prevent aircraft accidentally taxying into it.

A surprise arrival at Dyce in May 1943 was this Junkers Ju 88 which landed safely in spite of the fact that the airfield AA defences attempted to shoot it down! Belonging to IV/NJG.3, it had taken off at 1503 hours from its base at Aalborg in Denmark ostensibly for a mission over the Skagerrak. An hour later it dropped in to Kristiansund to refuel as it is believed that at least two of the three-man crew had decided to defect to Britain. It appears that the pilot, Oberleutnant Heinrich Schmitt and the wireless operator Oberfeldwebel Paul Rosenberger, had to hold a gun to Oberfeldwebel Erich Kantwill in order to carry out their plan. At 1710 hours, Rosenberger sent a message to the German night fighter headquarters reporting that they had an engine fire while Schmitt descended to sea level to avoid German radar. They then released three life rafts to make it look as if they ditched before making for Scotland. British radar detected an unidentified aircraft east of Peterhead and two Spitfires from No. 165 Squadron were ordered to intercept at 1750 hours. Flight Lieutenant Arthur Roscoe's report explained what happened next: 'I was flying Blue 1 when we were scrambled to intercept an "X" raid said to be 15 miles east of Peterhead travelling west at zero feet. We were vectored 030° and I flew at very high speed in order to intercept before bandit reached coast. When about half way to Peterhead, we were told the bandit was flying south about five miles out to sea. We turned east and flew out to sea for a few minutes and then orbited as bandit was reported due

north of us going south. We were then told to come closer in shore and orbit. We were then told bandit was west of us and orbiting so I flew slightly NNW so I could see to port. I then saw bandit about one mile inland on my port bow at about 300-400 feet. I approached from his starboard beam and noticed his wheels were down and he fired numerous red very lights. I identified it as Ju 88. He waggled his wings and I answered him back so I presumed he

wished to be led to an aerodrome. I positioned myself about 400 yards ahead of him and told Blue 2 [Sergeant Ben Scamen] to fly above and behind and to one side of bandit. The 88 raised his wheels and followed me back to Dyce. Upon reaching the aerodrome he lowered his wheels, fired more red lights, did a short circuit and landed. I followed him around during his complete run-in, just out of range. We then pancaked.'

This Ju 88 was a rare prize as it was fitted with the latest UHF-band radar which was eagerly examined when the aircraft was flown to the Royal Aircraft Establishment at Farnborough. The radar equipment was removed for examination which helped develop counter-measures. The fighter later became part of the RAF's No. 1426 (Enemy Aircraft) Flight. In the 1950s it was displayed to the public on Horse Guards Parade and since 1978 it has been a static exhibit in the RAF Museum, now fitted with replica radar array.

Departure from Dyce . . . then and now . . . the contrast could not be greater. Now, renamed Aberdeen International Airport,

it is also the world's busiest heliport with over 37,000 movements each year.

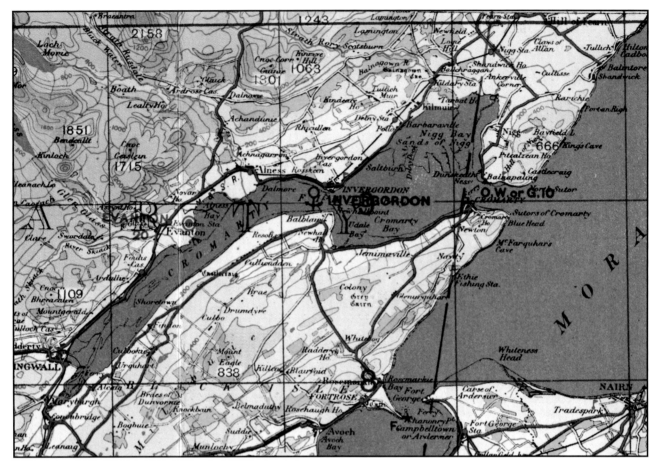

INVERGORDON/ALNESS

The 1943 edition of the Army/Air Quarter-inch map (Sheet 5 The Eastern Highlands) showing the location of the Invergordon flying boat base on Cromarty Firth. In February 1943 it was renamed RAF Alness after the site of the main camp.

The Cromarty Firth in north-east Scotland is acknowledged to be one of the finest natural harbours in the United Kingdom, comprising a 20-mile, deep-water channel with a sheltered entrance. It was employed as a naval base from the early 19th century and in the First World War seaplanes of the Royal Naval Air Service landed on the Firth from time to time and had a site for beaching.

During the 1920s and 1930s, flying boat moorings were established at Invergordon naval dockyard to cater for exercises and aircraft in transit, and one of the users in 1924 was the Flying Boat Development Flight. The alighting area comprised the whole of the Firth from the Sutors (the name given to the north and south jaws of its entrance) as far as Alness to the west. The east to west distance was notified as being about six miles and from north to south varied from one to three miles.

Operational procedures included the following advice: 'Approach should be from the east with the letter of the day being flashed to the Naval Signal Station on the North Shore. Visiting aircraft should circle Invergordon West Pier and flash their identification letter and receive acknowledgment before landing.The flarepath consists of three dumb [unpowered] dinghies with a pinnace at the windward end of the taxying area. Visiting aircraft will be lead to buoys allocated by marine craft, with four special night-flying buoys off Udele Bay. Forty-two RAF type moorings are situated on the North and South Shores to the west of Invergordon.'

At the time of the Munich Crisis in September 1938, Singapore, London and Stranraer aircraft of three squadrons were based here for a few days, their ground crews living in tents as no other accommodation was available. Then, just before the war began, steps were taken to prepare the area for active flying operations, and when most of the naval vessels left for their battle stations, Invergordon effectively began to come under RAF control. Buildings in the nearby town were requisitioned for stores and offices and Station Headquarters was set up initially in the Masonic Hall, later moved to an address on the main street. Most of the RAF personnel were billeted in private houses but some unfortunates still had to resort to tents.

No. 201 Squadron's Saro Londons arrived in November 1939 and began patrols to the Norwegian coast in an effort to locate blockade-runners, surface raiders and submarines heading out for the Atlantic. The obsolete aircraft were given up for Sunderlands in April 1940 and the squadron left in May for Sullom Voe from which they began ferrying supplies and personnel to Iceland. Another Saro London unit — No. 240 Squadron —

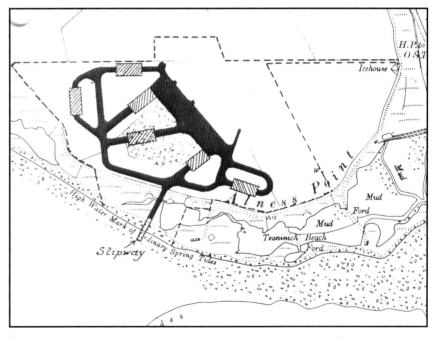

The maintenance area at Alness comprised six hangars bordering the shore.

flew patrols from Invergordon from February to April 1940. Detachments of several other squadrons, including Nos. 209 and 228, spent time at the station during the early months of the war.

Aldon Ferguson visited Alness in August 2105. There were seven accommodation sites, an instructional site, technical area, communal site and sick quarters but of these he found virtually nothing left. All the six hangars had gone and the area redeveloped as the Alness Point Business Park. *Above:* **This was how it appeared in 1971.** *Below:* **A similar angle looking south today with the positions of the hangars indicated.**

Above: **On November 10, 1941, a severe gale battered Alness and this Saro Lerwick (L7257) of No. 4 (Coastal) Operational Training Unit was swamped at its mooring.** *Below:* **The same gale badly damaged this Catalina (Z2141) visiting from Sullom Voe.**

Its wings were badly damaged as the ribs of the trailing edges and ailerons were covered with doped fabric.

The site is now occupied by the MSIS Waste Management Group.

One of the most unfortunate incidents to befall the station took place the following year when a Sunderland staged through to pick up the Duke of Kent, who was a Group Captain in the RAF's Welfare Branch. He was scheduled to visit bases in Iceland and had travelled north by rail to Invergordon, arriving on the evening of August 24. Sunderland W4026 of No. 228 Squadron was already at her mooring having arrived from Oban the previous afternoon. Although the weather was poor on the 25th, the Cromarty Firth was fairly clear with the cloud base at 800 feet.

The Sunderland took off at 1.10 p.m. with a total of 15 persons on board for its 900-mile flight. The planned route was to follow the coastline in a north-easterly direction for 85 miles, keeping out to sea, before turning north-west around the top of Caithness. However, for some reason, the pilot strayed inland with the result that the aircraft hit high ground and scattered itself across the landscape, killling all on board. (See *After the Battle* No. 37.) Author David Smith sought out the crash site in the 1980s with his friend the late John Finch-Davies, seen here.

On August 25, 1942 Invergordon saw the departure of a Sunderland of No. 228 Squadron that had flown in from Oban to pick up the Duke of Kent and his party and convey them to Iceland. However, soon after take-off, the aircraft crashed on a hillside in Caithness with only the tail gunner surviving. An element of mystery still surrounds this sad incident and, although unlikely conspiracy theories continue to circulate, the real reason is likely to have been an uncharacteristic navigational error by an experienced crew.

From the shape of the fin, this photograph would appear to have been taken by a Hudson, probably of No. 519 Squadron based at Wick.

Sunderland N9046, nick-named 'Flying Porcupine', after a sortie from Invergordon on April 3, 1940 when it fought off six Ju 88s.

With the arrival of No. 4 (Coastal) OTU from Stranraer in June 1941, Invergordon took up a training role with a mixed collection of flying boats which included Lerwicks and Sunderlands. Then in February 1942 it was decided that pilot training would be done at Stranraer while the operational training of crews would be concentrated at Invergordon. By now, the Officers' Mess and accommodation had been established in Dalmore House with huts nearby for any surplus. New hutted encampments had been provided for the other ranks, with the WAAFs based in a woodland setting.

To better describe its actual location, Invergordon was renamed RAF Alness on February 10, 1943, having been referred to semi-officially as Dalmore for some time. One of its major activities now centred around No. 5 Flying Boat Servicing Unit which had formed here in September 1942.

No. 5 FBSU disbanded in December 1944 but the OTU continued after the war until moving to Pembroke Dock in August 1946. Thereafter, Alness saw occasional visits by Sunderlands until the type was retired during the late-1950s. RAF marine craft continued to operate from Alness until 1986 when the station finally closed.

Dalmore House became the Officers' Mess, now sub-divided into separate apartments.

The peaceful scene 75 years later looking southwards across Cromarty Firth to the hills of the Black Isle.

Looking from the hardstanding towards the slipway which is slowly being reclaimed by the sea.

Although the RAF station area has been taken over for a business park, there is still a lot of evidence of wartime occupation, the most obvious being the ruined watch tower of local RAF design on the end of Dalmore Pier. The slipway near the mouth of the River Averon is another significant reminder. This was where the flying boats were pulled ashore after beaching wheels had been attached to each side of the hull at the water's edge, along with a dolly truck set under the rear of the hull. They were then wheeled up the concrete ramp with the aid of a very powerful tractor, although sometimes by manpower alone. Any work required was then performed on one of the hardstandings.

The Alness bomb store — a double compartment earth traverse — is still visible having avoided being lost when the A9 was upgraded. A number of Nissen explosive stores — single buildings with earth banks on both sides — also survive. There was a Bellman and five modified T2 hangars at Alness but only the remains of the floors can now be seen. The Airmens' Mess at the former RAF Marine Craft Unit is now known as 'Catalina House', while, at Alness Point, there is a fine memorial to the station and its personnel which includes images of the Sunderland and Catalina.

On the night of August 15, 1944, a Sunderland flew into high ground north-west of Dornoch, 15 miles to the north. Twelve of the 14 crew were Canadians with one Australian and one Briton. They were laid to rest in Rosskeen Parish Churchyard in Alness where there were already 61 burials from the First World War.

Fortunately David Smith has preserved this photo of a unique piece of aviation ephemera which has a direct bearing of the origins of Leuchars aerodrome. The father of the author's old friend, Dr Atholl Duncan, owned a garage at St Andrews and on occasion from 1913 onwards supplied petrol to the aeroplanes en route to and from the Royal Flying Corps aerodrome at Montrose. In the first volume of a biography *Notify Eric Rattray*, which draws heavily on a secret journal kept by her father as a prisoner of war in Japan, his daughter, Meg Parkes, writes: 'Atholl's love of aeroplanes was not merely that of many young boys of his time; it had been engendered from his early days when he would accompany his father to supply the fuel for visiting planes which landed and took off from the town end of the West Sands.' During Atholl's lifetime, these movements would mainly be made up of civilian aircraft carrying golfers to the local links, but there is some evidence to suggest that the suitability of the area to the north of the town for an aerodrome had been noted by the early RFC visits.

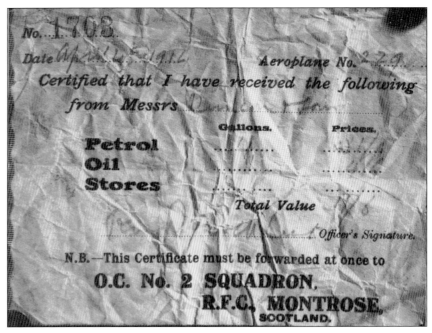

LEUCHARS

Classified as a School and Ships Aeroplane Base when it opened in July 1918, the original site of 220 acres was large for the period and had seven General Service hangars, four of which are still in existence today. The impressively named Grand Fleet School of Aerial Fighting and Gunnery was immediately formed. The station was transferred to RAF Coastal Area in September 1918 and in March 1920 the School was renamed Royal Air Force Base Leuchars to provide instruction in a variety of flying disciplines relevant to the maritime role. Strong naval links were retained and throughout the 1920s a succession of Fleet Air Arm squadrons formed and trained at Leuchars, some being based there for considerable periods.

Temporary Armament Training Camp, Leuchars formed here in March 1935, the 'Camp' designation being changed to 'Station' in April 1938. Meanwhile, No. 1 Flying Training School had formed out of its parent RAF Base Leuchars and replaced the latter in April 1935. With Leuchars about to be transferred to Coastal Command because of its eminently suitable position on the Scottish east coast for maritime operations, the School moved to southern England in August 1938. The Temporary ATS remained until the war started, whereupon it was absorbed by the Air Observers School at Evanton. No. 224 Squadron's Hudsons were here from September 1939 and during the first month of the war they flew 113 sorties; had four combats with German flying boats, and lost one crew. A U-Boat was bombed in December and in April 1940 the squadron became heavily involved in the Norwegian campaign, attacking harbours and shipping. Even after resistance was over, the squadron continued to operate in this area and also made strikes as far south as Heligoland.

The station was originally grass-surfaced but two runways of 816 and 800 yards were constructed by George Wimpey & Co during the summer of 1939. The longer of the two was later extended to 1,200 yards by the use of 50ft wide 'continuation tracks' at each end, often referred to as 'bat-handles'. Both runways were eventually extended to 2,000 yards to accommodate four-engined aircraft types and 50 frying-pan hardstandings were laid down, most of them being of steel mesh tracking. Four C Type hangars were pro-

vided, with two Bellmans and nine blisters being added later.

Craigie about three miles to the north was laid out as a 'Q/K' day and night decoy and Eden Mouth, only about two miles to the north-east, served as a night decoy only. An operational satellite airfield was located at Dunino on a very undulating site to the south-east of St Andrews. It had four grass runways, the longest being 1,150 yards, with a 10ft wide perimeter track of rolled ash for vehicle movement. It was used also by army co-operation squadrons until being transferred to the Fleet Air Arm in December 1942.

The other Hudson unit at Leuchars from September 1939 was No. 233 Squadron, although it was still in the process of re-

equipping with the type, so Ansons were used for initial operations. They were phased out by the end of the year but not before one had bombed a U-Boat, only to be hit by shrapnel and forced to ditch. On into 1940, the campaign in Norway was the main focus of action with shipping searches and bombing raids on Bergen and Stavanger. The squadron moved to Northern Ireland in December 1940, leaving No. 224 Squadron to continue convoy escort and patrols along the Norwegian coast. A move was made to Northern Ireland in April 1941.

In March 1941, No. 42 Squadron arrived from Wick with Beauforts, although some of its aircraft were detached as far away as Shetland and Lincolnshire. A torpedo attack

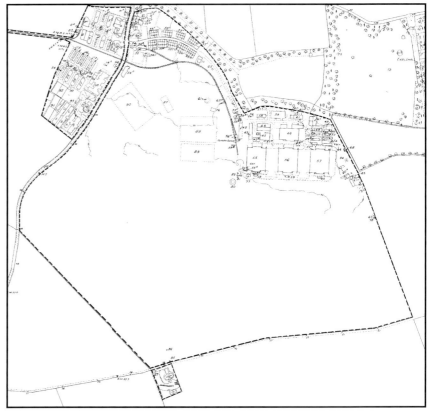

When Leuchars opened it was a simple grass aerodrome with the technical site on the northern perimeter.

This shot of Avro Anson K6323 of No. 48 Squadron was pictured by Dr Duncan on the station's Air Day in 1938. The look-out on the roof is believed to have been removed soon after the war although some of the brackets which supported the access ladder remain.

was made on the cruiser *Lutzow* off Norway on June 13, causing severe damage. The Luftwaffe's own anti-shipping efforts were countered by attacks on their Norwegian bases. Between March and May 1941 the Blenheims of No. 107 Squadron were attached to Coastal from Bomber Command in support of No. 42 Squadron's efforts. Searching a section of coastal waters, where a specific ship was believed to be, was carried out according to a standard 'Parallel Track' procedure. In the following example, six aircraft would fly a south-easterly course to southern Norway on six independent but

parallel courses, spaced 20 miles apart, and approach the coast at an angle of about 45 degrees. When within four or five miles from the coast, they would turn south for about 20 miles and then turn towards Leuchars.

The take-off times would be staggered so that each aircraft would make its appointed landfall on the Norwegian coast at the same time. Thus, in about seven minutes' reconnaissance some 120 miles of enemy coastline could be covered. The sudden appearance of six aircraft off the Norwegian coast at different points was calculated to confuse the enemy and thus increase the chances of the

RAF aircraft escaping fighter interception. If contact with a ship was made, a report of its position, course and speed would be radioed back to Group Headquarters before a torpedo attack was mounted.

It was a crew from No. 42 Squadron who featured in the well-known saga of 'Winkie' the pigeon. Out on patrol on February 25, 1942, their Beaufort suffered engine failure and unable to maintain height on one, they were forced to ditch. A carrier pigeon was always taken along on these sorties, but on this occasion the bird struggled free from its cardboard box without a message while the

The Belfast truss aircraft shed seen in Aldon's comparison is one pair of an original three pairs (see plan), now listed as Grade II. However, the centre pair were demolished and have since been replaced by a modern building for mechanical engineering.

No. 224 Squadron was based at Leuchars with Hudsons from September 1939 to April 1941.

as Cornwall and northern Scotland until the whole squadron was consolidated at Skitten in August 1942.

No. 455 Squadron had been transferred from Bomber Command and moved into Leuchars towards the end of April 1942. Its Hampdens conducted bombing and mining sorties along the Norwegian coast. At the same time it began to receive Hampdens equipped for torpedo dropping and much of its time was taken up with training in their use.

No. 144 Squadron was another Hampden-equipped transferee from Bomber Command in April 1942. Its first operation was to bomb Lister airfield in Norway on May 4 but then it began converting to the torpedo-dropping role. Aircraft from both squadrons were detached to northern Russia in September in order to attack German shipping threatening the convoys from Britain. For

airmen were launching their dinghy. The bird eventually arrived back with its civilian owner, exhausted, wet and oily. After some extensive deduction, based on the fact that the bird had almost certainly spent the night on a northbound tanker, hence the oil, the hitherto fruitless air search was extended much further out. The crew's dinghy was soon found and they were rescued. (This use of pigeons for operational purposes was finally discontinued in February 1944.)

A Royal New Zealand Air Force unit — No. 489 Squadron — formed at Leuchars on August 12, 1941, with the intention of equipping it with Beauforts. However, the demand for these aircraft in the Middle East took priority so the squadron had to make do with Blenheims until Hampdens became available in April 1942. These served as a stop-gap torpedo bomber and were detached as far apart

Looking south-south-west from the main hardstanding in front of the C Type hangars.

Leuchars pictured in August 1943 by No. 540 Squadron which was also based there at the time before moving to Benson.

The crews of No. 455 Squadron pictured with one of their Hampdens. The photograph appears to have been taken

looking north, away from the airfield, with the western end of the C Type hangar on the right.

the rest of the year, anti-submarine patrols and the occasional bombing raid were made from Leuchars. In January 1943, the squadron started converting to Beaufighters and began torpedo operations with these in March only to move to Tain a few weeks later.

On October 19, 1942, No. 540 Squadron formed from two flights of No. 1 Photographic Reconnaissance Unit which had been based here for almost a year. The new squadron's chief task was to monitor the activities of the German Navy with particular reference to those of *Tirpitz* as she moved from fjord to fjord. Appropriately, the squadron's badge depicted a mosquito, as it was the first operational user of the type. At various times aircraft were detached to Ben-

son and Gibraltar and in February 1944 the squadron's base shifted to Benson. Even then, aircraft were sometimes detached to Leuchars according to operational demands. A Mosquito flying from Leuchars on February 19, 1944, achieved the first wholly successful photo coverage of Berlin after some 40 previous abortive or only partially successful attempts.

During April 1943, No. 1477 (Norwegian) Flight whose flying boats operated from nearby Woodhaven, based six Mosquitos at Leuchars for shipping reconnaissance along the Norwegian coast. On May 10, 1943, the flight was expanded to full squadron strength and became No. 333 Squadron, continuing its unusual dual function. The Catalinas now operated with formidable fighter cover, the

Mosquitos accounting for at least five enemy aircraft before the end of the year. Into 1944, the pace increased with the Mosquitos now carrying depth-charges that they used to good effect. Several U-Boats were damaged and one destroyed. The Catalinas moved to Shetland in July and in September the Mosquito element joined the Banff Strike Wing.

The following month, No. 489 Squadron returned from Skitten, and began to re-equip with Beaufighters. The squadron became operational again in January 1944 and made torpedo attacks on a number of ships, sinking a minelayer before the month was out. The squadron began to operate by day and night and this produced three more ship victims in February. Further attacks followed until a move was made to Norfolk in April 1944.

The main runway has been extended at least twice and currently stands at 2,800 yards.

King Haakon VII of Norway, exiled in Britain since June 1940, paid a visit to the Norwegian No. 333 Squadron on May 7, 1943.

Here the King is pictured just inside the domestic site. The building on the right is now the Air Cadets' Regional Headquarters.

From July 1944 the station's main operational effort had been mounted by No. 206 Squadron's Liberators. Two U-Boat attacks were made that month and one submarine was definitely sunk in September. On the debit side fighters were beginning to take a toll of the Liberators. A second Liberator unit arrived in September: No. 547 Squadron. It, too, began operating off the Norwegian coast but lost three crews before the end of the year and only encountered one U-Boat. No. 206 Squadron received Leigh Light Liberators in November and most of its operations now took place at night. Many attacks were made on U-Boats and surface ships right up to the end of hostilities, the squadron leaving Leuchars in July 1945. No. 547 Squadron had done similar work with multiple shipping attacks and disbanded here on June 4, 1945.

On the subject of Leigh Lights, Liberator skipper, Jim Glazebrook, wrote that 'the apparently simple addition of a searchlight for night attacks involved more headaches than would at first seem possible. A phenomenal amount of intensive and arduous training was necessary to acquire the correct co-ordination between pilot, radar operator and the Leigh Light operator-cum-bomb-aimer. Night after night the training sorties continued, making practice runs across Bell Rock lighthouse, the 'Mark V' training buoy and any conveniently placed shipping in the area. Later exercises were arranged with an Allied submarine stationed at Dundee. Occasionally aircrew went out in the submarine, and members of the submarine's crew were carried in the exercise aircraft. Neither was attracted to the other's environment!'

Amidst all the warlike activity at Leuchars, British Overseas Airways Corporation (BOAC) had been running a service to and from Stockholm, Sweden since mid-1941,

A timeless 'then and now' scene . . . inspection on the main parade ground lined with the same unchanged barrack blocks.

The wartime Operations Block is now used for the station's telephone exchange.

142

first with Hudsons and then, from February 1943, with Mosquitos. Mail and one passenger were carried in the Mosquito bomb bay, along with limited cargoes of high quality engineering products, especially Swedish ball-bearings. Despite flak from ships and attempted fighter interceptions, it was believed that no aircraft were lost to enemy action, but several were destroyed in accidents. By the time the Mosquito service moved to London's Croydon Airport on May 17, 1945, the aircraft had flown 520 round trips.

An even more clandestine organisation was based at Leuchars in 1944, commanded by Colonel Bernt Balchen, a distinguished polar aviator who held dual Norwegian-American citizenship. It conducted the 'Sonnie' Project, and, from September the 'Ball' Project. The first was to fly back to the UK several thousand Norwegian aircrew trainees and American internees from Sweden, the second involved supply drops to the Norwegian Resistance. These trips were very hazardous and were usually undertaken when cloud cover was available. The cover designation for the B-24 Liberators, most of which carried civil registrations, was that they were a detachment of the 1409th Army Air Forces Base Unit at Prestwick. However, these undercover operations were only distantly related to the normal

In post-war years, Leuchars achieved a reputation for hosting Britain's quick reaction force to counter the frequent incursions by Soviet Bears. Initially, these actions were mounted by English Electric Lightnings and, from 1969, by McDonnell Douglas Phantoms.

work of a component of the European Division, Air Transport Command. Some of the aircraft involved were detached from the 'Carpetbaggers', the USAAF's 492nd Bomb Group which flew agent-dropping missions from Harrington in Northamptonshire.

With the contraction of the RAF in peacetime, life at Leuchars returned to a more gentle pace, hosting a School for General Reconnaissance and the St Andrews University Air Squadron. In 1950 Leuchars entered the jet age as it passed from Coastal to RAF Fighter Command and became the home of the Gloster Meteors of No. 222 Squadron. The next generation of jet fighters to be stationed at Leuchars were the Hawker Hunters of No. 43 Squadron and the Gloster Javelins of Nos. 29 and 151 Squadrons. They in turn were superseded by Lightnings and Phantoms. The Tornado F.3 took over the air defence role in the Eighties, continuing to

monitor the movements of Soviet aircraft operating close to British airspace.

The final QRA (Quick Reaction Alert) function at Leuchars was performed by the Eurofighter Typhoon from September 2010, the Tornados being retired soon afterwards. Following the 2010 Strategic Defence and Security Review, it was announced that the RAF would transition to a single Main Operating Base in Scotland — RAF Lossiemouth — which would continue the growth of the Typhoon force and provide Quick Reaction Alert for the northern United Kingdom. On April 1, 2015 Leuchars was transferred to the Army.

A granite pillar stands at the main gate of the station, inscribed 'This stone commemorates the brotherhood in arms between British and Norwegian airmen who fought from these northern shores in World War II 1939-1945. We honour those who gave their lives.'

The Phantoms gave way to the Tornado and then the Typhoon when No. 1 (Fighter) Squadron reformed at Leuchars in September 2012, providing defence of the northern UK with No. 6 Squadron, until it was announced in 2010 that the Quick Reaction Force was to be concentrated at Lossiemouth. On April 1, 2015, Leuchars ceased to be an RAF station and was instead transferred to the Army.

MILLTOWN

In 1976 Aldon Ferguson took this photo on a visit to Milltown just before it closed to flying, so he was very interested to see how the intevening years had treated the airfield, particularly bearing in mind its historic role in the destruction of the *Tirpitz*.

Used operationally by Coastal Command for only a relatively short period, Milltown in Morayshire (now Grampian), started its career as a 'Q' site or dummy airfield for RAF Kinloss, about three miles to the north-west. It was sited on a flat area of farmland, which soon gave rise to suggestions that it had the makings of an excellent airfield in its own right. For once, officialdom took notice and the 'Q' site was abandoned in October 1941 and given over to airfield development. Three runways were built; a main of 1,900

yards and two subsidiaries of 1,540 and 1,400 yards. Hangarage consisted of single examples of the T1 and B1 and 27 loop hardstandings were constructed off the perimeter track. Domestic sites were dispersed in the fields to the south.

Early completion does not seem to have been a priority, as the new airfield was not brought into use until June 1943. It had been intended to house a Coastal Command OTU but this changed to a role as a satellite for Lossiemouth's Bomber Command OTU.

Wellingtons from this unit flew from Milltown until the beginning of September 1944. At this point there was an urgent need for a suitable airfield to accommodate aircraft to combat the U-Boats now operating from Scandinavia, owing to the loss of their French ports. Liberators of No. 224 Squadron arrived from Cornwall the same month and started patrolling in Norwegian and Danish waters. Two U-boats were sunk and two damaged by the squadron during September and October.

Aldon reported back that 'Milltown is a typical wartime temporary airfield with three concrete runways which after the war became a satellite to nearby Lossiemouth. Later an aerial farm was installed, still within the RAF base but I understand the aerials were removed approximately ten years ago and the site sold to the owners of Innes House, a very substantial house/castle located approximately one mile from the airfield. The aerodrome

itself has been virtually cleared of all buildings including the tower, all hangars except one, dispersals, living and technical sites and dispersed sites. The runways and taxiways remain intact plus an aircraft dispersal in front of the remaining T2 hangar. The spectacle hardstandings are extant but overgrown due to lack of use. The MOD constructed the existing buildings for the aerial farm so virtually all remaining buildings are from the 1960s.'

Aldon: 'The whole airfield is used by grazing sheep which also have access into most buildings which therefore are in a poor state. However, the hangar is in fair condition even though there has been little or no maintenance since the RAF pulled out. There has been considerable interest from potential users including the museum at Kinloss Barracks for static aircraft, and another party is seeking its use for adventure training.'

Milltown's subsidiary function had been that of advanced base for Bomber Command and thus it played a part in the final destruction of *Tirpitz* in November 1944. A total of 32 Lancasters of Nos. 9 and 617 Squadrons took off for Norway from Milltown, Kinloss and Lossiemouth. The same month, No. 224 Squadron lost a Liberator to enemy fighters. The squadron's final action resulted in sinking a U-Boat on May 5, 1945; then in July it moved to St Eval.

When Lossiemouth was transferred to No. 17 Group, Coastal Command at the end of July 1945, Milltown once more became its satellite. In August, No. 111 OTU's Liberators arrived here from the Bahamas and soldiered on until disbandment in August 1946. Thereafter, both airfields were taken over by the Royal Navy. Milltown was returned to the RAF and saw limited use until closed for flying in 1977 becoming a radio transmitter site. Three runways and the perimeter track remain intact but there are now only traces of the loop dispersals. A single hangar survives on the south side next to a typical oblong Navy parking apron of post-war vintage.

It was on November 12, 1944 that a final operation was mounted by Bomber Command to seal the fate of the *Tirpitz*, the German sister battleship to the *Bismarck* sunk in May 1941. An earlier operation had to be mounted from Archangel in the Soviet Union, because the range from Scotland to Altenfjord *(left)* was too great, but a smoke-screen led to inaccurate bombing and the ship was only damaged. Conveniently, the Germans then moved *Tirpitz* south to Tromsö from where it was accessible from Scottish bases using specially modified Lancasters with extra fuel tanks. The attack from Milltown, Lossiemouth and Kinloss by Nos. 9 and 617 Squadrons achieved one direct hit from a 12,000lb Tallboy and two near misses which caused her to turn turtle.

Part of the Oban complex was the flying boat servicing area at Ganavan Sands, now used as a yachting marina.

OBAN

Oban Harbour on the west coast of Scotland is sheltered from strong winds in all directions, chiefly by Kerrera Island to the west but also from low hills to the north, east and south. This position proved ideal as a flying boat base and it played a key role in the Battle of the Atlantic. Its potential was recognised as early as 1928 when four Supermarine Southamptons of No. 481 Coastal Reconnaissance Flight operated from here on a temporary basis. As a result of this detachment, Ardantrive Bay on Kerrera was equipped with six mooring buoys and a supply of aviation fuel. Use remained spasmodic until war approached and the need for advanced bases to cover the North-West Approaches became apparent. Dungallan House in the town was requisitioned as Station Headquarters and on October 2, 1939 the new base opened under No. 18 Group, Coastal Command.

Facilities were rapidly improvised, beginning with a hut constructed in the rear garden of the house to serve as the Navigation Office, with a path leading down to a boathouse that became the Orderly Room. Here, a new jetty was built to enable aircrew to reach aircraft moored offshore. The meagre amenities over at Ardantrive were greatly expanded to include an enlarged slipway so that flying boats could be brought ashore for maintenance.

An explosives storage area, a gas decontamination centre, and other buildings were constructed, including at least a dozen Nissen huts. In Oban town, support functions were established in various locations and most of the local hotels were taken over to house their personnel, the Esplanade Hotel being used as the Officers' Mess. For defence of the base, an anti-submarine net was laid across the south end of the Sound of Kerrera, mined and controlled by switches in an observation building that still exists.

The published details for flying operations included the following: 'Landings can be made inside Oban harbour in a north-east south-west direction, but it is advisable to land outside the harbour in other directions and if landing at Oban for the first time. Take offs can be made inside in the south-west north-east direction, but must be made outside in all other directions.

'The north channel only should be used for entering and leaving the harbour. On entering the harbour from the landing area leave Irar Beacon on the starboard side and proceed through the middle of the channel into Ardantrive Bay, taking care to follow the buoyed channel.

'A total of 24 RAF moorings are available. They are situated in Ardantrive Bay and along either side of Kerrera Sound. Fuel and oil can be obtained from RAF Oban. A slipway and workshops are available in Ardantrive Bay, where aircraft of any size can be beached and repaired. There is an additional slipway at Ganavan, two miles north-east of Oban.'

A Saro Lerwick (L7257) of No. 209 Squadron — the picture was taken looking across the bay at the Isle of Kerrera. The house, Mount Pleasant, which still stands, was used as a squadron office in 1939-40 before it was taken over as a billet for Italian POWs working on the island. The wartime photo must have been taken on a misty day as the Ben Buie mountain is completely hidden.

Left: **Officers of No. 210 Squadron gather at Dungallan House where the terrace became a popular venue for group photos.** *Right:* **The crew of Catalina AH547. The picture was taken on the departure of the skipper, Flight Lieutenant Wheeler, on his** transfer to Gibraltar at which point the second pilot, Sergeant Doughie Baker was to take over as captain. Four of the crew shown here were killed in January 1941 when the aircraft crashed on take-off in the Firth of Lorn.

Early in September 1939, No. 209 Squadron brought in its Supermarine Stranraers from Invergordon. These outmoded aircraft soon began to be replaced by the new Saro Lerwick. The type failed to live up to its promise, however, being unable to maintain height on one engine, along with a number of other shortcomings. Despite this, the squadron made its first operational Atlantic patrol with the Lerwick on Christmas Day 1939. A shortage of spare parts and two serious accidents meant that Stranraers did most of the operational flying until March 1940. With considerable modification, the Lerwicks were greatly improved but still left much to be desired. The squadron moved to Pembroke Dock in July 1940.

It was replaced by No. 210 Squadron which had already detached one of its Sunderlands to Oban from Pembroke Dock in May to reinforce its sister squadron. The whole squadron now moved to Oban to concentrate on anti-submarine and convoy patrols. On August 16, a surfaced U-Boat was attacked and claimed as damaged and two weeks later another — according to the escorted convoy — was considered to have been sunk. Mostly uneventful patrols were flown. In April 1941, the squadron began to re-equip with Catalinas, instruction being

provided by four US Navy pilots under covert secondment. The USA, of course, had yet to enter the war but her military were anxious to share expertise and also to gain experience for a conflict that many considered inevitable. In February 1942, No. 210 Squadron moved to Shetland.

March 1942 saw the arrival of No. 228 Squadron's Sunderlands from Stranraer, with operations beginning almost immediately. On the 13th, a U-Boat was attacked but without any apparent result. The average monthly sorties rate was 30 but there were four fatal accidents between May and September, including the one that killed the Commanding Officer and the Duke of Kent (see page 135). The squadron moved to Northern Ireland at the end of 1942.

A Royal Canadian Air Force (RCAF) unit, No. 423 Squadron, had formed here on March 18, 1942 but it was some months before the first of its Sunderlands were delivered. The first operation — a routine patrol — took place on August 23 but progress with crew training and aircraft acquisition was slow before the unit left for Northern Ireland in November 1942. Another RCAF Squadron, No. 422, moved into Oban the same month having recently partially converted from Catalinas to Sunderlands. However, its work-

ing up was badly affected by awful winter weather, so much so that operations did not start until March 1943. No submarines were sighted before a move was made to Bowmore in May.

The Norwegian-crewed No. 330 Squadron arrived from Iceland in January 1943 and began to convert onto Sunderlands. Once fully operational, the unit moved to Shetland in July. In 1943, the RAF took delivery of a small number of Martin Mariners, an American twin-engined flying boat. A new squadron — No. 524 — formed at Oban on October 20, 1943 with the task of gaining operational experience on the type. Unfortunately, in the opinion of many pilots, its performance was somewhat lacking, with limited range and inadequate safety margins when flying with one engine inoperative — a throwback to the Lerwick, some considered. It was soon deemed unsuitable for operational service and the squadron was disbanded on December 7, 1943.

By mid-1943, Oban had reverted to a mainly training role, with No. 302 Ferry Training Unit (FTU) moving in from Stranraer in late July. Its job was to train crews to ferry flying boats to overseas units, using Sunderlands and Catalinas. Many thousands of hours were flown but the accident rate was

Neil Owen kindly visited Dungallan House for us to picture the former terrace overlooking Oban Harbour.

considerable. For example, two virtually intact Catalinas are known to lie in the Firth of Lorn and the wreckage of another Catalina can still be seen on the island of Vatersay. Far out in the Atlantic, the mountainous island of St Kilda claimed one of the unit's Sunderlands and its crew. (The story behind this and other crashes on the island and one of its sea stacks can be found in *After the Battle* No. 30.) The Ferry Training Unit moved base to Northern Ireland in April 1945 and RAF Oban was reduced to Care and Maintenance at the end of that month.

Ganavan Sands, about two miles northeast of Oban, was used mainly by No. 4 Flying Boat Servicing Unit, which formed here September 9, 1942 and disbanded in April 1944. The site, which was effectively a satellite station for RAF Oban, was shared by No. 302 FTU and also the Mariner squadron during its short life. The area where a T2 hangar once stood has now been covered by a small

The Lerwicks were unsuccessful and had been phased out by May 1941.

In their place came the Short Sunderland which had an endurance range of around 16 hours. Neil Owen told us that the chap up the ladder on the rudder was a local man, Tom Lennox, who came back to Oban after the war. Servicing of the flying boats at their mooring was always a risky business, the fitters being ferried from the shore to machine in pinnaces.

housing development, but the slipway remains, along with a large concrete hardstanding now adapted as a car park. A fine memorial stands nearby with the dedication 'To the memory of all air and ground personnel of 18 Group Coastal Command who served at RAF Oban' and lists the units which flew from here. The wrought iron gate to a cycle track at the end of the car park bears an attractive head-on rendition of a Sunderland. Over on Kerrera Island and reachable by ferry, the bomb stores and other buildings remain intact. The slipway is still used by fishing and pleasure craft.

In the town, the Regent Hotel, once the Sergeants' Mess, contains a small RAF display and Dungallan House is now a hotel. Standing on the Esplanade just to the north of Oban's North Pier is the excellent Oban War and Peace Museum. Apart from covering many aspects of the story of the town and surrounding area, there is much on the flying boat involvement. A one-eighth scale model of a Sunderland, depicting an aircraft serving with No. 228 Squadron at Oban in 1942 is an outstanding exhibit.

It remains to give a mention to the former RAF Connel, five miles north-east of Oban and known locally as North Connel. It was built as a forward fighter base chiefly to defend RAF Oban, but also to serve as an Emergency Landing Ground in an area devoid of airfields because of terrain. Connel's curious configuration of two runways only 12 degrees different in direction was dictated by its cramped position on a narrow coastal plain. The longer run was 1,400 yards and the other was 1,050 yards. High ground up to 1,000ft only one mile to the north and north-north-east was not encouraging. In the event, its main use was for communications aircraft visiting Oban, but it also hosted aircraft taking part in combined operations exercises in the area. Today, this remarkably scenic site has been greatly modernised as Oban Airport and is used for club and private flying, as well as gliding. Only the longer of the two runways remains in use.

RAF Connel, five miles north of Oban, was squeezed into a narrow strip of land on the edge of the loch. Its main purpose was to provide fighter cover for the flying boat base but all went sadly wrong on February 6, 1944 when three Hurricanes of No. 516 Combined Operations Squadron took off on a training exercise. At the end of the session, thick cloud rolled in from the west. The Hurricanes broke formation as each pilot attempted to find somewhere to land. Pilot Officer Larry Figgis was about to bale out when he spotted a break in the cloud and made a safe belly-landing west of Stirling Castle but the other two pilots were not so fortunate. Warrant Officer John Stephen crashed on the island of Coll, and Flight Lieutenant Arthur Woodgate, a New Zealander, crashed on the Ardnamurchan peninsula, north of the Isle of Mull.

In 1967 Connel was purchased by Oban Council for conversion into their local airport and in August 2013 a marvellous piece of history was re-enacted there when Australian Jeff Boyling landed his Consolidated Catalina at Oban to commemorate the *Daily Mail* Circuit of Britain air race held in August 1913.

Then there was only one entry, the Sopwith floatplane, but it failed to complete the course after the biplane crashed. The Catalina had an endurance of up to 30 hours enabling Coastal Command to extend its patrols far out in the Atlantic and by the war's end they had some 600 on their books.

SKITTEN

This station in Caithness in the north-east of Scotland was planned as a satellite for RAF Castletown's day fighter squadrons. It had a secondary role as night fighter satellite to RAF Skeabrae in Orkney, although this function failed to materialise. Construction began in 1940 in the rolling treeless country alongside the road from Wick to Castletown. Three runways were laid down; a main of 1,590 yards and two subsidiaries of 1,350 and 1,120 yards. Seven double fighter dispersal pens were spaced around the perimeter along with four blister hangars, a total eventually raised to nine. The aerodrome took its name from the farm on whose land much of it was built.

RAF fighters continued to use Skitten, along with a temporary presence of Royal Navy fighters early in 1941 to plug a gap in RAF coverage. Meanwhile RAF Wick was showing an interest in the airfield as a satellite for Coastal Command operations, so a preliminary survey of the available accommodation was carried out in May 1941. The plan came to fruition in July when No. 404 Squadron's Blenheims arrived for convoy escort. These duties continued until October when No. 48 Squadron's Hudsons took over before moving to Wick in January 1942. Beauforts of No. 217 Squadron were the next residents but only briefly as they were transferred to Leuchars after a month or so.

For a station designed to accommodate a single fighter squadron, Skitten was becoming seriously overcrowded. At one time in February 1942, the Sergeants' Mess was catering for almost 200 men with staff to serve only 38! The runways, too, were marginal for the safe operation of medium-sized aircraft and all three were extended during 1942, the longest strip becoming 2,000 yards. These extensions served the secondary purpose of allowing emergency use by Bomber Command if operations against naval

GB 10899 b
Nur für den Dienstgebrauch
Bild Nr. 8/40-26 (Lfl. 5)
Aufnahme vom 8. 12. 40

Kilmster
Flugplatz (im Bau)

Länge (westl. Greenw.): 3° 09′ 43″   Breite: 58° 29′ 47″
Mißweisung: − 13° 40′ (Mitte 1941)   Zielhöhe über NN 28 m
Maßstab etwa 1 : 20 700

Genst. 5. Abt.   Juni 1941
Karte 1 : 100 000
GB/Sc 7

The Luftwaffe had no means of knowing the names that the RAF had adopted for their new airfields and, in the case of Skitten photographed in June 1941, they gave it the name of the nearby village, although the correct spelling should be Killimster.

anchorages in Norway were called for. No. 86 Squadron's Beauforts were in residence from March to July 1942, during which period they carried out an exercise with US Navy carrier aircraft temporarily land-based at Hatston, Orkney.

Based at Skitten from August 1, 1942 to October 1943, this flight of Hampden Mk Is of No. 489 Squadron of the Royal New Zealand Air Force were pictured on a flight somewhere over northern Scotland.

In 1942 there was a real fear that Germany was developing nuclear fission, Churchill explaining after visiting President Roosevelt that June, that 'we both felt painfully the dangers of doing nothing. We knew what efforts the Germans were making to procure supplies of "heavy water" — a sinister term, which began to creep into our secret papers. What if the enemy should get an atomic bomb before we did?' Intelligence arrived from Norway which indicated that production of heavy water was being increased at the Norsk Hydro Electrisk plant at Vermork, near Rjukan in the central southern part of the country, where excess power was used to electrolyse natural water leaving a concentrate of deuterium oxide. In October 1942, four Norwegians were dropped by parachute to reconnoitre the factory complex which led to the proposal to use glider-borne troops from the Royal Engineers to mount a raid to destroy the installation. Two Horsa gliders were to be towed by Halifaxes the 600 miles from Skitten, one from No. 295 Squadron, the other from No. 297. The whole force assembled at the airfield on November 17, but the operation mounted two days later was a disaster. One of the Halifaxes and both Horsas came to grief, all aboard being killed, either in the crashes or were subsequently executed by the Gestapo.

In 1942 the airfield became associated with a gallant failure — Operation 'Freshman' — the attack on the heavy water plant at Vermork in Norway. Bombing had been tried to deprive the Germans of the means to manufacture material for an atomic bomb but the plant was well protected by mountainous terrain. The answer seemed to be a ground assault by a force of 32 volunteer soldiers in two Horsa gliders towed to Norway by a pair of Halifaxes. Skitten was chosen because of its long runway and relative proximity to the target. The aircraft took off on November 21 but the navigation equipment malfunctioned and it proved impossible to locate the radio beacon which had been placed on the ground by Norwegian agents.

The Halifaxes and their gliders flew around for a while in some confusion until the tow-rope snapped on one of the Horsas and it crash-landed in the mountains north of Stavanger. The tow-plane just managed to reach Skitten on its last drop of fuel. The other combination flew into high ground killing all on board, including the Skitten Medical Officer who had volunteered at the last moment to fill a vacant crew position. The survivors from the force were executed by the Gestapo but the plant was later destroyed by SOE agents and the Resistance.

A follow up sabotage operation was mounted in February 1943, successfully crippling production, and a massive raid by the US Eighth Air Force in November caused the Germans to abandon production altogether and save what heavy water was left, but the ferry on which it was being transported was sunk (see *After the Battle* No. 45).

This picture shows the plant when it was featured in the 1964 film *Heroes of Telemark*, starring Kirk Douglas and Ulla Jacobsson. The heavy water building was decommissioned and demolished in 1977.

151

Skitten pictured in November 1942, the month that Operation 'Freshman' took place on which 41 men lost their lives.

Early in 1943, Skitten was officially designated as a reserve base for Bomber Command, holding up to 24 heavy bombers, which meant that the Coastal Command units would have to move elsewhere at short notice. Although the aerodrome had good flat approaches, the prevailing wind often favoured the shortest runway so plans were made to extend it to 1,400 yards.

In April 1943, Skitten saw the formation of a very hush-hush unit for 'anti-submarine duties' under No. 18 Group. Titled No. 618 Squadron, it was in fact created primarily for dropping modified bouncing bombs on the *Tirpitz*. This operation was to take place the day before its sister unit, No. 617 Squadron, was to attack the Ruhr Dams. Loch Striven on the Scottish west coast was selected for practice drops because of its resemblance to the Norwegian fjord where the ship was anchored.

Two spherical mines were to be carried in tandem, back spun to nearly a 1,000 rpm by a belt drive connected to an air turbine. The aircraft was to descend to 25 feet before releasing the weapons about a mile from the target. The mines would then bounce along the water behind one another, leaping nets and booms protecting the ship. On striking its hull the mine would rebound and sink and, at a pre-selected depth beneath the hull, the 600lb Torpex charge would be detonated by a hydrostatic pistol. However, problems with the weapon, as well as delays with crew training for this precision task, resulted in the project being abandoned. No. 618 Squadron conducted further trials but the weapon still proved unsatisfactory and the unit moved south in September 1943, pending further development.

One of the final units to be based at Skitten was No. 519 Squadron with a mixture of

Today only the odd ruined building remains to mark the existance of the technical site.

The runways and taxiways have not been taken up but a quarry in the middle of the airfield has rendered them useless.

Hampdens, Spitfires, Hudsons and Venturas for meteorological flights. The focus of operations was the North Atlantic and North Sea, especially one route code-named 'Recipe' which ran well north of the Arctic Circle before turning back. The twin-engined aircraft were used for the long and medium range sorties and the Spitfires for high altitude ascents. The squadron moved to Wick at the end of November 1944 leaving Skitten little used until the war ended. Soon afterwards it was abandoned and returned to farmland.

Despite a quarry dug out of the centre of the airfield, considerable sections of the runways are still in place although in very poor condition. Until the quarrying became very obvious, the UK Air Pilot (the official procedures and navigation manual now renamed prosaically as the Aeronautical Information Publication), warned: 'There is a disused wartime airfield [Skitten] three nautical miles NW of Wick aerodrome. The approach path to Runway 14 at Wick passes directly over this airfield and aircraft have touched

down there in error on occasion in conditions of poor visibility'.

Today the hangars and fighter pens are long gone but many subsidiary buildings, including the gas decontamination centre, have survived. Beside the B876 at the original airfield entrance is an unusual circular defence structure whose dished roof has been cleverly converted to grow flowers. It also supports a stone bearing the name Skitten, the farm having long been reinstated.

The station cost £356,000 to build (about £14½ million today), by George Wimpey, which during the war years had their own 300-man construction unit in the Army. 'Wimpey' 608 General Construction Company, Royal Engineers', had to return to Skitten in November 1941 to strengthen the runways for use by Bomber Command at a cost of £53,000 (£2 million).

153

SULLOM VOE

The two bases in the Shetland Isles were vital for No. 16 Group's task of attempting to block access to the northern Atlantic. Here a Saro London from No. 240 Squadron approaches the base in the winter of 1939-40.

The most northerly wartime air station in the British Isles and certainly the bleakest, Sullom Voe dated from the summer of 1939, 'Voe' being an Orkney and Shetland term for a small creek or bay and is derived from Old Norse via Norwegian. The support ship SS *Manela* brought in the work parties detailed to build proper quarters, as well as a slipway and maintenance area at Sellaness. When a hutted camp had been completed in April 1940, the ship departed and soon took up similar duties in Iceland.

The landing area from north-west to south-east was notified as one square mile and from north-east to south-west as two square miles. In Garths Voe there were 22 moorings described as '40-inch Short buoys' and dispersal moorings in Heinkel Gap (three), Voxter Voe (three) and Haggrister (four). The name 'Heinkel Gap' presumably refers to the occasion when four bombs were dropped harmlessly during November 1939. Marine craft consisted of three pinnaces, three seaplane tenders, three propelled refuellers, three dumb refuellers and two bomb scows. Accommodation was provided for 104 officers and 1,158 men and the prevailing weather was described ominously as 'wet and windy'. There were no hangars until later in the war when two TFB types were erected.

Derek Gilpin Barnes, an RAF intelligence officer and author of the memorable book *Cloud Cover* (Rich and Cowan 1943) described Sullom Voe as a place haunted by 'the clash of remote Scandinavian swords and the grinding of Norse keels upon forgotten sands'. His striking pen picture captures the atmosphere perfectly: 'The station lay like a sullen explorer's encampment by the deserted shores of a black and evil loch. Yet in that austere landscape there was the utmost beauty as well as forbidding gloom. One sensed that the noise of aircraft and the prolonged shouting of a thousand men were but a momentary echo in the long Northern silence that would again irrevocably descend. We'd built a town by the Voe. Our shouts and aero-engines, guns and launches bring to this forgotten valley the bustle of a city. Yet, three hundred yards outside the boundary, the eider duck are feeding and the white Arctic hares leap in the heather.'

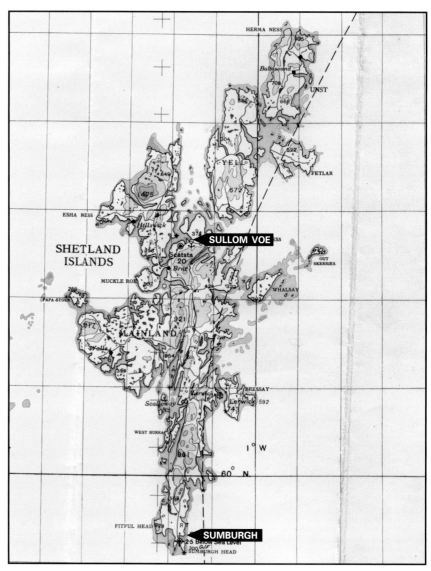

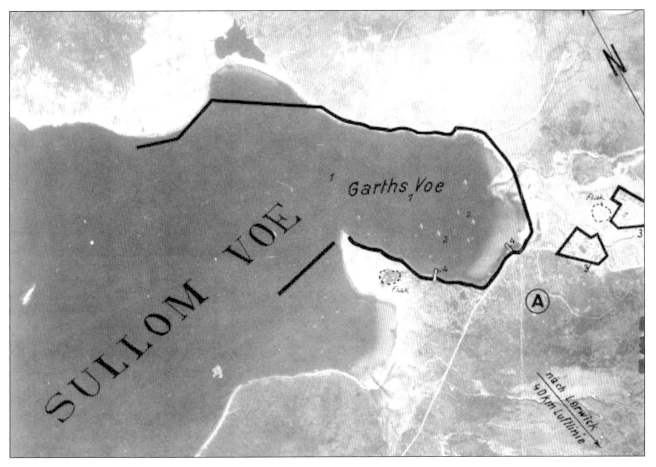

By the middle of 1938, the Luftwaffe had already prepared target maps listing Sullom Voe [A] as Target GB 10314. [1] Water landing areas. [2] Anchorage for seaplanes with anchor-buoys. [3] Accommodation huts under construction. [4] Landing stages. Note that Scatsa aerodrome has not yet been built south-west of the seaplane base.

SCATSA AIRFIELD

Armed with the wartime plan, Sammy Sjoberg explored the site for us and found a number of the camp buildings still standing. This is the Flight Office (No. 233a) which lay between the two hangars 137a and 137b.

He goes on to say: 'The sullen waters of the Voe, ablink with the riding lights of aircraft at their moorings. In the camouflaged huts, huddled on that desolate shore, were many young men all dreaming of trams and girls, fish bars, pictures, "the dogs" and home and all shouting or singing or turning on radios to drown the thin, insistent voices of an earlier age.'

The first based squadron was No. 201 from southern England, sent here as its war station in August 1939. It operated a mix of Saro Londons and Supermarine Stranraers and began to fly as far as Norway searching for German surface-raiders and submarines. The Londons soldiered on until April 1940, by which time two had been lost, one to enemy action. The same month the squadron began converting to Sunderlands and subsequently flew many of its operational patrols from Invergordon. In November 1939, the London-equipped No. 240 Squadron moved into Sullom Voe. On December 19, it saw action for the first time with a fight against an He 111, during which the captain was killed but the crew managed to return to base. The squadron transferred to South Wales in May 1940.

The Sunderlands of No. 204 Squadron had been here since April 1940 flying patrols over the Norwegian coast. They were attacked on occasion by Ju 88s, resulting in the loss of one aircraft. In one encounter a Sunderland fought off six Ju 88s and shot down two of them. A Bf 109 was accounted for on June 21 while two Sunderlands were shadowing the *Scharnhorst.* A detachment was sent to Iceland that month and the rest of the squadron followed in April 1941.

On the morning of March 23, 1941, two Me 110s made a low-level attack on the camp but it was Sullom church and village which took most of the fire. One aircraft was hit by Bofors gun-fire and crashed in flames into the water. The pilot's body was later washed ashore, along with the auxiliary fuel tanks which had made the long flight from Norway possible. An unexploded 250kg bomb was defused, mounted with an inscription and surrounded by a small fence!

No. 201 Squadron left for Northern Ireland in October 1941, the Canadian No. 413 Squadron taking over. Its Catalinas began a routine of convoy escorts and anti-submarine patrols over the North Atlantic. These continued until March 1942 when the squadron left its aircraft in Shetland and began the long journey to Ceylon. No. 210 Squadron's Catalinas took over its duties, extending them to covering the Russian convoys, during which many U-Boats were found and

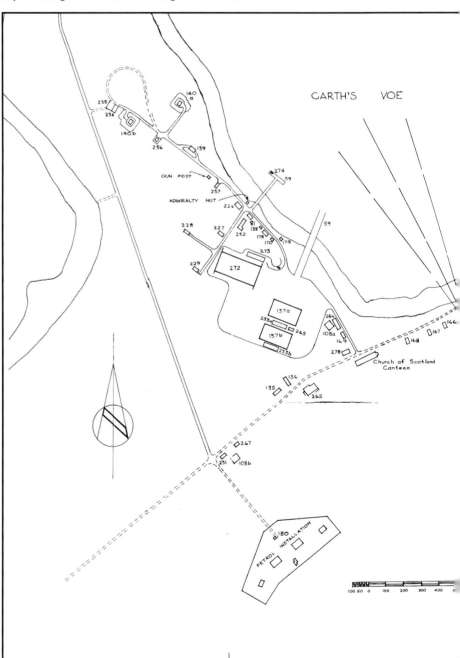

This was the Officers' Mess (Building 245) which for a time after the war served as a hotel.

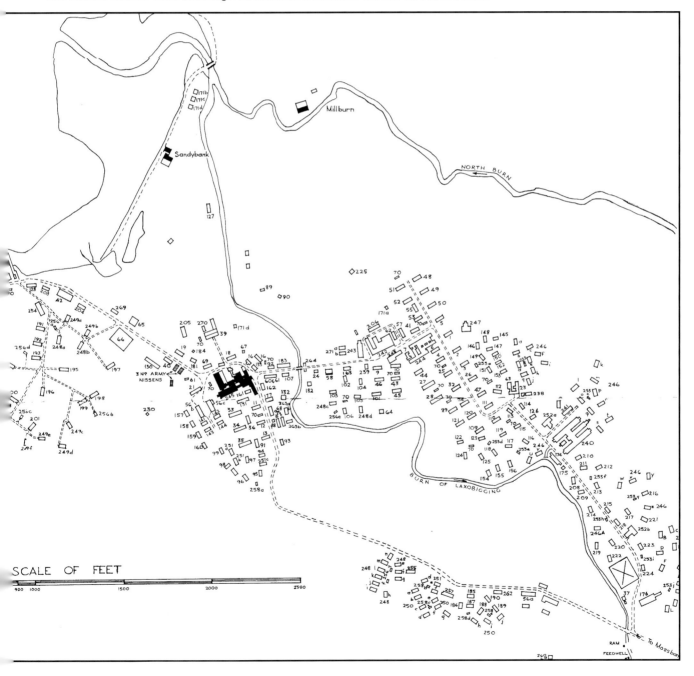

SCALE OF FEET

A surprise was in store in the Eduction Hut (Building 183); beer was still 1/3 per pint — about 6 pence today!

attacked. On September 21, *U-253* shadowing convoy QP.14 was sunk, but with a change in operational needs, the following month the squadron moved to South Wales.

A new Catalina squadron — No. 190 — formed at Sullom Voe on March 1, 1943 for Atlantic patrols and almost immediately began operations. Before the month was out it had sunk its first U-Boat when Pilot Officer J. Fish's crew made two attacks, despite being damaged by flak. No. 190 disbanded here at the end of December 1943 and reformed the following day by being re-numbered as No. 210 Squadron. The latter had just disbanded in southern England with its aircraft and crews being dispersed to other squadrons. There was no doubt a reason for these bureaucratic changes but it is not obvious!

The Catalinas of No. 210 Squadron carried on the usual convoy escort and anti-U-Boat patrols. They were mostly uneventful but on February 25, 1944, a radar contact turned out to be *U-601* and it was swiftly sunk. This was claimed to be the first U-Boat kill north of the Arctic Circle. In May 1944 the last Russian convoy was safely escorted and thereafter the squadron concentrated on the U-Boat war. By the end of May, two more U-Boat kills were obtained and in July another two. The one on the 17th resulted in Flying Officer John Alexander Cruickshank being awarded the Victoria Cross. On his first run the depth-charges would not release but on the second against heavy AA fire the U-Boat was bracketed, although the navigator was killed and the captain severely wounded. He maintained command of the aircraft on the five and a half hour flight back, though sometimes lapsing into uncon-

The crew of this Catalina of No. 210 Squadron made the last attack of the war on a German submarine. In the early hours of May 7, 1945, they depth-charged the *U-320*, west of Bergen, Norway. The U-boat was badly damaged and, despite an attempt at repairs by the crew, it sank off the Norwegian coast two days later. The crew are: Front row L-R: Flying Officer C. Humphrey (navigator), Flying Officer F. Weston (3rd pilot), Flight Lieutenant K. Murray (captain), Flight Lieutenant W. C. Robertson (2nd pilot), Flight Sergeant D. Fowler (1st wireless operator/air gunner). Rear row L-R: Flight Sergeant G. Swift (air gunner), Flight Sergeant P. G. A. Alway (Flight Mechanic), Flight Sergeant L. W. Rose (Wireless Operator/mechanic) and Flight Sergeant I. W. Evans (2nd Wireless Operator/Air Gunner).

The slipway at Sullom Voe today with the installation of the oil terminal across the bay.

John Cruickshank enlisted in the Royal Artillery in May 1939 but transferred to the RAF in 1941. He earned his wings in July 1942 and was posted to No. 210 Squadron at Sullom Voe in March 1943. On July 17, 1944, he was piloting his Catalina when a U-boat was spotted on the surface. The *U-361* immediately opened fire, killing the navigator and injuring four of the crew including the second pilot and Cruickshank himself but on their second pass they straddled the U-Boat, sinking it with all hands! Despite being severely wounded, Flying Officer Cruickshank maintained control and set course for the Shetlands but when the RAF medical officer boarded the aircraft he had to immediately give him a blood transfusion before it was considered safe to move him to hospital. Cruickshank's injuries were such that he never flew in command again. His award of the Victoria Cross was announced on September 1, 1944. After the war he returned to his pre-war job in banking, later becoming Vice-Chairman of the Victoria and George Cross Association.

sciousness. He insisted in helping his inexperienced and wounded second pilot, Flight Sergeant Jack Garnett, with the landing at Sullom Voe after which they had to run the aircraft onto a beach before it sank. On reaching hospital he was found to have 72 different wounds but made a full recovery.

In August 1944 No. 210 Squadron commenced an intensive Leigh Light and radar training programme in preparation for the long winter nights to come. A detachment of Catalinas of No. 202 Squadron was sent from Northern Ireland to help with the operational commitments. A summing up of Sullom Voe's achievements during 1944 showed 14,080 operational flying hours and a total of 1,064 sorties. The closing months of the war saw little action with only two inconclusive U-Boat attacks.

The mainly Norwegian-crewed No. 330 Squadron had operated Sunderlands from the Voe, beginning in July 1943. It flew anti-submarine patrols to north Norway and beyond to cover Russian convoys. These were mainly uneventful until May 16, 1944 when a Sunderland front gunner was killed in an attack which left a U-Boat damaged. The unit went on to fly regular patrols until the war ended but there were few actions and no successes. At the end of May the squadron flew to Norway and was taken over by the Royal Norwegian Air Force.

The station and nearby Scatsta reverted to Care and Maintenance in 1946. Natural deterioration and storm damage made conditions very primitive when both locations were

St Clair's House (Building 16) was requisitioned for the Station Headquarters.

used for Exercise *Mainbrace* in the summer of 1952. No. 201 Squadron's white-painted Sunderlands contrasted with midnight blue PBM Mariners of the US Navy, together with the seaplane tender, USS *Timbalier*. When the flying boats left, the Americans took with them at least three Shetland ponies!

Soon after the first oil was discovered in the North Sea in 1969 construction began on an oil terminal which became operational in 1975, engulfing the former RAF camp although several wartime buildings still remain standing. There is also a fine memorial to the station and its personnel, particularly those lost flying from here.

Stand down at Sullom Voe in May 1945 . . . then and now.

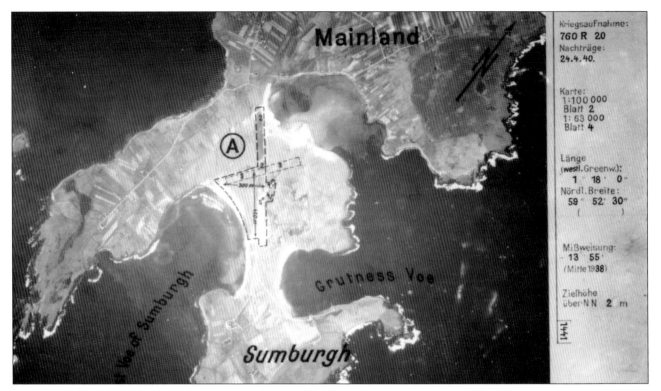

Kriegsaufnahme:
760 R 20
Nachträge:
24.4.40.

Karte:
1:100 000
Blatt 2
1: 63 000
Blatt 4

Länge
(westl.Greenw.):
1° 18' 0"
Nördl.Breite:
59° 52' 30"
( )

Mißweisung:
-13° 55'
(Mitte 1938)

Zielhöhe
über NN **2 m**

1441

SUMBURGH

Photographed by the Luftwaffe in April 1940, prior to the building of the hardened runways, a NW-SW landing strip has been given as 450 metres (1,500 feet), but when pictured again four months later, two runways had been constructed although on different axes.

This airfield on the southernmost tip of Shetland had been established pre-war on Sumburgh golf links and scheduled services to the mainland had begun in 1936. Its location was far from ideal, but in view of the lack of other potential airfield sites on the islands, reconstruction began in the early part of 1940. As Captain E. E. Fresson described it in his book *Air Road to the Isles* (David Rendel Ltd, 1967): 'It was a difficult airfield to develop as its level area was very limited. Consequently, it amounted to a major engineering job and costly alterations had to be made to the surrounding country. On the north side, the Pool of Virkie, which was a tidal basin, had to be filled in to a great extent, and a great number of high sand dunes levelled. To the south lay the beach alongside the North Sea and to the east, Sumburgh Head rising to 300ft with a lighthouse on the top of it. To the west lay Fitful Head towering to over 900ft some four miles away, with the ground sloping up gently from the airfield. So to construct the north-east/south-west strip, a cutting of 200ft wide and some 40ft deep had to be made, through the sloping ground to the sea coast at the southern end of the site.'

A Station Headquarters was established in May 1940 to administer the Blenheim-equipped No. 254 Squadron and the 'Sumburgh Fighter Flight' with its Gloster Gladiators, which formed Shetland's air defence. RAF Sumburgh's Operations Record Book notes the following: 'There is one runway running north-west to south-east to be 1,200 yards when completed. Two others are under construction. Accommodation consists of bell tents and marquees and one corrugated iron hangar for the Fighter Flight. Water is being laid on, but for the time being, has to be carried from Ward Hill about a mile away. Fortunately the weather was fine and the work of erecting tents was carried out very quickly.'

When completed, the runway lengths were 1,330, 1,120 and 980 yards, respectively. Hangarage consisted of three Bellmans. Two 'Q' site decoys were laid out at Quendale, three miles to the north-west, and Scatness about two miles south-west where the

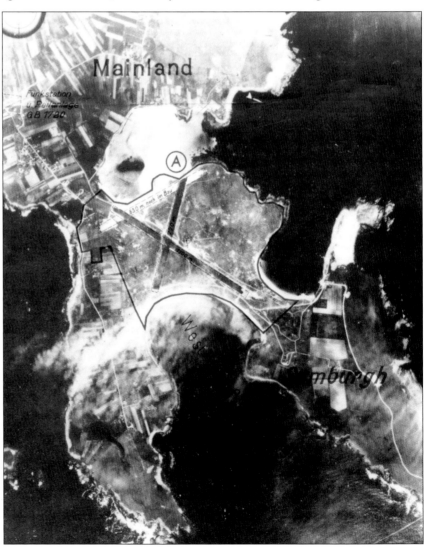

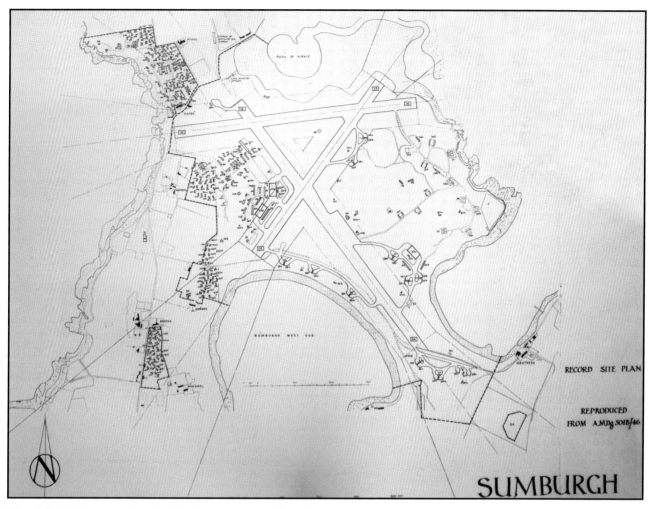

RECORD SITE PLAN

REPRODUCED
FROM A.M.Dg.5016/46

SUMBURGH

The airfield when completed with three runways, the main NW-SE with the secondaries NE-SW and E-W. After the war, the discovery of oil east of Shetland in the Brent field, resulted in Sumburgh becoming the fastest growing airport in the United Kingdom with a new terminal building being opened in 1979. The main runway was extended at the eastern and western ends in 2006 which meant that the A970 road crossed the runway, neccessitating closure when aircraft were using it.

control bunker can still be seen. RAF Sumburgh's Battle Headquarters bunker was emplaced near the road on the south-west perimeter of the airport. It remains in good condition, as does a quite rare Allan-Williams Turret beside the road just to the north of the airport.

When the Gladiators were sent to south-west England in July 1940,'B' Flight of No. 3 Squadron was detached from Wick to maintain the fighter presence, this time with Hurricanes. It soon became a new squadron in its own right — No. 232 under the Wick Sector. For the most part flying convoy escort, it was scrambled on occasion and on August 23 accounted for an He 111 off Fair Isle. No. 232 Squadron left for the mainland in September 1940, No. 254 Squadron having already gone to Dyce in July. No. 248's Blenheims took its place and flew anti-shipping patrols off Norway until early in January 1941, when No. 254 returned and stayed until the end of May.

There was rarely a complete fighter squadron available for service in Shetland, so detached flights of Hurricanes from mainland units filled this gap in the northern defences. They included parts of Nos. 3 and 17 Squadrons. In addition, Sea Hurricanes of the Fleet Air Arm's 880 Squadron were here during the autumn of 1941. Beaufighter long-range fighters were based for the first time in September 1941, when No. 143 Squadron arrived from Dyce. A total of 156 sorties were flown during October on convoy escort, fighter patrol and Faroes patrol. On the 19th a Ju 88 was claimed as probably destroyed; the unit's first success.

Although the Luftwaffe sent a single Ju 88 to raid Sumburgh in February 1942, it was an 'own goal' on March 20 that caused the most damage when the offices of No. 235 Squadron were accidentally torpedoed by No. 42 Squadron! Wing Commander Hugh Garlick explained what happened in his self-published book *One Life Left*: 'On our first night at Sumburgh, we had experienced a trauma. Having arrived late in the afternoon there was time only to pile the equipment we had brought with us into our squadron office — a wooden hut standing not far from the edge of the main runway. Having settled into my new quarters, a half a Nissen hut heated by a free standing solid fuel stove whose chimney disappeared through the centre of the roof, I was asleep when the Tannoy, of which I had a loudspeaker in my room, announced, "Everyone is to get at least 400 yards from 235 Squadron offices — the torpedo is due to explode in seven minutes". Putting aside such questions as who would want to torpedo our office, I rang the Ops. Room with the important question: "Is my room 400 yards from my office?" After the assurance that it was, there was nothing to do but wait for the bang, a satisfyingly loud one, which momentarily changed the shape of my Nissen hut so that several inches of outside chimney appeared inside. Once that was over it was a case of finishing dressing and going to view the hole that had been our offices.'

On February 1, 1942, a Ju 88 strafed the airfield, riddled a hangar with cannon fire and damaged some Blenheims, killing two airmen and injuring another six. The following month, a Beaufort with engine trouble swung on landing and ran into the squadron offices. In the resulting fire, the torpedo exploded soon afterwards, completely wrecking the offices and crew rooms. Fortunately, the crew had got clear in time and a warning had been broadcast on the Tannoy enabling ground staff to get well away. In the aftermath, the squadron engineering officer declared that the cubic capacity of the hut was insufficient to hold all the gear claimed as destroyed!

By August 1942, the station had been increased in size until it was capable of accommodating three Coastal squadrons. These were No. 248 with Beaufighters (here since the end of May), No. 404 with Blenheims and a detachment of No. 608's Hudsons. Targets off the Norwegian coast were attacked and convoys on their way to northern Russia were escorted. During August, Sumburgh was used as the starting point for Hampdens of Nos. 144 and 455 Squadrons. With fuel tanks topped off, they set off for Russia but several were lost en route. Well over 30 years later, one of them was found on a Lapland mountain with the remains of some of the crew still in the wreckage (see *After the Battle* No. 16).

Notable visitors on September 25, 1942 were three Mosquitos of No. 105 Squadron refuelling on the way back from the celebrated precision raid on the Gestapo HQ in Oslo.

The fighter detachments had continued in 1942, the last being Spitfires of No. 602 Squadron which was replaced by No. 234 Squadron. On March 24, 1943, one of the latter's pilots shot down an Me 210 off Fitful Head. This detachment left in April, being relieved successively by Flights of Nos. 313, 310 and 453 Squadrons. For anti-submarine patrols, Hudsons of No. 48 Squadron were here from September to November 1942.

Sammy Sjoberg works in the control tower and knew the location where the Wing Commander's office had stood.

This is the gaping hole left where the office had stood. Wing Commander Garlick commented that 'this was carrying inter-squadron rivalry too far! A hole caused by the explosion of a torpedo carried by a Beaufort which had swung off the runway on landing, embedded itself in our wooden hut, and caught fire. Luckily the crew escaped without damage, which is more than could be said for our equipment. What had not been burned or blown up had just disappeared and I was forced to recall that there was a resident squadron — now on Blenheims — that I had visited the previous year as President of a Court Martial of some of their postal staff who had been accused of "diverting" parcels of goodies. It seemed that it was not the postal staff alone who were light-fingered. As certain items belonged to an officer who had gone missing a few days before, and some of these could have been sufficiently embarrassing to require a Court of Enquiry, I went on the Tannoy and broadcast a heart-throb appeal for their return with no questions asked. Either conscience, or lack of a market for sale, caused a change of heart and these items mysteriously reappeared. Our Engineer Officer claimed that the cubic capacity of our late office was insufficient to take the volume of items we claimed for write-off, but this did appear to be the ideal opportunity for clearing the books of shortages which had been bothering me since taking over the squadron.'

Flying from Sumburgh, especially at night, was a hazardous business because of the nearby hills. One Beaufort pilot lost control trying to avoid high ground and spun in. On another occasion, a Mosquito of No. 143 Squadron was forced by a hill to make a right-hand circuit with, rather than against, a dead engine as was, and is, standard practice. To maintain control, the landing had to be fast but resulted in over-running the runway and a collision with a brick wall that killed one of the crew.

Life for ground personnel had its disadvantages too. The Station Medical Officer recorded in April 1942 that he had treated an abnormal number of airmen for anxiety neurosis . At that time, 12 months on the island was reckoned to be the maximum before a mainland posting was deemed to be desirable, and some of the cases had well exceeded this. He also suggested, somewhat ambiguously, that the presence of WAAFs on the camp would do much to improve the general happiness of the men! Another domestic problem was the shortage of green vegetables and it was arranged that Harrow transports would fly them up regularly from the mainland, the flying boat base at Sullom Voe also taking advantage of this service.

From June 1944, the Ansons of No. 1693 (General Reconnaissance) Flight began close-in anti-submarine patrols to the west of the Orkney Islands. This was almost certainly the last operational use of the type and the Ansons remained at Sumburgh until May 1945. Mosquitos, including those from No. 333 Squadron, used Sumburgh as an advanced base for reconnaissance of the Norwegian coast. It was also a convenient staging post for photo-recce aircraft based at Wick and Leuchars. No. 540 Squadron's first operational sortie had been launched from Shetland, during which *Tirpitz* and *Admiral von Scheer* were photographed in Ofot Fjord. In 1944, Cansos of the Canadian No. 162 Squadron based at Reykjavik were flying armed transits between Sumburgh airfield and Iceland on the lookout for submarines.

VE-Day saw the immediate end of Sumburgh's strategic importance. The Coastal Command operations room closed on June 4, 1945 and the only visitors that month were two Spitfire squadrons in transit to Norway. At the end of August the station was reduced to Care and Maintenance status, parented by Sullom Voe.

The wartime civil scheduled services to the mainland were continued and expanded and, in the late 1970s, the rapid expansion of oil related traffic saw the airport become the fastest growing in the UK, with a peak of 685,000 passengers and 51,000 aircraft movements in 1978. A new terminal was built and the runway was further extended.

Airport expansion has meant the removal of many wartime structures but the wartime watch office has been retained, albeit greatly altered and with the addition of a modern visual control room.

Some scattered buildings and many hut bases can be seen in the vicinity of the airport, as well as the defence structure described above. Apart from the legacy of the airport, other benefits of the war included the construction of paved roads on the island.

The airports cramped position is evident from this angle. The other slightly longer runway stretches from left to right beyond the terminal and a short helicopter strip is just visible above the sea inlet in the foreground.

TAIN

The Canadian press officer released this photo with the caption that 'these boys of a RCAF Beaufighter squadron have just returned from a "rescue" trip over the North Sea, and appreciate the tea and buns being dispensed from this Church of Scotland van.'

This airfield's links with military aviation date back to 1913 when the area was surveyed by the War Office for possible use as an aerodrome for the defence of naval installations around the Cromarty Firth. Records also indicated that the area often had favourable weather conditions for flying and, although no action was taken on the original plan, the Tain Bombing Range was established between the wars and used by both RAF and naval aircraft before the start of the Second World War. A grass landing ground was laid out to serve the range and it was this that became the basis for a Fighter Sector station that opened in September 1941. It was intended to bridge the defensive gap between Scapa Flow in the Orkneys and the northern edge of the Turnhouse Sector. Satellites were planned at Fearn and Elgin, but instead Fearn was soon transferred to the Navy and Elgin became a satellite for Lossiemouth's OTU of Bomber Command.

In June 1942, with construction recently finished, the station's Operations Record Book commented that 'a strong west wind made the aerodrome rather like the Libyan Desert with flying sand. There is no doubt that completion of the station and its efficient appearance has reacted favourably on general morale and discipline. A few months ago it was nothing more than a contractor's dump; there was no incentive for smartness. Flaming June is something of a joke in the North. Despite rumours of heat-waves in southern England, there is snow on the hills north of Dornoch and the airmen have to look at their diaries to reassure themselves that it really is summer. The airfield is still without aircraft and the staff are beginning to wonder if Tain is marked on the maps at Whitehall and Kingsway.'

Future allocation to Coastal Command was heralded by the arrival of Coastal Command Development Unit in mid-June 1942 for a posting that was to last until April 1943. The airfield was also earmarked for operations to Norway by USAAF heavy bombers if this proved necessary. To support the plan, a party of American engineers arrived at the end of October 1942 to lay down extensions to the NE-SW runway and at the same time gain experience in airfield construction. Two of the three runways had now been extended to 2,000 yards with a subsidiary of 1,460 yards. Hangarage consisted of three Bellmans and eight blisters.

The New Year saw some activity when detachments from three separate squadrons began operating from here: No. 254 with Beaufighters and Nos. 311 and 547 with Wellingtons. After Tain was officially transferred to the control of Coastal Command on February 22, 1943, there now followed a rapid succession of strike and shipping recce squadrons being based there for varying periods. On March 11, for example, the Hampdens of No. 415 Squadron flew an armed recce off the Norwegian coast, carrying torpedoes. Although no enemy ships were sighted, one aircraft failed to return and five diverted to Dyce on the way back.

During April, No. 404 Squadron's Beaufighters made their first sorties from Tain, attacking shipping with cannon fire. They were joined by the Beaufighter-equipped No. 144 Squadron which stayed until October 1943 when they moved north to Wick. April 21 saw a typical example of the squadron's activities. Four Beaufighters were airborne on a patrol when they sighted a motor vessel of 4,000 tons with two escorts. After raking the target with cannon fire, it was left listing and pouring smoke and steam and many hits were also observed on the escorts. Two more Beaufighters were despatched in the afternoon with the intention of finishing the job but were intercepted by two Bf 109s. One of the Beaufighters, too late to gain cloud cover, was hit badly, the radio being wrecked and the navigator wounded. The fighters finally broke off and the Beaufighter made it back to Tain, only to have the undercarriage collapse on landing. The crew just managed to escape before it caught fire.

As was usual with wartime captioning, the squadron was not identified, and no code letters are visible, but research indicates that it was No. 404 who were based at Tain in April 1943 and that this was the mount of Flying Officer Ivor Johnson which he had named *Morning Glory*. Aldon Ferguson, who visited the former airfield in August 2015, explains that 'it has been derelict since the end of the war having been reconfigured as an air-to-ground gunnery and bombing range covering the area of Morrich More. Most of the runways and taxiways remain but are very overgrown and totally unused.'

In January 1943, No. 1 Torpedo Refresher School formed at Tain to provide training facilities for torpedo bomber crews, including Fleet Air Arm personnel returning to operations with new equipment. It also trained Wellington crews destined for torpedo bomber co-operation squadrons in the use of bomb-sights and ASV radar, and further included a section converting crews to rocket-projectile attacks. When the school was disbanded in January 1944 it left Tain somewhat under-used for the first months of that year.

During this time, the E-W runway was further extended by an RAF Works Flight, using pierced steel planking (PSP). Loop hardstandings were also laid down to prepare for the possible stationing of Coastal Command Liberator squadrons there. No. 86 Squadron had already been operating a Liberator detachment from Tain for a week in July 1944 to deal with a concentration of U-Boats off Norway, and even before that a squadron aircraft flying from the base had sunk a U-Boat on June 26. The remainder of the squadron now moved in, soon to be joined by the Czechoslovak-manned No. 311 Squadron.

During October 1944, while on patrol off Norway, one of No. 311 Squadron's Liberators was shot down by a Bf 110. The same month, another Liberator flew back to base after two engines failed and, when the news reached representatives of the Pratt and Whitney engine company, they found it hard to believe that the other two engines had been successfully operated at full power for almost three hours! At the end of October, Liberators mortally damaged a U-Boat with rocket-projectiles and depth-charges, leaving it be finished off by Halifaxes. No. 311 Squadron's final U-Boat sinking of the war took place in the Kattegat, the strait between Denmark and Sweden, on May 5, 1945.

The changing face of Tain . . . from 1945 to 2015.

The majority of the wartime buildings were demolished in 2006 but fortunately the control tower was spared.

And the Operations Block has been preserved in the ownership of Miss Claire Armstrong who once hoped to convert it into her home. She kindly gave Aldon a guided tour where he was able to record the signs still visible on the walls.

The gunnery tower was demolished soon after this photo was taken in 1989 to be replaced by a state-of-the-art structure.

In March 1945 No. 86 Squadron began to use the Mk VIII Liberator, with its absolute maximum endurance of 11 to 12 hours. Patrols were mostly uneventful until May 5 when three surfaced U-Boats were spotted off Denmark, one of which was being attacked by a Wellington. This aircraft was hit by flak and dived into the sea, leaving one survivor clinging to a dinghy. Two of the submarines had by now submerged but the third was straddled by depth-charges and it was soon sinking stern first, with about 40 survivors in the water. A lightship about a mile away lowered a boat to pick them up and the circling Liberator was able to direct attention to the Wellington crewman, who was also rescued.

The next few days were spent in shadowing surrendering U-Boats and in June No. 311 Squadron was transferred to Transport Command, leaving for East Anglia. No. 86 Squadron followed them in August, to be replaced by No. 519 Squadron's Fortresses for a few months. After some further use for torpedo training with Beaufighters, Tain reverted to Care and Maintenance in November 1946 and later became part of the Tain Bombing Range which extended to the north. Now controlled by Defence Training Estates and known as an Air Weapons Range, it remains in use by the RAF and other NATO air forces.

Many of the derelict buildings still dotted around were demolished in 2006 but some survive on the dispersed living sites to the south-east. The real gem is the former Operations Block, originally planned to control a Fighter Sector, which in the 1990s still retained many of its fittings.

Ordnance now acts as an unusual 'Gate Guardian' at the entrance to the operational enclosure. The Tain Air Weapons Range is the largest live bombing range in Europe where weapons up to 1,000lbs can be dropped. It is also used by the USAF. The entire range is visible from the tower which operates like a conventional control tower to control the aircraft using the range.

THORNABY

Thornaby was once a vital base for No. 18 Group covering operations over the North Sea. Here we see it in September 1943, during the period when air-sea rescue by No. 281 Squadron was its primary role.

The aeronautical use of this site in north-east England dated back to 1912 when a farmer's field was utilised for an air show featuring pioneer aviator Gustav Hamel. The same field was adapted in the First World War as a Night Landing Ground for a Home Defence squadron. It later became the basis of the very much larger RAF Thornaby which opened in 1930 as the base of No. 608 Squadron, Auxiliary Air Force, equipped with Westland Wapiti light bombers. In 1937 it converted to a fighter role with Hawker Demons but it was eventually decided to bring the squadron into line with other Thornaby units. Thus in March 1939 it adopted a general reconnaissance role, and re-equipped with Ansons. The station transferred to Coastal Command soon afterwards. The other Anson units at Thornaby prior to the war were Nos. 224, 233 and 269, although all had gone elsewhere by the end of 1938. No. 185 Squadron's Fairey Battles, soon replaced by Hampdens, were here from October 1938 until moving south in August 1939.

The clay and grass landing area was frequently waterlogged, hence Thornaby became one of the first airfields to receive concrete runways; three were constructed, the longest being 1,250 yards. These were upgraded in 1942 to near Class 'A' standard. Drem lighting was installed and the 1,980-yard main runway was equipped with Contact Lighting and the Standard Beam Approach, though this necessitated aircraft landing from the south-west due to industrial haze obstructing the more usual north-east approach. Later the superior Air to Surface Vessel (ASV) Beam Approach was added to the 1,410-yard east-west runway which greatly assisted aircraft returning from over the North Sea.

Thornaby had two steel aircraft sheds dating from the 1930s. Around 1936 two short C Type permanent hangars and a number of prototype canvas Bellman hangars had been added. Unfortunately very heavy snowfalls severely damaged the roofs of all the Bellmans which led to a complete redesign. All were demolished, eventually being replaced by a single standard steel Bellman, and the more recent Ministry of Aircraft Production A1 shed.

A large semi-circular dispersal track led off into the fields from the south-east perimeter, with many frying-pan hardstandings spaced along it. Storage was provided for a total of 224 tons of bombs. Since the station had been built long before notions of dispersal, the main camp was concentrated to the north-west. The balloon barrage one mile to the north protecting the heavy industries of Middlesbrough and Stockton-on-Tees was obviously a major hazard. Two decoy sites were laid out, Grangetown being a 'Q/K' for day and night use with dummy aircraft, the other, Middleton, three miles to the north, was a night decoy only.

The nominated operational satellite was West Hartlepool, also known as Greatham and which had been the local municipal airport since 1938. It does not seem to have been used very much by the RAF, apart from training circuits and landings and occasional forward-based fighter detachments from RAF Catterick. It remained grass-surfaced throughout its life, with a longest runway of 1,400 yards and returned to civil use after the war. A flying club was established and limited scheduled services operated by the then fledgling BKS airline, including one to London's Northolt airport using Dakota aircraft. When the airfield eventually closed, a steel works was built on the site and in recent years a business park has been established where the technical

The years have not been kind to Thornaby and, of all the Coastal Command bases featured in this book, it lives up to the phrase 'expunged from the map' with virtually no trace remaining today.

site once stood. The only evidence of wartime use is a line of three pillboxes guarding what was once the southern edge of the airfield, and an original wartime wooden hut on a nearby farm.

On the outbreak of war, No. 608 Squadron took up anti-submarine and air-sea rescue patrols, as well as convoy escort. Conversion onto the Blackburn Botha began in the summer of 1940, the squadron being the only one to use the Botha operationally. However, the type was found to have serious deficiencies and all were withdrawn in November. Ansons were a stop-gap until replaced by Blenheims in the spring of 1941. The usual patrols continued until Hudsons were acquired in July, giving the squadron a far better offensive capability. In September an enemy convoy was bombed and a Ju 88 was claimed as damaged.

In November 1939, the King arrived in a Hudson of No. 220 Squadron; one wonders what he would have made of the base today.

169

Thornaby New Town takes shape in 1965. Fortunately the Thornaby Aerodrome Memorial Committee were able to persuade Stockton-on-Tees Borough Council and Thornaby Town Council to put preservation orders in place on certain RAF buildings.

With the greater range available, the squadron now began operating over Denmark, bombing the ports of Aalborg and Esbjerg in October, as well as attacking shipping. In January 1942 a move was made to Wick in the north of Scotland and later that same year the squadron flew out to North Africa to take part in the Mediterranean campaign, not returning to the UK until 1944.

Another Anson Squadron, No. 220, was based at Thornaby from August 1939 and soon converted to Hudsons, extending its operations to Norway and the Dutch coast. During one such patrol in February 1940 the German prison ship *Altmark* was located off the Norwegian coast and as a result was intercepted by a Royal Navy boarding party which released the 299 British sailors on board.

No. 114 Squadron was present between March and May 1941 using its Blenheims for anti-shipping strikes.

Thornaby assumed a training role in July 1941 for No. 6 (Coastal) Operational Training Unit's Hudsons and Ansons. The OTU was joined by Czech and Polish flights with Wellingtons, supporting Nos. 304 and 311 Squadrons after their transfer from Bomber to Coastal Command. The whole unit was by now Wellington-equipped, with West Hartlepool used for circuits and landing practice. In March 1943, No. 6 OTU exchanged bases with another Coastal OTU, No. 1 at Silloth. The latter unit moved into Thornaby with Fortresses, Liberators and Halifaxes until transferring to Northern Ireland in September 1943.

Thornaby's main duty now became air-sea rescue (ASR), with No. 281 Squadron's airborne lifeboat-equipped Warwicks in residence until February 1944, when they moved to Tiree. A sister Warwick squadron, No. 280, was also resident between October 1943 and May 1944. From October 1944, No. 279 Squadron's Warwicks were at Thornaby, providing detachments in northern Scotland to cover the activities of strike and patrol squadrons. ASR duties continued to be

flown by Warwicks until June 1946. Post-war also saw No. 608 Squadron re-formed at Thornaby as a night fighter unit with Mosquitos. It went over to a day fighter role with Spitfires, followed by Vampires from December 1949. In October 1958, after a Hunter squadron, No. 92, had left at the end of a year-long stay while the runway at its home base Middleton St George was extended, Thornaby closed to flying, with No. 608 Squadron disbanding and laying up its standard in York Minster.

In the years since then, the airfield has been slowly encroached upon by housing and other development. Progress accelerated sharply in the past decade with the demolition of nearly all buildings and the redevelopment of the whole flying field with housing, leaving only one or two stretches of taxiway and a small portion of the east-west runway in use as a car park. A fine memorial featuring a statue of an airman stands in Thornaby Road and a stained glass window was dedicated in St Paul's Church in 1976. Stockton Borough Council is well aware of the site's historic past and has issued a leaflet providing a self-guided aviation walk. This starts and finishes at the full-size replica Spitfire in the markings of No. 608 Squadron which was dedicated in April 2007.

More than that, they asked David Thompson to supply photographs and background information to produce a walking tour of the preserved buildings. Here Geoff Green, David and Ron Young launch the trail leaflet beside the replica Spitfire which was sited as a focal point in April 2007. RAO were the post-war code letters for No. 608 (North Riding) Squadron based at Thornaby from 1948-50.

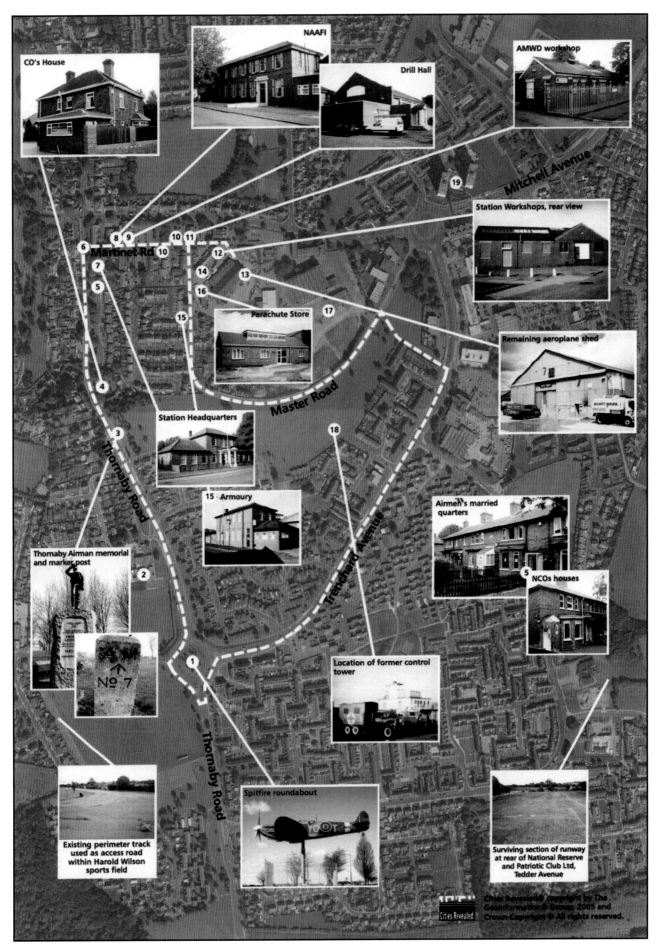

CO's House

NAAFI

Drill Hall

AMWD workshop

Mitchell Avenue

Station Workshops, rear view

8 9 10 11
6 Martinet Rd 10
7 12
14
5 13
16 17
15

Remaining aeroplane shed

Parachute Store

Master Road

4

Station Headquarters

18

3

15 Armoury

Airmen's married quarters

Thornaby Road

NCOs houses

Thornaby Airman memorial and marker post

2

No 7

1

Location of former control tower

Thornaby Road

Existing perimeter track used as access road within Harold Wilson sports field

Spitfire roundabout

Surviving section of runway at rear of National Reserve and Patriotic Club Ltd, Tedder Avenue

This plan and the associated explanatory leaflet with much other interesting detail can be obtained from the Countryside & Greenspace Team on 01642 526871 or downloaded from the Borough Council's website, www.stockton.gov.uk.

WICK

Although this town near the north-east tip of Scotland already had a rudimentary pre-war airfield at Hillhead Farm, the RAF built a new aerodrome on a more suitable site just to the north-west. It was planned to house two general reconnaissance squadrons, with hutted technical and domestic buildings to accommodate approximately 750 personnel. Until proper accommodation at the airfield could be provided, RAF personnel were billeted in the town at hotels and private houses. The newly completed North School was requisitioned for use as the airfield's operations centre and the Bignold Hospital for the treatment of the wounded and the sick.

At first the airfield was grass-surfaced but the folly of this was revealed when it became a quagmire soon after becoming operational in September 1939. The construction of three runways, each of 1,000 yards, was rapidly put into effect. These were extended at a later date, the longest being 1,570 yards. Four C1 Type hangars — an austerity version of the original C Type — were built, with two Bellmans added later in the war, along with 43 frying-pan hardstandings and bomb storage totalling 110 tons.

Wick's first operational aircraft were Skuas of the Fleet Air Arm's 803 Squadron for fighter patrols to protect the fleet anchorage at Scapa Flow. Thereafter, there were a succession of RAF fighter squadrons, mostly detachments, apart from No. 111 Squadron's Hurricanes which were here from before the war until May 1940. The airfield was attacked on several occasions, notably on April 8, 1940 when three He 111s were shot down by No. 43 Squadron and two damaged. One of the bombers crash-landed on the aerodrome with two dead crew members. Two days later, Hurricanes from Wick shared the destruction of seven bombers with Scapa's AA defences, during a great air battle over Orkney.

Wick had become a Sector Station in December 1939 under No. 13 Group, Fighter Command. Initially the station was shared between Fighter and Coastal Commands, but in October 1940 Fighter Sector HQ moved to Kirkwall, Orkney, leaving Wick solely to Coastal Command. No. 269 Squadron's Ansons had been stationed at Wick since October 1939 and by January 1940 they were flying 150 patrol sorties a month. During February, the squadron made six attacks on U-Boats, one being claimed as probably destroyed. The intensity of enemy activity is measured by the fact that patrol sorties by No. 269 Squadron rose to 200 in March, a month which also saw the arrival of the squadron's first Lockheed Hudson.

On March 21, 1940, Flight Lieutenant C. Price prepared to take off for an anti-submarine patrol. Unfortunately the temporary runway being used had a Hurricane and fuel bowser parked at the far end, and the heavily-laden Anson failed to gain sufficient lift. Price aborted and N9673 flopped to the ground. There were no fatalities but two crew members were hospitalised.

The onset of the Norwegian campaign saw the Hudsons in the thick of the action. They attacked shipping and U-Boats in the fjords and bombed Stavanger airfield in May with the loss of one aircraft. On June 11, 12 of the squadron's Hudsons attacked *Scharnhorst* in Trondheim Fjord. They carried out a pattern bombing attack from 15,000ft, dropping 36 250lb armour-piercing bombs. *Scharnhorst* was probably missed but two cruisers and a supply ship received direct hits. Two Hudsons were lost, one to anti-aircraft fire and the other to an enemy fighter. The Norwegian coast remained the operational area until the summer of 1941 when No. 269 Squadron moved to Iceland.

No. 42 Squadron was also a strong presence at Wick between June 1940 and March 1941, flying Beauforts against the German Navy. Three aircraft were lost when *Scharnhorst* was dive-bombed on June 21. The first ship sunk was a naval transport in a fjord on October 26, 1940. Two Beauforts were shot down but so was a Bf 109. At that time the Photographic Reconnaissance Unit based a Flight of Spitfires at Wick to cover the Norwegian coast. It was from Wick on May 21, 1941, using Sumburgh, Shetland, as a refuelling stop, that one of the most famous of all the early photographic sorties took place. Pilot Officer Michael Suckling returned with the shocking news that the *Bismarck* was on her way out to the Atlantic. As a direct result of this, the battleship was sunk six days later, but tragically Suckling was lost flying from Cornwall exactly two months after his epic discovery.

However, far worse was the operation to Norway on April 23. Two weeks earlier the Germans had invaded the country and on the 23rd No. 224 Squadron despatched three of its Hudsons to cover the British landings at Andalsnes. It would appear that the forces on the ground had not been informed of the RAF participation which resulted in HMS *Curacoa* opening fire as the aircraft approached. N7249 was shot down and while Pilot Officer A. Pearson was rescued, Pilot Officer Hector Webb was never found. A second Hudson, N7264, was also hit by anti-aircraft fire but managed to limp home to Wick with this large hole in its wing.

An air raid on June 4, 1941 resulted in severe damage to one of the C Type hangars, along with the destruction of a Whitley, plus damage to three others of the same type. From January to August 1942, No. 608 Squadron's Hudsons flew mainly shipping strikes in the fjords, known as Operation 'Bluebeard'. They also bombed Bergen on January 7. When it moved to Shetland, the squadron was replaced by No. 415 Squadron equipped with Hampdens. No. 48 Squadron's Hudsons were also based for much of 1942 for attacks on shipping off Norway. No. 179 Squadron formed at Wick in September 1942 for anti-submarine patrols before moving to Gibraltar in November.

Moving on into 1943, No. 612 had been at Wick since the previous September flying Whitleys. The type was slowly replaced by Wellingtons which escorted Russian convoys and mounted shipping patrols in Norwegian waters until leaving for Cornwall in April. No. 1406 Met Flight had been flying Hampdens and Mosquitos from Wick since early in 1942 and in August 1943 it became the nucleus of the new No. 519 Squadron. The unit transferred to the satellite at Skitten a few months later to help relieve congestion at the parent station. Between October 1943 and May 1944, Beaufighters of No. 144 Squadron were based for 'Rover' patrols, with varied results. These were armed reconnaissance flights with attacks on opportunity targets.

During May, No. 162 Squadron, Royal Canadian Air Force, brought its Cansos (the amphibious version of the Catalina) into Wick from Iceland. The squadron had been seconded to Coastal Command since January 1944 to cover the mid-ocean portion of the North Atlantic convoy routes. Its new task was to support the Normandy invasion by intercepting Norwegian-based U-Boats trying to head round the so-called Northern Transit Area. The squadron sank four German submarines, and shared in the sinking of a fifth. One of the pilots, Flight Lieutenant David E. Hornell, was awarded a posthumous Victoria Cross for sinking *U-1225*,

This early-war photo shows the four hangars intact but the raid on June 4, 1941 virtually destroyed the easternmost of the C Types.

despite heavy flak which forced the aircraft to ditch. It soon sank and the single dinghy recovered was insufficient to hold the entire crew. After 24 hours, either in or clinging to it, they were rescued, but Flight Lieutenant Hornell and two his crew died from the effects of exposure.

By the time No. 519 Squadron returned to Wick at the end of November 1944, the Hampdens had long been replaced by Hudsons and Venturas. In November 1944 Fortresses were received for long-range duties. The weather flights ventured out into the North Atlantic, the North Sea and north towards the Arctic Circle. Wellingtons were at Wick once more in August 1944, flown by No. 407 Squadron on anti-submarine patrols. Apart from three U-Boats depth-charged in October, there was little action and a move was made to Chivenor in November 1944.

This oblique from the 1950s shows that the remains of the hangar had still not been cleared although the two Bellmans which occupied the two white concrete bases on the left have gone. The wartime tower and signals square are still in use.

Wick transferred to No. 13 Group, Fighter Command, in August 1945 for Polish Mustang squadrons, a use which continued until March 1946. Although reverting to civilian use, it was retained as a reserve station for fighters in the event of war. With jet aircraft now in service, the main runway was extended to the north-west in 1954-55, despite poor ground quality. The reserve function was dropped a few years later and Wick has carried on being a civil airport ever since. In March 2013, it was officially renamed Wick John O'Groats Airport in order to promote local tourism and thus attract passengers. Only the longest NW-SE runway remains in use.

Today, two of the massive C Type hangars still stand, along with the wartime control tower, the functions of which have been transferred to a modern new building.

Most of the technical and administrative hutting survived until the late 1980s as industrial units, but a big clean-up saw the whole area re-developed and all these buildings were demolished to make way for modern accommodation.

Reverting to civilian airport use after World War II Wick was officially reopened in August 2005 with a new upgraded terminal by Prince Charles in his position as the Duke of Rothesay. Of the four 'austerity' C Type hangars, only two now remain and most of the wartime buildings have gone save for the tower, now used as offices, as it has been replaced by a new rescue and fire-fighting section.

An interesting survival is the bomb stores area on the northern boundary, the buildings retaining their huge steel doors and protective blast walls, as well as the gantries for lifting bombs and depth-charges. They are a stark reminder of the airport's aggressive past.

It remains to mention Wick's dummy airfield site at Sarclet, about five miles south of Wick and about 70 per cent the size of the real airfield. Nominated a 'Q/K' site, it was intended to be noticeable by day as well as by night. It was equipped with dummy Blenheim bombers, buildings were simulated with wood and canvas, and even time-expired vehicles were strategically parked. There are still a small control bunker and personnel shelters dotted around the site and on Google Earth the outline of one of the runways is prominently visible. Faint stretches of

perimeter track are also just discernible. So realistic was the effect that a Blenheim landed and crashed here in daytime, despite attempts to warn the pilot off!

The control bunker lies on the west side of the road from Thrumster to Mains of Ulbster, and is constructed to a standard design of brick and concrete with a corrugated iron roof, which would originally have been protected by an earth banking. Internally, the bunker was provided with two rooms placed on either side of an access passage. A metal ladder provides access to the roof. One room would have served as an operations room, while the other, smaller, would have housed the electrical generators used to power the decoy lighting. All the effort involved was worthwhile because the Luftwaffe dropped bombs on the decoy on a number of occasions during 1941.

Most airfields were provided with decoy sites to try to divert the attention of enemy bombs, but the Luftwaffe had already got Wick down in their target folder as GB 10244. Nevertheless this dummy site at Sarclet did receive some attention.

WOODHAVEN

Woodhaven lies on the south bank of the River Tay between Wormit and Newport-on-Tay, directly opposite Dundee. It was an extremely small Coastal Command base accessed by a steep approach road comprising a main jetty and slipway.

Originally known as Tayport, it was described in contemporary RAF documents as 'a sheltered anchorage situated three quarters of a mile to the east of the south end of the Tay Bridge. Stone slipway and landing pier accessible at all except lowest spring tides. Sheltered from all sides except west, whence only partial shelter.'

The landing area in the Tay Estuary extended from north to south for 1½ miles (¾ miles at low water) and east to west for five to six miles. Eight 'Short' type buoys and two metal buoys for tenders were available. A refuelling vessel with a capacity of 2,100 gallons of fuel and 200 gallons of oil was held at RAF Marine Craft Section, Tayport, three and a half miles away, for use at the moorings.

The Tay had seen occasional use by flying boats before the war, notably in October 1938 when the Short Mayo Mercury composite aircraft took off from here. The Mercury seaplane was positioned on top of the Mayo so that it could be taken aloft with a greater fuel load. The aircraft separated to the north of the city and Mercury flew on to Alexander Bay in south-west Africa, a distance of 6,041 miles and a world seaplane record. There is a

In 1943, No. 333 Norwegian Squadron arrived at Woodhaven with three Catalinas (and a Heinkel 115 seaplane brought over from Norway in 1940), and before Aldon Ferguson travelled to Scotland to cover the Coastal Command stations north of the border he tracked down a unique collection of photos taken there by the Norwegians. These are just some of the many shots showing a mix of aircraft at the moorings and/or being serviced.

very fine commemorative plaque on the Dundee waterfront, close to the historic Antarctic research ship *Discovery*. Also on the north bank of the Tay is the site of Stannergate, a very active World War I seaplane base. Its large concrete apron appears to survive amidst oil industry development.

At the time of the Munich Crisis in September 1938, No. 210 Squadron sent six of its aircraft to Tayport, which had been nominated as its war station. Further detachments followed in the first months of the war, which resulted in five attacks on U-Boats but with no confirmation of kills. There were no permanent units until February 1943 when a Norwegian detachment formed at Woodhaven in No. 18 Group. The detachment was

soon designated No. 1477 (Norwegian) Flight and equipped with three Catalinas to carry out clandestine flights to Norway, as well as anti-submarine patrols. These were often far-ranging, as shown by an ice reconnaissance to the North Cape and from there to Iceland, following the edge of the ice as far as Jan Mayen Island.

In May the flight was expanded to full squadron strength as No. 333 Squadron. It was a dual-purpose unit in that part of it was based at Leuchars with Mosquitos and the other at Woodhaven with Catalinas. Both parts operated in the same area, flying shipping reconnaissance, convoy escorts and anti-submarine patrols over the North Sea and Norwegian coastline. In addition, the

squadron flew so-called 'Specials' to Norway, co-operating with the Resistance and landing or picking up secret agents and saboteurs. At least one former Royal Norwegian Navy Air Service Heinkel He 115 floatplane featured in these exploits. It is also known that a Norwegian pilot flew a Heinkel under the Tay railway bridge to the horror of passengers on a passing train. It was quite a large aircraft so there couldn't have been much clearance between bridge supports and wingtips and the tide must have been out as well!

The squadron's first U-Boat kill came on June 17, 1944 when Lieutenant Karl Crafft depth-charged and sank *U-423*. Another U-Boat was heavily damaged by a Woodhaven Catalina a month later. On the debit

side, a Catalina had been lost on May 17 when it sank in the Tay after returning to base heavily damaged by U-Boat flak and carrying a dead gunner. In July 1944, the Catalinas moved to Shetland and RAF Woodhaven closed the following year. No. 333 Squadron remains an elite unit of the Norwegian Air Force and some of its P-3 Orion maritime patrol aircraft carry the names originally painted on the wartime Catalinas.

A very obscure operation described as 'Top Secret' was conducted from Woodhaven from mid-September 1944 until the end of November that year. Catalina JX363 was loaned by the RAF to the US Navy's Fleet Air Wing 7 which in turn transferred it to 'Special Air Unit 5'. Its duties were described as 'special operations in collaboration with US Army planes under the general direction of Colonel Bernt Balchen'. This officer was in charge of the clandestine operations outlined in the entry for Leuchars.

Rock House, the wartime Norwegian Headquarters, still stands, as does the pier constructed to serve the flying boats. It is now the base of the Wormit Boating Club and a commemorative stone just to the west of its clubhouse bears the Norwegian squadron badge and the inscription: 'These laburnum trees were planted in July 1944 to

King Haakon VII visited Woodhaven on several occasions. Here he is seen approaching the station headquarters.

commemorate the visits of King Haakon VII of Norway to No. 333 Squadron Royal Norwegian Air Force which was based at Woodhaven during World War II.'

Although it is now split into separate apartments, Rock House still stands, virtually unchanged . . . but for the loss of the 'HQ' sign!

The Heinkel 115 was reputedly used for transporting agents to Norway, but the name of the pilot (previously thought to be lost to history), who took it for a joy ride and flew it under the railway bridge is now revealed as Lieutenant Knut Skavhaugen.

In 1944 on May 17 — Norway's National Day — Lieutenant Hartmann carried out an attack on a U-Boat in a Catalina named *Jøssing* but return fire hit his aircraft and mortally wounded his gunner, Kvartermester (Quartermaster) Kyrre Berg. Hartmann managed to get the machine back to base but the damage was so severe that the Catalina, FP121, sank at its mooring.

No. 19 GROUP

BRAWDY

Brawdy was opened in 1944, nominally as a satellite for St Davids, although in post-war years the roles were reversed as it was singled out as one of the three dispersed sites for Britain's nuclear V-bomber force.

Brawdy, along with Haverfordwest and Templeton in the same area of south-west Wales, was planned originally for use as an Operational Training Unit for Bomber Command. However, requirements had altered by the time of its official opening as an independent station in February 1944. Halifax squadrons based at nearby St Davids had been using Brawdy as a satellite for some time prior to this for operational sorties. Whenever cross-winds at the parent station rendered take-offs with a full fuel load potentially dangerous, aircraft were flown over to Brawdy 1,000 gallons short to have their tanks topped up. Brawdy's runways were longer and much better aligned with the prevailing winds in these parts.

In February 1944, No. 517 Squadron moved its meteorological reconnaissance Halifaxes over from St Davids, the crews being proud to claim that they 'even flew when the birds were walking'! Their usual weather sorties were code-named 'EPICURE', the aircraft turning for home at a point to the west of mid-Portugal.

These flights were never entirely routine. For example, in June 1944 a Halifax suffered

In February that year, No. 517 Squadron moved in from St Davids. They were one of Coastal Command's meteorological squadron and their work was featured in a 1944 RAF documentary titled *Survey of Coastal Command Meteorological Squadron*.

The film opens with an artistic shot of a Halifax overflying Roch Castle which must be artistic licence on behalf of the film makers for the cameraman as it lies some three miles to the south-east of the aerodrome.

One of the most spectacular sequences, illustrated overleaf, is the return of this Halifax, filmed from the control tower.

Flying ceased at Brawdy when it was given to the army in 1992 at which point it was renamed Cawdor Barracks. Unfortunately the tower was demolished soon afterwards.

later with Hawks. The RAF withdrew in 1992 whereupon Brawdy was renamed Cawdor Barracks, becoming the British Army's main electronic warfare base. At the time of writing it was announced that this function would move to St Athan in 2018.

Originally, Brawdy was built with three runways with a central intersection, two of 2,000 yards and a third of 1,400 yards. There were three T2 hangars which still survive, along with 30 loop type hardstandings. A blister hangar is also still in evidence. The three T2s moved post-war from St Davids by the Navy appear to have been replaced by parking areas. The bomb stores were located to the north of the airfield while the technical site and dispersed accommodation were to the south-west of it. There have been various subsequent phases of development with the naval and renewed RAF use of the site. In the early 'sixties, the station became one of many around the United Kingdom designed to operate dispersed elements of the V-Bomber force in time of war. Most notably, hardstanding pads were built at the northern end of the lengthened main runway to enable bombers parked at readiness to get airborne without delay.

An interesting post-war aspect of Brawdy's career was the presence between 1974 and 1995 of a top secret US Navy 'Oceanographic Research Station'.

an engine fire 800 miles out over the Atlantic and there was no other option but to ditch. The whole crew escaped into their dinghy and after three days adrift were very lucky to be picked up by an American ship and taken to its ultimate destination — New York! Others were less fortunate. In November 1944 a Halifax was found wrecked in the sea with no sign of its crew. Other aircraft were simply never seen again. Weather and mechanical trouble were the main hazard and the only enemy aircraft encountered that far out over the ocean were Focke-Wulf Condors on similar duties. A former Halifax pilot told the author that there was an unspoken agreement with the German crews that neither would interfere with the other in the event of a chance encounter.

No. 517 Squadron left in September 1945, having shared the station for a short period with a Spitfire detachment which towed target gliders for trials. There was also a detachment of Spitfires and Mosquitos from No. 8 OTU at Haverfordwest for photographic reconnaissance training. In January 1946 the airfield was taken over by the Admiralty and used by various squadrons, flying such types as the Sea Hawk, Hunter and Gannet. Then in February 1974 the RAF regained its old base for a fighter Operational Conversion Unit, later renamed No. 1 Tactical Weapons Unit and equipped first with Hunters and

Approaching from the south, the Halifax touches down, the undercarriage suddenly collapses and the aircraft slithers along the ground for several hundred yards. The camera pans from right to left until it finally comes to a halt and the crew clamber out.

Brawdy's main runway lies on a ridge of high ground, and is invisible from the technical site. So with no control tower to give us the necessary height, we had to resort to taking our photograps from the runway itself.

CAREW CHERITON

Canvas Bessonneau hangars — reminiscent of the First World War — give shelter for the Hornet and Tiger Moths of No. 5 Coastal Patrol Flight. Attached to No. 217 Squadron, they patrolled the Bristol Channel until disbanded in May 1940.

Situated half-way between Pembroke Dock and Tenby in south-west Wales, it was built in the 1930s on the site of a World War 1 airship base, known as Royal Naval Airship Station Pembroke but also referred to as Milton, after a nearby village. As well as non-rigid airships, conventional aeroplanes also flew from here in the later stages of the war. The station was disposed of in 1920 but with the expansion of the RAF, the same area was selected for revival as an aerodrome. It was to be named after another local village to avoid confusion with other RAF locations. Note that Carew is pronounced 'Care-oo'.

The aim was to complement Pembroke Dock's long-range flying boats by using Ansons for coastal patrol and shipping defence. The boats would then be free to roam further afield. Construction started in 1938, but initially the airfield was grass surfaced. This was soon remedied by the building of three runways, one of 1,040 yards and two of 965 and 765 yards, respectively. No perimeter track was provided on the south side and the shortest runway stood in for another missing portion to the east. The hangarage consisted of two Bellmans, four canvas Bessonneau and eight blisters. Dispersed parking areas were simply of Som-

merfeld Tracking and storage for 35 tons of bombs was emplaced on the southern edge of the airfield.

Detachments of Nos. 206 and 217 Squadrons moved in during August and September 1939. The Ansons carried a very small bomb load but one did attack a submarine off Lundy Island on September 20. Months of mainly uneventful convoy escort followed but the deterrent value was incalculable. At the same time, No. 5 Coastal Patrol Flight's Tiger Moths and Hornet Moths patrolled inshore between Bideford Bay in Devon and Carmarthen Bay to the north, until the unit was disbanded in May 1940.

Although the construction of a new bypass for the A477 has bisected the former technical site, fortunately the bases have survived.

In May 1940 a new squadron — No. 320 — was created with Dutch personnel who had escaped when their country was invaded. Here airmen are removing the chocks from one of their Anson Mk 1s. This particular aircraft (K6175 ex-No. 48 Squadron) was destroyed at Carew in a Luftwaffe raid on October 1, 1940.

That month, personnel of the Royal Netherlands Navy Air Service who had escaped when their country was overrun were attached to No. 217 Squadron to gain Anson experience. Dutch crews formed No. 321 Squadron in May 1940 and began convoy escort over the Irish Sea during July. The detachment of No. 217 Squadron then moved to St Eval.

The Dutch squadron left in January 1941, having just been re-equipped with Hudsons. Its replacement was No. 236 Squadron with Blenheims. Their role was still convoy escort and, with their better armament, they were more than capable of driving off any attackers. Several combats occurred with Condors and Ju 88s but no claims were made. Three air raids in 1940 had resulted in the death of one airman and the destruction of a Bellman hangar and two Ansons. On April 15, 1941, six enemy aircraft bombed the airfield, causing 12 fatalities and damaging seven Blenheims and an Anson. After a runway was repaired, the station was fully operational within 12 hours. Carew hit back a few days later when three of its Blenheims intercepted four Ju 88s off southern Ireland and claimed one as damaged. The airfield's decoy site at Begelly to the north-east attracted a stick of bombs in October and this was probably the last time that Carew attracted the Luftwaffe's attention.

Looking out across the former flying field. At certain times of the year, the ghostly outline of the hangar base of the Royal Navy Airship Station shows through the grass.

Beaufighters began to replace the Blenheims in August 1941 and were frequently used for night intruder patrols over the Brest airfields, until the squadron moved to East Anglia in February 1942. No. 254 Squadron's Blenheims took over the escort duties until May when they returned to Scotland. In the meantime, a detachment of the other Dutch unit, No. 320 Squadron, had been operating Hudsons from Carew between October 1941 and April 1942. These were the last operational aircraft to be based here and the airfield was transferred to the control of Flying Training Command towards the end of July 1942, followed by a further change to Technical Training Command in October.

The airfield ceased operations in 1946, the ensuing years seeing the destruction of many of the wartime buildings. *Left:* The control tower — technically a Fighter Station Watch Office — fell into a sad state of repair . . . that is until the

Carew Cheriton Control Tower Group approached the landowners in 2000 with a request to take the building over and restore it to its former glory which, it must be said, has been carried out magnificently.

Carew Cheriton photographed by No. 540 Squadron on July 8, 1946 as part of the United Kingdom survey — see page 81.

The newly formed No. 10 Radio School went on to train hundreds of wireless operators, using Oxfords and Ansons. The five-week course prepared them for postings to Operational Training Units and from there to the squadrons. The good safety record of the unit was marred on September 3, 1943 when two Oxfords collided at a runway intersection, killing six aircrew. The work continued until the unit disbanded in November 1945, and the airfield closed at the beginning of May 1946.

It remains to mention one other important organisation; Coastal Command Development Unit which was formed at Carew in October 1940 with examples of the Whitley, Beaufort and Hudson. Pembroke Dock was conveniently near for flying boat involvement. CCDU's initial tasks included the service trials of the new airborne radar apparatus for use in the Command. By the time it moved to Northern Ireland a year later, activities had expanded to embrace a whole range of new equipment and tactics against the U-Boats. One of the scientists and pilot of the unit's Whitley aircraft was Michael Weizmann, whose father was to become the first President of Israel.

The airfield soon returned to agriculture and many buildings have been demolished over the years. The runways, however, are largely intact, although adapted for various activities, including a large industrial complex, a go-kart track and a caravan park. Some interesting buildings can be found in

However, on September 3, 1943, an horrific accident occured at Carew. At that time the main unit in residence was No. 10 Radio School, training wireless operators on the unit's Anson and Oxford aircraft, two of which collided right here at the intersection of the two runways. Killed in Oxford X6813 were Pilot Officer Bert Price and Sergeants Alan Taylor and Ken May, while Flight Sergeant Frank Leslie and Sergeants Wifred Louden and George Wareham perished in Oxford V3976.

The A477 bypass now carves its way through the former technical site. A caravan park and scrapyard now occupy part of the runways.

the area, such as a single bay Turret Trainer, the Main Stores and workshops, the explosives stores, pillboxes and air raid shelters. The real gem is the very unusual control tower which is said to be based loosely on the type known officially as the Watch Office for Fighter Satellite Stations, but with a bay window and a small observation room on the roof.

This later wartime structure was built to replace the original watch office, which was situated 50 yards to the west on the opposite side of the taxiway. The brick and concrete base of the original building can still be seen today and one can see the outline of the timber structure that formed the watch office. Remarkably, this had once been the wheelhouse that came from the ship *Montrose* remembered for its connection with murderer Dr. Crippen and the radio message from the ship that sealed his fate!

To restore and maintain the later building, the Carew Cheriton Control Tower Group was formed in 2000 after the landowner kindly offered the building on a long-term lease at a peppercorn rent. The project is based on achieving three main aims: a lasting memorial to all who served on the airfield through two world wars, particularly to the airmen who made the supreme sacrifice during those years; a structure for educational use focused on school and group visits who are studying this period of modern day history, and a tourist attraction offering a wartime experience.

The restoration of the Watch Office has been carried out by an enthusiastic band of volunteers masterminded by John Brock and his son Deric. An ancillary canteen-cum-museum building has also been erected nearby and a complete Stanton shelter was dismantled and moved some 200 yards to avoid being lost when the bypass was constructed. School parties are encouraged to experience the period by donning authentic uniforms and taking their places in the shelter. All a magnificent achievement.

CHIVENOR

In a very pleasant situation on the north bank of the River Taw estuary, RAF Chivenor originated from the snappily-named Barnstaple and North Devon Aerodrome. This opened on June 13, 1934 and, apart from club flying, regular services were flown to and from Lundy Island in the Bristol Channel. The site had come to the notice of Air Ministry as very suitable for development and, after requisitioning, work began in the spring of 1940. George Wimpey & Co Ltd was the contractor and the new airfield was built immediately to the west of its predecessor, absorbing it as a dispersed site. At this stage, the runways were grass-surfaced but were soon replaced by three concrete strips of 1,450, 1,200 and 1,160 yards, respectively. Four Bellman hangars and four of the lesser known Hinaidi type were erected.

The station's initial role was envisaged to be Coastal Command operational training and No. 3 (Coastal) Operational Training Unit duly formed here on November 27, 1940. Its duty was the training of Anson and Beaufort crews with the intention of extending this to crews for the Whitley and Wellington. Plans changed, however, and No. 3 OTU moved to Lincolnshire in July 1941, leaving its Beaufort section at Chivenor. This was now re-designated No. 5 OTU and remained in residence until May 1942 when it moved to Scotland.

The station's first squadron, No. 252, arrived here in December 1940 to equip with Beaufighters. When declared operational, a move was made to Northern Ireland at the beginning of April 1941. Another squadron — No. 272 — then moved in for conversion to Beaufighters prior to leaving for the Middle East at the end of May 1941. For the rest of that year and into 1942, various squadrons detached aircraft to Chivenor. For some time two Bomber Command Whitley squadrons were temporarily transferred here to reinforce Coastal's efforts over the Bay of Biscay.

Above: **An early shot of Chivenor but by 1944** *(below)* **the main E-W runway had been extended to 2,000 yards and the NW-SE to 1,460 yards.**

Airborne radar (ASV) in the Wellington had enabled homing in on surfaced U-Boats with a maximum detection range of seven miles. The big problem was that frequently with a rough sea, contact was lost in the last mile owing to wave returns on the radar screen. Hence the Leigh Light which was installed in the Wellington's mid-under turret position. This airborne searchlight had been devised by Squadron Leader Humphrey de Verde 'Sammy' Leigh, hence its name. After Coastal Command Development Unit at Carew Cheriton had proved the concept of the Leigh Light for illuminating submarines, No. 1417 (Leigh Light Trials) Flight was formed at Chivenor in January 1942. The next four months were devoted to

intensive training but this was not without its dangers. The Helwick Light Vessel in the Bristol Channel served for practice detection but one night a crew homed in on what they took to be the vessel. Unfortunately the blip was an American tanker and the alert crew opened fire, sending the Wellington down in flames with no survivors.

On April 4, 1942, the flight was expanded into a full squadron — No. 172 — and by early June 1942, the Wellingtons were ready to be tested in battle. The first attack took place on June 2 when a U-Boat was straddled with four depth-charges but only damaged. Three more submarines were attacked in July and on another occasion a Wellington had a running battle with two Arado Ar 196s, during which

RIVER TAW

A Beaufighter (X8084) of No. 235 Squadron comes a cropper on the main runway in October 1942. This Beau, X8084, was declared 'Category B', indicating that it was beyond repair on site but repairable at a maintenance unit or at a contractor's works. It survived the war and was finally struck off charge on July 6, 1945, having later served with No. 236 Squadron and No. 9 OTU.

one was shot down, but two of the bomber's crew were mortally wounded. An unusual incident occurred on July 24, 1944 when a Wellington was shot down during an attack and actually crashed onto *U-459*. The crippled submarine was then attacked by another Wellington and subsequently abandoned. The survivors and a sole Wellington crew member in his dinghy were soon picked up by a Polish destroyer.

Even though its first use was on such a small scale, the new weapon had had an instant effect on the German crews. Liable to be suddenly transfixed by a dazzling glare that heralded a salvo of depth-charges, they found that darkness was no longer a protection. Their growing resistance to breaking surface at night soon presented daylight patrols with more targets. Reacting swiftly to the double threat, Admiral Dönitz ordered all U-Boats in the Bay of Biscay to proceed submerged both by day and night. If they surfaced it must only be to charge batteries. The result was that life for the German crews became not only more dangerous but more uncomfortable.

In July 1942, No. 235 Squadron's Beaufighters transferred from Norfolk in order to escort Whitleys patrolling the Bay. In August they shot down three Arado Ar 196s and damaged two Condors at no loss to themselves. Offensive sweeps in September accounted for five Ju 88s and a Condor. One aircraft was lost that month but three in

Above: **Before the squadron left for Leuchars in January 1943, they had this group photograph taken.** *Below:* **In May 2014, when Aldon Ferguson visited Chivenor — which has changed considerably since the war — he felt that this shot had been staged on the airfield looking towards the gap between two rows of Hinadi hangars.**

October. This pattern of operations continued until January 1943 when the squadron moved to Scotland. Their replacement for similar duties was No. 404 Squadron, having just re-equipped with Beaufighters. They departed to Scotland in April.

Leading Aircraftwoman Felicity Lambert moves a Wellington XIV of No. 602 Squadron. This particular aircraft, HF 385, appears to have had a charmed life as it survived the war, only to be scrapped in May 1947.

A Wellington Squadron, No. 407, was based at Chivenor between March and September 1943 for anti-submarine patrols over the Western Approaches. Three U-Boats were attacked with unconfirmed results during April and more were to follow, but the squadron was losing roughly one crew per month. Also based on the airfield was No. 547 Squadron from March to June 1943. Its Wellingtons were employed on similar duties until moving to Cornwall. A third Wellington unit, No. 612 Squadron, was based in 1943 between May and November. Its duty was mainly night patrol over the Bay, and a detachment was maintained at Davidstow Moor in Cornwall. Two crews failed to return in July and another two in August but six U-Boats were found and three attacked.

The Royal Marines took over Chivenor in 1994 and with the assistance of Major Gil Perry, Aldon recreated the photo with a Sea King of No. 22 Squadron, based there on air-sea rescue duties. The pilot is Flight Lieutenant Tamsyn Ryall. 'A' Flight operates out of Chivenor; 'B' Flight is based at Wattisham in Suffolk and 'C' Flight is stationed on Anglesey, although the squadron's duties are due to be handed over to HM Coastguard at the end of 2015.

The third Polish squadron, No. 304 under Wing Commander Jerzy Kranc, arrived in February 1944, these photographs being taken when General Mateusz Izycki, in his role of Inspector of the Polish Air Force, visited for its Squadron Day on April 25.

September that year saw a disastrous flood that left the camp underwater.

erally slightly below the surface of the sea. The other vent in the *Schnorkel* was an air intake pipe which brought in fresh air for the crew's breathing and also for the diesel engines. A special pump and plug took care of any water that inadvertently entered the air intake. The U-Boat crews took several months to gain experience in operating the *Schnorkel* but ultimately it obviated the need for surfacing for the purpose of charging batteries.

No. 14 Squadron had been flying Marauders in the Mediterranean until its personnel were posted to Chivenor in October 1944. It now flew Wellingtons on anti-submarine patrols and anti-shipping work in the Western Approaches and over Biscay. Disbandment came at Chivenor on June 8, 1945. No. 407 Squadron had returned in November 1944 and maintained about 100 sorties per month up to the end of the war in Europe. In the final months before the squadron's disbandment in June 1945, its prime targets

In February 1944, No. 304 Squadron brought in more Wellingtons and was soon averaging two U-Boat attacks per month. However, as they were night ops with the aid of Leigh Lights it was hardly ever possible to determine the results. As the invasion came closer, the squadron concentrated on preventing U-Boats entering the Channel and on June 18 one was confirmed as destroyed. A move was made to Scotland in September 1944. No. 36 Squadron arrived the same month and began to fly anti-shipping box patrols off the Channel Islands, as well as attempting to find *Schnorkel*-equipped U-Boats. It left for the Hebrides in March 1945.

The *Schnorkel* was a truly revolutionary device that consisted of a pipe attached to the deck of a U-Boat and slightly shorter than a periscope. When a U-Boat was proceeding at periscope depth, the *Schnorkel* would be raised. This pipe contained two vents; one which ended about six feet from the top, expelled exhaust gases and was gen-

Today the doors of the Hinadi hangars have been replaced by fixed cladding.

The Leigh Light — an airborne 22 million candle-power searchlight — was proposed by Squadron Leader Humphrey Leigh, thus giving it its name. Fitted under the wings of Catalinas and Liberators *(left)* or in retractable underslung turrets in the Wellington, the aircraft would detect U-Boats charging their batteries on the surface using their ASV radar and then suddenly illuminate their quarry during the final approach. *Right:* The Canadian No. 407 Squadron were exponents of the weapon at Chivenor.

were the midget submarines operating along the Dutch and Channel coasts. Meanwhile No. 172 Squadron had continued and perfected its pioneering Leigh Light operations, sending detachments to Gibraltar and the Azores. The entire squadron moved to Northern Ireland in September 1944.

There was an interesting development in April 1945 when the US Navy held conferences on the use of non-rigid airships (blimps) in the inshore waters of the United Kingdom. This led to a decision to send four Goodyear K Type blimps of ZP-42 Squadron to join Fleet Air Wing 7. It was influenced by the fact that the continuing successes of enemy submarines called for the augmentation of the forces deployed against them. Radar detection by blimps had been found by experience to be relatively more successful than from aircraft. Magnetic Anomaly Detection (MAD)-equipped blimps were also to be experimented with, the relatively shallow inshore waters appearing to offer desirable conditions for MAD operations. RAF Chivenor was chosen as the base, with support from the barrage balloon centre at

Cardington in Bedfordshire. Preparatory work for the accommodation of 'Blimpron 42' was undertaken at both locations early in May by an advance party working in co-operation with the RAF. The blimps were well on the way from Bermuda when the war ended and they were recalled.

It was planned initially that the station would remain with Coastal Command after the war but after a few months' residence by the Halifaxes and Fortresses of two Met Squadrons — Nos 517 and 521 — Chivenor was transferred to Fighter Command in October 1946. The first resident in the new role was No. 691 Squadron, an anti-aircraft co-operation unit equipped with a mixture of types, including Martinet and Spitfire. No. 203 Advanced Flying School moved in from Wiltshire in October 1947 to train fighter and reconnaissance pilots on Spitfires. After the AFS left for East Anglia in July 1949, the station's main use was for target-towing units supporting ranges in the Bristol Channel.

In November 1950, Chivenor was selected as the base for No. 229 Operational Conversion Unit to provide opera-

tional training for fighter pilots. The OCU began flying its Vampires from here at the end of March 1951 but jet blast erosion from the low-mounted engines soon began to damage the runways. During the summer of 1951 the runways were reconstructed and two large Aircraft Servicing Platforms (ASPs) were built either side of the control tower. No. 229 OCU remained the primary user until it moved to Brawdy in 1974, operating the Vampire, Sabre and Hunter in succession.

During 1979-80, the main runway was again rebuilt and the temporary wartime buildings finally replaced for a new arrival: No. 2 Tactical Weapons Unit equipped with Hawks. In 1994 the TWU left for RAF Valley when Chivenor was transferred to the Royal Marines. The runways are still used for support flying and an RAF Air Cadet Gliding School. In wartime it must have been a spartan place with constant operational pressures, but in the words of a more recent airman, 'It was by far the best RAF station in the UK. Not for nothing was it known as "Heaven in Devon".'

For a brief period in 1943, Coastal Command dispensed with squadron codes. Each station was allotted the numbers 1, 2 and 3 which were then allocated to squadrons on the station. Unfortunately, this resulted in confusion when identically marked aircraft were positioned to another base for operational purposes.

The Strike Wings did not like it either because reforming squadrons after an attack was much easier with letter codes. Consequently, the scheme was abandoned during 1944 and the squadrons reverted to letter codes. No. 14 Squadron aircraft carried the letters 'CX'.

Today very few World War II buildings survive at Chivenor; even the control tower has gone and its successor is no longer in use . . .

. . . so it was a real treat to find this blister hangar still standing north of the east end of the main runway. It is used by the resident Air Cadet gliding school whose headquarters lies alongside with this fitting memorial.

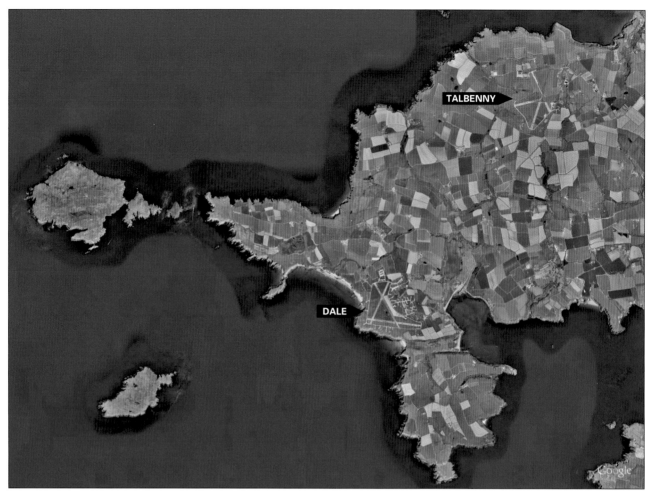

DALE

Strangely enough, aircraft from this satellite station saw as much action as those based at its parent, Talbenny. Perched close to 150-foot cliffs in south-west Wales, it had three runways, one of 1,400 yards and two of 1,100 and 1,300 yards, respectively. A single T2 hangar served for heavy maintenance, but most of the routine work had to be carried out in the open air on the 36 frying-pan hardstandings dispersed around the perimeter.

Manned and opened up on June 1, 1942,

Exactly two months later the vulnerability of runways facing the sea was demonstrated when seven Wellingtons were assigned to an anti-submarine patrol over the Bay of Biscay. The operation on the evening of August 11 entailed a night take-off at a time when the aerodrome had no night-flying facilities. The weather was appalling with a strong south-westerly wind and, to further complicate things, the runway that should have been used was unserviceable due to construction works. Departure had been scheduled for 2100 hours but due to the strong and gusty wind it had to be postponed, flying control finally giving permission for take-off at 0230 on the 12th. Wellington HX384 was the first to go and began its take-off run in a cross-wind. The aircraft rose into the air in a faltering rising curve to the right before falling below the cliff top and crashing into the sea below. Shortly afterwards there was the sound of a large explosion as the depth-charges exploded. Despite courageous rescue attempts, there were no survivors from the crew of six. Flying Control immediately cancelled the mission.

Dale, Talbenny's satellite, first became the base for the Polish No. 304 Squadron, formed in 1940 within Bomber Command. However, in May 1942 it was transferred to No. 19 Group of Coastal Command, the squadron moving to Dale on June 11.

Dale's first aircraft were the Wellingtons of the Polish No. 304 Squadron which arrived from Tiree on June 15 to support No. 311 Squadron's Wellingtons at neighbouring Talbenny. No. 304's first operation came on the night of June 25/26 when seven aircraft took part in the Thousand Bomber Raid against Bremen, operating from an advanced base on the East Coast. Coastal loaned 102 Wellingtons and Hudsons to make up the numbers, five of them being reported missing. Patrols then began from Talbenny, a U-Boat being attacked on July 11 with unknown results..

The nearby cliffs saw a particularly tragic accident on the night of August 11/12, 1942 when a Wellington was taking off for an anti-submarine sweep. The into-wind runway was unserviceable so one with a strong cross-wind had to be used instead. The heavily-loaded aircraft failed to get airborne and plunged over the cliff into the rough sea.

With only one hangar, which obviously could not accommodate over 20 Wellingtons, so much servicing had to be carried out in the open.

An indication of the squadron's work can be gained from a breakdown of the flying hours for February 1943: 484 hours on anti-submarine patrol, six hours on bombing operations against a German-occupied port, 14 hours on convoy escort and 13 hours on general reconnaissance. In spite of hazardous operations such as shipping raids in the Gironde estuary in France, all of No. 304's losses were due to bad weather or mechanical failure. At the end of March 1943 the squadron was transferred to Docking in Norfolk.

The next resident was the Coastal Command Development Unit from Tain in north-east Scotland which arrived during April 1943 with a variety of aircraft types engaged in service trials of new equipment. They were joined for a short period that summer by No. 303 Ferry Training Unit while a Drem lighting system was installed at Talbenny. A complete change of role came in September 1943 when the Royal Navy exchanged its airfield at Angle for RAF Dale. Angle was very close to the

RAF's domain of Pembroke Dock and Carew Cheriton and it is said that naval signals and flying control procedures were causing confusion. Dale, now known as HMS *Goldcrest*, was home to a target-towing unit for a while before housing a twin-engined conversion unit. This was because of the Fleet Air Arm's perceived need for larger aircraft and as few Royal Navy stations had runways long enough to take types such as the Beaufighter and Mosquito, Dale was an ideal choice.

Although the T2 hangar has long gone, the base remains. The burned-out skeleton is the remains of one of the post-war navy buildings.

197

Engine mechanics had to brave the elements on the exposed dispersals. This Wellington is being serviced just off the northern perimeter track as Little Marloes Farm is visible in the distance on the left.

Post-war occupants included a night fighter school and the Fighter Direction School, which operated in conjunction with the ground training station at nearby Kete. Dale finally closed in December 1947. Runways, perimeter track and dispersals remain intact, although almost all the buildings on the airfield have been cleared, a notable exception being the underground Battle Headquarters near the cliffs. In contrast, a living site just off the north-east perimeter is virtually intact. In the Navy era it was primarily the WRNS's quarters, so was aptly dubbed the 'Wrennery'.

Tie-downs can still be found in the concrete.

According to a letter from the Squadron Adjutant dated October 1942, it is believed that the airfield was first called RAF Marloes.

Engine servicing on the most westerly airfield in South Wales.

Looking towards St Ann's Head and the entrance to Milford Haven.

DAVIDSTOW MOOR

This rocket-equipped Beaufighter of the Canadian 'Buffalo' Squadron was pictured at Davidstow Moor, No. 404 having moved south from Scotland in May 1944 for three months to support the landings in Normandy — hence the invasion stripes.

Planned originally as an advanced base for Bomber Command anti-shipping operations over the Bay of Biscay and the Western Approaches, it was used initially for US Eighth Air Force raids on French ports. Allocation as a Coastal Command operational parent station came somewhat later.

The airfield was located about three miles north-east of Camelford in Cornwall and, at 970ft above mean sea level, had the distinction of being the highest aerodrome in the United Kingdom. Unsurprisingly, its weather record was to prove poor, with frequent hill fog. Contractors Taylor Woodrow Construction built three runways; a main of 2,000 yards and two subsidiaries of 1,400 yards. Fifty frying-pan hardstandings were dispersed off the western and southern perimeter tracks and, at a later date, three T2 hangars were provided.

Opening was planned for early 1943 to support a spring offensive against U-Boats in the Bay of Biscay. However, such was the demand for airfields in south-west England to support Operation 'Torch', the invasion of French North Africa, that it opened in October 1942. Although the runways, perimeter track and dispersals were complete, accommodation was not yet ready, nor was a water supply laid on.

November 1942 saw the first operational flying when 18 Liberators of the US Eighth Air Force were detached here to begin raiding the submarine pens of St Nazaire, La Pallice and Lorient. With much of the manpower and equipment being shipped by sea from the USA, it was hoped that this bombing campaign would hinder the submarines' activities against the Allied convoys. After the foothold in North Africa was secured, the job of completing and equipping the station resumed.

The first Coastal Command squadron to arrive was the Whitley-equipped No. 53 in February 1943 but they only stayed for a few weeks and were followed by further detachments of a few aircraft at a time. In April, No. 612 Squadron was present, converting onto Wellingtons from its ageing Whitleys. Some lingered on for a while until June 5 when the squadron sent out Coastal Command's last operational Whitley patrol. The aircraft was BD680 and it had to return early owing to engine problems.

That same month the Wellingtons of Nos. 304 and 547 Squadrons were stationed on the airfield for anti-submarine operations over the Bay. The poor weather often experienced at Davidstow was no doubt the reason why Air Ministry selected it for trials of the new and secret American GCA (Ground Controlled Approach) radar. The work began in August 1943 but was soon transferred to St Eval. The pioneering efforts in Cornwall are very well described in Arthur C. Clarke's novel *Glide Path*, which is based on his own experiences.

Meanwhile, a Wellington of No. 547 Squadron sank a U-Boat during July and patrols continued until a move to Thorney Island in October. No. 304 Squadron relocated to Predannack in February 1944 and No. 524 Squadron re-formed here with Wellingtons in April. Its duties included anti-E-Boat patrols off the coast of northern France and the illumination of targets for Beaufighter strikes, all with the emphasis on stopping enemy movements in the Channel during the build-up to invasion.

Beaufighters at this time were based at Davidstow with No. 404 Squadron and, during their three-month stay that summer, carried out many successful sorties, damaging at least three destroyers and probably sinking another.

A significant detachment was that of No. 279 Squadron based at Davidstow between April 1942 and December 1943. One of this rescue unit's Hudsons had the distinction of carrying the first airborne lifeboat operationally on February 17, 1943. The lifeboat, dropped on parachutes, carried the equipment and supplies needed for survival and communication until a rescue could be affected or the occupants were able to make their way home under their own power. On June 1, 1943, an aircraft from Davidstow was airborne in a fruitless search for survivors from a civilian Dakota shot down in the Bay of Biscay. It had been on a regular service from Lisbon to Bristol which the Luftwaffe usually left unmolested. One of the passengers was the celebrated film actor, Leslie Howard.

Aldon Ferguson visited the airfield — now wide open to the public.

Also resident at that time was the Polish No. 304 Squadron which had arrived at Davidstow Moor in June 1943 equipped with Wellingtons. This series of pictures was taken by Wojtek Szczepanik on Friday, August 13 that year — Polish Soldiers' Day — when the Polish President Wladyslaw Raczkiewicz visited the station to present members of the squadron with decorations. *Left:* Here the Commanding Officer, Wing Commander Mieczyslaw Pronaszko welcomes the President. *Right:* Squadron Leader Colin Pomeroy, RAF (Retd), stands in for the President.

With German naval forces now driven from the Bay, Davidstow's operational days were over and it was put on Care and Maintenance in September 1944. The RAF Regiment had been using it as a training camp for some months but it finally left in October 1945. The Royal Navy considered taking over the airfield but soon abandoned the idea, hastening its closure in December.

After the war it became a motor racing circuit, and in the early 1950s three Formula One races were held here (the Cornwall MRC Formula 1 Races) which included the first success for the Lotus marque.

A minor road, closed when the airfield was built and now reopened, runs straight across the site. All three runways, considerably shortened in useable length but more than adequate for light aircraft, are used by the

Davidstow Flying Club. Although the T2 hangars have gone, apart from their concrete floors, many derelict buildings remain. They include the Watch Tower, Bombing Teacher and Turret Buildings. The machine gun test butts and bulk fuel storage installation are some of the other surviving structures. Almost all the dispersal hardstandings are still intact, as are the roads serving the bomb storage area to the south.

Left: Just over a week later the crew of Wellington H2576 failed to return from an operation on August 22. Here Flying Officer Porebski is pictured with his flight and ground crews shortly beforehand. *Right:* The memorial outside the museum remembers all those who lost their lives flying from the airfield. No. 304 suffered a loss of 106 aircrew killed or missing from its several operating bases.

An early Air Ministry schematic overlaid on the land proposed for the airfield.

Two large aerial masts stand beside the road just to the north-west of the perimeter. They provide air traffic control radio coverage for south-west England and beyond and are a remote feed for the London Area Control Centre at Swanwick in Hampshire.

There are two museums here. The Davidstow Moor RAF Memorial Museum is located in the former Sergeants' Mess ablution block and associated buildings, plus two new structures and concentrates on this station, squadrons, aircraft, people and its operations and activities, whilst the Davidstow Moor Airfield Cornwall at War Museum covers Cornwall and many other subjects. It houses personal collections of former personnel based here with a huge collection of memorabilia, uniforms, models, press cuttings etc. Entrance is free. Cornwall at War is larger and both have good, unrestricted car parking. Also nearby is the factory producing the famous Davidstow Mature Cheddar Cheese.

Compare with the plan of December 1944 showing all the dispersed sites: [2] Administration. [3] HF/DF Station. [4] Communal Site No. 1. [5] Communal Site No. 2. [6, 7, 8, 9, 10, 13, 14] Personnel quarters. [11] WAAF Communal site. [12] WAAF quarters. [15] Sick quarters. [16] Sewage disposal No. 1. [17] Sewage disposal No. 2. [18] W/T Station. [19] Water Pumping Station.

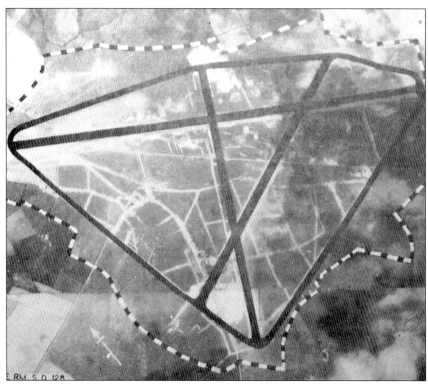

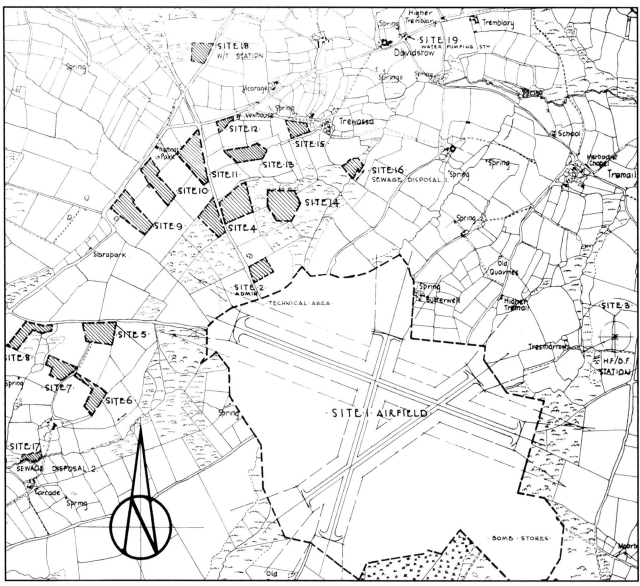

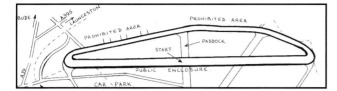

In May 1951, the Cornwall Vintage Car Club staged a rally on the airfield and the following year the Plymouth Motor Club joined them to organise racing at Davidstow, the first meeting taking place on Saturday, August 9. A circuit of 2.6 miles was prepared using the east-west runway and northerly perimeter track *(above left)*. Although the weather that day was awful, nevertheless Ken Watkins reached more than 120mph on the straight, crossing the chequered flag in his Cadillac Allard at an average speed of 83.71 mph. However, the layout of the track was considered too ordinary so a chicane was added for 1953 and the eastern end reduced to make it a 1.8475 circuit. Races were held in May and August that year in the Sportscar category and Formula 3 and 2. The next year's fixtures featured Formula 1 races — the first to be held in Cornwall — won in the rain by John Riseley-Prichard in a Connaught A3 at 74.20 mph. Two months later J. Coombs won the August 2 Formula 1 race in a Lotus.

The last motor race at Davidstow was on May 30, 1955. Here, Leslie Marr in the winning Connaught accelerates along the back straight, finishing at an average speed of 85.84 mph. Sadly Peter Collins and Tony Rolt due to take part were absent.

HAMWORTHY

RAF Hamworthy, home of No. 461 Squadron of the Royal Australian Air Force from August 1942 to April 1943. This is EJ134 on the reinforced slipway looking towards Dorset Lake. It ended its days on the beach at Praa Sands in Cornwall after fighting off eight Ju 88s.

In 1942, congestion at both the flying boat stations of RAF Pembroke Dock and Mount Batten caused Coastal Command to cast around for another site and, despite persuasive arguments about its unsuitability because of existing heavy use, Poole Harbour was the eventual choice.

The major problem was that the naval and army authorities had already taken over all the best sites and accommodation. In addition, British Overseas Airways Corporation already had a marine terminal on the eastern side of the harbour and therefore used the best-sited water runways. The RAF's selected location, still far from ideal, was flanking the Wareham Channel. Work began in June on what was to become

RAF Poole, although the name was altered to RAF Hamworthy just a week after opening on August 1. There were four 'runways'. No. 1 in the narrow Wareham Channel for limited use only (NW-SE) at 1,300 yards, while No. 2 (WSW-SSE) at the neck of the Channel at 2,000 yards became the main runway. No. 3 (NNW-SSE) at 3,000 yards had to be 'shared' with BOAC, and No. 4 (SSW-NNE) at 2,500 yards used jointly with the Fleet Air Arm.

There were a total of 18 flying boat moorings, laid on trotlines in sets of six and described as the 'Short' type. A slipway and hardstanding for up to four flying boats was available and an adjacent property was converted to serve as control tower/watch office.

As there was no room for hangars or any other buildings, a large marquee was erected and all maintenance had to be done there or at the moorings.

A number of chalet bungalows in the Lake Estate district were requisitioned as workshops. The RAF also used space at the Poole Harbour Yacht Club soon joined by BOAC. Group Captain R. L. Ragg, the Station Commander, was very unhappy with the dispersed nature of the base and secured approval to move operations to Parkstone Road, near Salterns Pier in Lilliput. This had its advantages but the big drawback was that the aircraft moorings were now anything up to four miles away.

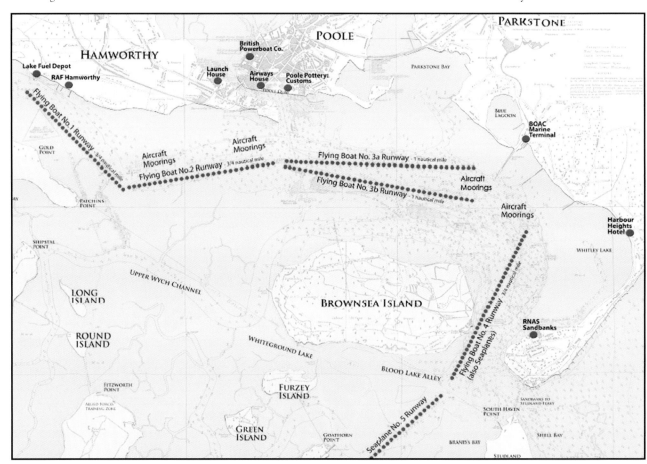

The site of RAF Hamworthy in Poole Harbour was very dispersed with operations based at the Lake Estate and Lake Pier for unloading fuel; the administration at Salterns at Lilliput (where BOAC also had its terminal), with the Officers' Mess way over in the Harbour Heights Hotel. This plan, produced by Aimee Alexander of Poole Flying Boats Celebration illustrates how spread out it was.

Beaching wheels being manhandled up the Hamworthy slip-way. In the background stands the station watch office.

The building still stands, now converted into a private house on Lake Drive.

The same Sunderland, 'N' for Nuts, is now firmly on dry land. Because the facilities were so spread out around Poole

Harbour, bicycles were provided, becoming essential transport for the ground crews.

LAKE ESTATE

CONTROL TOWER

AVIATION PIER

FORMER RAF HAMWORTHY

The present day view of the former station. There were no hangars so a large marquee was erected at the base although aircraft could only be serviced at their moorings and, if a major overhaul was needed, they had to be flown to other stations.

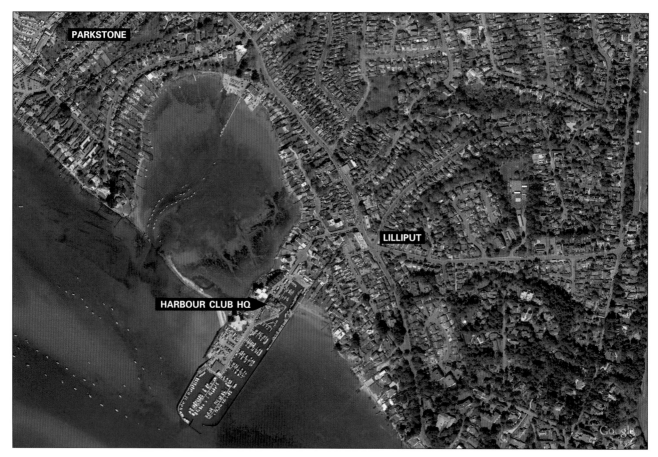

When it was opened on August 1, 1942 the base was known as RAF Poole but a week later the name was changed to RAF Hamworthy. The area was sparsely populated and although several properties in Lake View were requisitioned, the initial occupation was only temporary as it was eventually decided to move the station four miles away across the bay to Parkstone.

Operations started with the arrival on August 21 of Sunderland T9111 (UT-C) of No. 461 Squadron of the Royal Australian Air Force, the unit's operational strength being seven aircraft. Bay of Biscay patrols were the main activity, with aircrews having to fly to Mount Batten when operational night take-offs were required. Eight attacks were made on U-Boats and a blockade-runner was severely damaged and forced to return to La Pallice for lengthy repairs.

At first, officers stayed at the Haven Hotel in Sandbanks before the newly-requisitioned Harbour Heights Hotel near Canford Cliffs, was taken over as the Mess (alongside VIP passengers of BOAC staying there overnight). With RAF personnel numbers set to rise to more than 1,200, accommodation gradually concentrated around the Lilliput

area, and the Station HQ was relocated there from Parkstone Road, occupying the Salterns site and many adjacent properties.

When No. 461 Squadron's establishment increased to 12 aircraft it was obvious that the limited facilities were inadequate. Therefore the squadron was moved to Pembroke Dock in April 1943 in exchange for No. 210 Squadron, which had Catalinas, although perhaps the only benefit they gained from this move was the far better social opportunities in Bournemouth! The squadron became involved in a new tactic helping to set up patrol lines across the Bay designed to force the U-Boats to transit submerged and thereby exhaust their batteries.

In January 1944, the station was transferred to RAF Transport Command, and became the base for 24 Sunderland Mk. IIIs

that had been demilitarised for the carrying of passengers and freight. In 1946 these became the Hythe Class. They operated on long-distance routes to the Middle East, India, Burma and Singapore.

Although RAF Hamworthy officially ceased to exist on May 1, 1944, Combined Operations of the Royal Navy occupied the Lake site (as HMS *Turtle*) until the end of the war, after which the base was taken over for BOAC, but mixed use still continued. During the early 1950s, the hardstanding was used for storage of surplus ex-BOAC flying boats awaiting sale or to be scrapped. Then in 1954 the site reopened for military purposes as the Royal Marines' Amphibious School and, after a succession of name changes, the Royal Marines remain in occupation today.

Headquarters was located in the Harbour Club, known as Salterns, where RAF Flying Control combined with the BOAC terminal.

Fuel had to be brought ashore from oil tankers via Lake Pier which became known as Aviation Pier, where petrol was pumped into underground fuel tanks. This site was bombed by the Luftwaffe on June 3, 1942 and one tank received a direct hit resulting in a major contamination of the ground which lasts to this day.

The first . . . and most probably the last! The first Australian Sunderland to arrive was T9109, seen here coming ashore at Hamworthy.

The month before No. 461 quit the base, T9111 had a bad accident when it broke up on take-off! It veered off the marked lane and ended up in shallow water — all the crew being unharmed. When the matter was investigated, it appeared that the Sunderland had been assembled from two machines and had experienced structural failure once under full power.

HOLMSLEY SOUTH

Two years separate these two photographs. One of the photographic reconnaissance squadrons took the shot *(above)* on April 12, 1942, as Holmsley South was under construction and the one below on March 15, 1944.

In May 1934, the Air Ministry Aerodromes Board was formed within Air Ministry Works Directorate. Its job was to find suitable sites across Britain on which airfields could be built at some future date. One of the many hundreds of selected locations was Holmsley South, an area of the New Forest about five miles north-east of Christchurch, Hampshire. The Fleet Air Arm had its own requirements for airfields and there was liaison between the Admiralty and the Aerodromes Board. In November 1938, the yet-to-be-built Holmsley was allocated to the FAA although the option was not taken up.

During 1941-42, a Class A airfield was constructed, with a main strip of 2,000 yards and two subsidiaries of 1,400 yards. A total of 38 frying-pan hardstandings led off the perimeter track, to which three loop types were added at a later date. Two T2 hangars were erected, one of 23 bays and a smaller one of 13 bays Three more T2s were added later in the war.

Initially, it was intended primarily as a Bomber Command advanced base for anti-shipping operations over the Bay of Biscay and the Western Approaches. However, this role soon passed to Coastal Command and accommodation was to be built for two four-engined general reconnaissance squadrons. The main site was alongside the road on the southern perimeter, while the living sites were dispersed to the south of the airfield. A bomb storage area was built in the forest to the north of the airfield and a 'Q' site decoy was laid out at Ridley Plain, about four miles to the north.

The main runway at 2,000 yards was ideal for crew training for conversion to Halifaxes.

Holmsley was opened on September 1, 1942 well ahead of schedule in order to accommodate Coastal Command squadrons in support of Operation 'Torch', the invasion of French North Africa. The domestic sites were far from complete when the first RAF personnel moved in, but a flying unit did not arrive until mid-October. This was the newly-formed No. 547 Squadron which began to receive its Wellingtons the following month, only to leave for Chivenor in December, having barely become operational. Meanwhile, B-24 Liberators of Eighth Air Force's 330th Bomb Squadron moved in for anti-submarine patrols over the Bay of Biscay. Although sightings were made there were no successes and when 'Torch' was over, they returned to their East Anglian base.

No. 58 Squadron repositioned from Scotland in December 1942 and began conversion from the Whitley to the Halifax, after which they went to St Eval in March 1943. Holmsley's long runway was very suitable for Halifax conversion training, one of the squadrons being No. 295 that was working up during May and June in preparation for towing Horsa gliders in the pending Sicily operation. No. 58 Squadron returned in July 1943 and was joined at the same time by No. 502

Most of the concrete from the runways and taxiways has been lifted save for the dispersal areas used for caravan parks. This is the intersection of the long NE-SW runway where it crosses the N-S runway.

Squadron's Halifaxes for intensive anti-U-Boat patrols. Increased activity by Ju 88s over the Bay claimed three of No. 58 Squadron's aircraft during August and two more were lost in accidents. On September 27, 1943, *U-221* was sunk but its attacker caught fire and was forced to ditch. Six of the crew took to a dinghy and were very lucky to be found by two destroyers 11 days later. No. 502 Squadron scored a U-Boat kill on July 30 and in October the squadrons went over to night operations, using flares to illuminate the targets. Both units moved to west Wales at the end of 1943.

Being situated just 100 miles from the Normandy coast, Holmsley South became a forward base for four Typhoon squadrons.

Here is Wing Commander Charles Green in his personal machine bearing identification stripes and coded 'CG'.

Weed-covered dispersal located close to the memorial erected by the Friends of the New Forest Airfields to remember all those units which flew from the 12 aerodromes established in the area — Beaulieu, Hurn, Christchurch, Calshot, Stoney Cross, Winkton, Needs Oar Point, Bisterne, Sway, Ibsley, Lymington and Holmsley South.

Three Canadian squadrons — Nos. 441, 442 and 443 — worked up on Spitfires as No. 144 Wing from mid-March to early April 1944. They were then replaced by No. 121 Wing, which consisted of rocket-armed Typhoons of Nos. 174 and 175 Squadrons. They spent D-Day in direct support of the beach-head. Once the troops were established, the Typhoons attacked road transport immediately behind the German front line. They were soon reinforced by two more Typhoon squadrons — Nos. 184 and 245.

And of course there were the inevitable crashes. *Left:* No. 245 Squadron and *(right)* a machine from No. 175 that has turned turtle.

Meanwhile, No. 418 (RCAF) Squadron had begun flying night intruder operations until they turned their attention to patrols against V1 flying bombs. The squadron moved to nearby Hurn during July. After the Typhoons left for France in mid-June they were replaced for a very short period by RAF and Polish Mustang squadrons of No. 133 Wing for armed reconnaissance.

Towards the end of July 1944, the 394th Bombardment Group of the US Ninth Air Force moved its B-26 Marauders to Holmsley from Essex so as to be nearer the action in France. With three other groups based temporarily in the New Forest area, it continued to concentrate on destroying rail and road bridges and other transport targets. On the Group's final mission from Holmsley on August 9, the formation leader, Captain Darrell R. Lindsey, pressed on with the bomb run despite a burning engine. Having made sure that the rest of the formation had dropped their bombs on his signal, he ordered the crew to parachute from the now

Mosquito Mk VI of the Canadian No. 418 Squadron. It was while they were at Holmsley South that they chalked up their 100th victory.

The hardstandings at the south-western end of the main runway are now utilised for a caravan park.

blazing bomber. He held the B-26 as steady as he could while they did so, but a fuel tank exploded before he could follow and the aircraft dived into the ground. For his supreme courage which saved the lives of all but one of his seven crew, Captain Lindsey was awarded a posthumous Medal of Honor.

After the 394th Bomb Group left for a continental base, Holmsley was devoid of a flying unit until October 21, when No. 167 Squadron re-formed here with Warwicks under Transport Command. Serviceability was a major problem and it was December before the aircraft were ready for operations. They were used for fairly long transport routes within Europe and moved to Blackbushe, Surrey, in March 1945. Meanwhile, No. 246 Squadron had moved in from Lyneham, Wiltshire, employing its Liberators and Avro Yorks on services to the Middle and Far East. The unit proved to be Holmsley's last occupant, continuing operations until October 1946 when it went back to Lyneham.

Although abandoned soon after the war, the airfield remained virtually intact for many years. Its position about seven miles out from Bournemouth Hurn airport's similarly aligned main runway was an on-going source of confusion, and perhaps the largest aircraft to land here in error was a Lockheed Constellation in the early 1950s. In 1947,

faced with a serious housing crisis, Christchurch Town Council, converted some of the large buildings on the former Communal Site into flats. These were finally demolished in 1960 and by the end of that decade the runways had been torn up, leaving only short stretches of concrete. Several public camping sites and a caravan park have been created

on the former hardstanding groupings along the north-east side of the perimeter track, as well as both sides of the former runway on the south-west of the airfield. Parts of the perimeter track have been adapted as service roads and a fine memorial to all the New Forest airfields stands alongside one of them on the west side of the site.

Looking across the airfield towards the technical site where the hangar once stood.

MOUNT BATTEN

RAF Mount Batten at Plymouth was an established seaplane base long before the outbreak of hostilities. In this view taken prior to 1939, we are looking north-west across the Cattewater, with what appears to be a Short Singapore on the slipway.

In the words of the wartime pilot's brief, 'The air station is situated at the north-eastern corner of Plymouth Sound in the Cattewater, which affords shelter from all winds. The Cattewater is two cables in width [about 400 yards], the air station and mooring area lie on the southern side inside Mount Batten breakwater. Plymouth Sound itself affords comparatively good shelter from all winds but a strong southerly or south-westerly wind will cause a swell to run into the Sound. Owing to the restricted area of the Cattewater and the presence of shipping, fishing vessels and numerous small craft, especially during the fishing season, aircraft should avoid landing in the Cattewater unless compelled to do so by sea conditions in the Sound.'

The landing area is described as follows: 'Plymouth Sound is roughly one and a half miles square, giving ample landing area. On the water are several marking buoys, indicating channels for surface craft. These are plainly visible in daylight, while those likely to cause any obstruction to aircraft at night are illuminated. Owing to the presence of rocks, aircraft should not attempt to land between Drake's Island (in the north-west corner of the Sound) and the mainland to the westward of it.'

The details continue: 'All aircraft must approach Plymouth Sound on a direct course (024 degrees True) from Eddystone to the breakwater. All aircraft will be met by an RAF motor boat which will direct the aircraft to a mooring buoy. There is every facility for refuelling and repair of aircraft at the RAF base. Refuelling is usually carried out afloat from motor-driven petrol lighters but

A lovely comparison courtesy of the Plymouth Yacht Haven.

In April 1937, the resident squadron, No. 204, took delivery of this Saro London (K5911) from Saunders-Roe but in June 1939 it began re-equipping with Sunderlands.

Aldon Ferguson found the tide out on his visit to Mount Batten — this is his comparison taken from the slipway looking north.

aircraft can be refuelled ashore if necessary. Boat facilities comprise power boats, dinghies, petrol lighters and bomb scows. There are two slipways — No. 1 Slipway (western) is complete and can be used at all tides. This has an electric winch capable of handling 30 tons. No. 2 Slipway (the easterly one) is incomplete and should not be approached.'

As early as 1913, the sheltered Cattewater in Plymouth Sound was used for seaplane trials and in 1916 plans to establish a Royal Navy seaplane station were agreed. In February 1917 Royal Naval Air Station Cattewater was opened just opposite to Plymouth Hoe. It had a hangar for aircraft storage and maintenance and a stone pier with a railway track that enabled a steam crane to lift the seaplanes in and out of the water. The first aircraft based here were Short 184s and these were soon followed by other types. Operational flying, mainly coastal patrols, was carried out from what became RAF Cattewater in April 1918. In 1919 there was a notable arrival — a Curtiss NC-4 flying boat making the first aerial crossing of the Atlantic. It had made many stops en route, however, and the feat was eclipsed two weeks' later by Alcock and Brown's non-stop achievement.

Short Sunderlands became the mainstay at Mount Batten, this photo being a Mk III of the Australian No. 10 Squadron. This unit was the only one in the Royal Australian Air Force to continually serve in Europe for the duration of the war. A small group of squadron personnel arrived in Britain in August 1939 to begin training on the Sunderland but when war was declared the following month, the Australian government ordered the squadron to remain in the UK, becoming operational on February 1, 1940.

The aftermath of the Luftwaffe attack on November 28, 1940, when two of the Australian Sunderlands were wrecked.

Sunderland. Plymouth was soon well within reach of the Luftwaffe in Brittany and became the target for a number of German air raids, including the destruction of one of Mount Batten's hangars and two Sunderlands on November 28, 1940. More raids followed during the first few months of 1941 causing further damage to aircraft and the detachment of most of the squadron to various other bases. Congestion on the water and the proximity of barrage balloons forced the rest of the unit to move to Pembroke Dock in May 1941.

For a time, Mount Batten served only as a forward operating base for several flying boat squadrons until No. 10 Squadron returned in January 1942. In April some of its personnel helped form No. 461 Squadron here with Sunderlands. After some air-sea rescue work, it was declared operational in July and began patrols over the Bay of Biscay. In subsequent weeks, the crews of two Whitleys were picked up and an Arado 196 floatplane was shot down. At the end of August, the squadron moved to Hamworthy.

Meanwhile, No. 10 Squadron continued its patrols but ever-increasing numbers of long-range fighters over the Bay and increased

From 1923 the station was rebuilt and extended and was reopened on October 1, 1928 as RAF Mount Batten. The change of name was said to have been suggested by a certain Aircraftman Shaw, better known as T. E. Lawrence. He was then serving a little known career in the Marine Branch of the RAF where he was instrumental in developing the RAF's fast rescue boats. By the end of the Second World War, these craft had saved some 13,000 lives.

Several flying boat squadrons served at Mount Batten during the 1930s, and on the outbreak of war the resident unit was No. 204 Squadron, which had recently re-equipped with Sunderlands. At dawn on the following day, the first operational anti-submarine patrol was carried out in the Western Approaches. Within days, submarines were attacked on numerous occasions and one was claimed as a probable on September 18. The same day, about 120 miles west of Land's End, a Sunderland found the entire 35 crew of the sunken merchant ship, the *Kensington Court*, landed and picked them up.

At the beginning of April 1940, No. 10 (Royal Australian Air Force) Squadron, now under RAF control, flew in its Sunderlands from Pembroke Dock, while No. 204 left for Sullom Voe in Shetland. In July No. 10 Squadron scored the first U-Boat kill by a

No. 10 Squadron, RAAF, ceased operations on June 1, 1945 having six U-Boats to its credit. The previous month one of their machines was pictured about to take to the water after an overhaul.

This is the same northern slipway but the area to the north-west side has been filled in since the war so the gap seen in the wartime photo no longer exists.

U-Boat armament were taking a toll of all anti-submarine aircraft. The heavily armed Sunderland, however, proved a formidable adversary and the combats were not always one-sided, several U-Boats being destroyed. No. 10 Squadron sank a total of six U-boats between February 1940 and May 1945. It also set a Coastal Command record in February 1944 for the most patrol hours flown in a single month: 1,143. The unit lost 25 aircraft during the war, 19 from enemy action and six in flying accidents, but had sunk six U-Boats and damaged eight more, sent a ship to the bottom and damaged eight others.

In October 1945, the Australian squadron departed for home and the station became a Maintenance Unit and also housed the Marine Craft Training School. RAF Sunderlands continued to visit on occasion until the last UK-based boat squadron disbanded in 1957. From 1961 Mount Batten became the main base of the RAF Marine Branch with the closure of No. 238 Maintenance Unit at Calshot. In turn, the Marine Branch closed in 1986 and the site was taken over by the Plymouth Development Corporation in 1992.

The former RAF station has since been extensively redeveloped and is now home to a hotel, apartments, restaurants and a pub. Two big F Type hangars remain in excellent condition and they now house boats. The old Warrant Officers' and Sergeants' Mess is now a water sports training centre and the two imposing married quarters — named 'Port' and 'Starboard' — still flank the road which runs down the hill to the water.

On the headland walk is a propeller on a steel column with an adjacent engraved marble plinth, while on the castle wall are two plaques commemorating No. 204 Squadron and also the Australian units based here.

Mount Batten then . . .

. . . and Mount Batten now

215

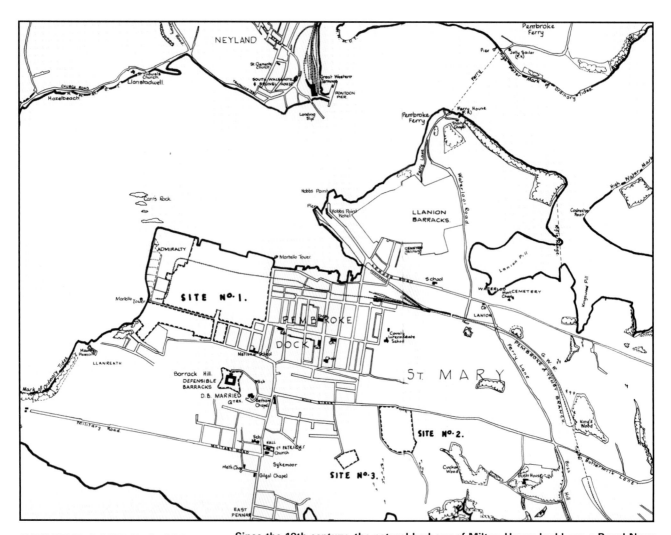

PEMBROKE DOCK

Since the 18th century, the natural harbour of Milton Haven had been a Royal Navy base but four years after the Admiralty closed the dockyard in 1926, the Royal Air Force took over and for over 30 years Pembroke Dock became a vital RAF base.

A wartime flight information document describes this base in south-west Wales thus: 'Milford Haven is a large natural harbour running east and west and forming the seaward end of the estuary of the Cleddau river. Its entrance is at the western end, facing south-west. Pembroke Dock RAF Station, which occupies part of the site of the former Royal Dockyard, is situated on the southern side of the estuary about eight miles from the entrance, and is well protected from all winds. The town of Pembroke Dock adjoins the RAF station.'

The safe operation of a flying boat base was a complicated business governed by a number of factors, winds and tides being the most significant. Although Castle Archdale in Northern Ireland was sited on an inland lake and so of course immune to tidal effects, it had its own problems, as can be read in the appropriate chapter. Pembroke Dock's procedures were more complex than most and are worth recording in some detail:

'Position and extent of alighting area at high water. By night a flare path for night flying is laid in the area north of Angle Bay which is a large inlet on the south side of the Haven some four miles west of the RAF station. The estuary here is about one mile wide and at high water Angle Bay provides a much greater width. The flare path consists of three boats, each carrying a conspicuous cluster of lights. During air raids the flare path is extinguished unless it is necessary for an incoming aircraft to alight immediately. When endurance permits, incoming aircraft are warned and sent out to sea until such time as the flare path may safely be relit.

'Position and extent of alighting area at low water. The alighting and taking-off areas are practically the same as for high water, but great care must be taken to avoid Carr Rocks and also the mudflats which are very extensive in places. Whenever possible a chart should be consulted or local knowledge sought; failing these aids, alighting and taking-off should be performed as far as possible in the buoyed channel (or at night, on the flare path).'

The main aircraft moorings were north of the station in the centre of the river. There were also dispersed moorings along both banks of the river stretching about a mile to the east. The ones on the north bank were the Neyland and Burton trots, those on the south bank were known as the Hobbs Point trots. There was also an onshore dispersal area with a slipway at the GWR yard at Neyland. Since the actual alighting area was about two miles west of PD, the taxying instructions from there to the moorings were unusual, to say the least.

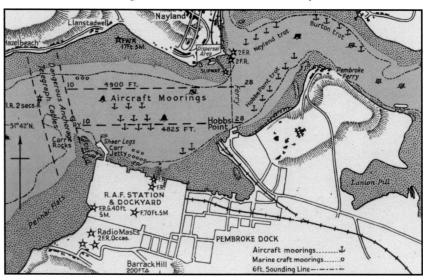

This photo of the main RAF entrance was taken in 1957, the year the station effectively closed when the Sunderlands departed.

The gateway still stands, minus its propellers and leads to what is now a commercial port.

Personnel of No. 10 Squadron of the Royal Australian Air Force arrived in the United Kingdom in July 1939 with the intention of flying six brand new Sunderlands back to Australia, but before they could depart war was declared. As a result they remained in Europe for the duration. They spent two spells at Pembroke Dock: October 1939-April 1940 and June 1941 to January 1942.

It continues: 'Taxi into harbour until town of Milford is passed. When past Milford keep to the buoyed channel to the northern side of the estuary as extensive mudflats lie to the south. Past the south side chequered buoy at Wear Point, turn northeast so as to round the starboard buoys off Spit. Taxying from the night flying flare path opposite Angle Bay is difficult at night without local knowledge and it is advisable for visiting pilots to do so only when guided by an RAF pinnace or seaplane tender. Weather permitting, aircraft may be moored at RAF buoys on each side of the estuary opposite Angle Bay. Aircraft proceeding to the RAF station are frequently towed by RAF pinnace in order to save fuel and still more to spare the aero-engines.'

Unfortunately the slipway was lost during the post-war alterations.

The view looking in the opposite direction showing the easternmost of the two hangars. The floatplane is a Dutch Fokker T-VIIIW of No. 320 Squadron, one of eight flown to Britain when Holland was invaded.

Also serving at PD from the autumn of 1939 was No. 10 Squadron of the Royal Australian Air Force, equipped with Sunderlands. They flew shipping escorts and moved to Devon in April 1940. No. 210 Squadron continued its patrols with occasional attacks on U-Boats but no confirmed results. The unit moved to Oban in July 1940, being replaced by the Saro Lerwicks of No. 209 Squadron. These aircraft were proving very troublesome and unserviceability severely limited flying. The squadron left for Stranraer in December 1940.

It was therefore fortunate that No. 320 Squadron had also been at Pembroke Dock, having formed here on June 1, 1940. It was composed of members of the Royal Netherlands Naval Air Service who had escaped from Holland when Germany invaded. They had brought with them a collection of 26 aircraft and nine of them (eight Fokker T-VIIIWs and one C-XIVW) became the squadron's immediate equipment. The floatplanes were put to good use for convoy patrols and anti-shipping sorties in the South-West Approaches. Two

Although the base had been open since the previous year, when No. 210 Squadron arrived in June 1931 there were still no hangars or slipways. The unit's two Southamptons were moored out in the Haven and servicing had to be carried out by placing the aircraft in a small floating dock, anchored offshore. It was well into 1935 before two large B Type hangars and a slipway were constructed. By that time, No. 210 Squadron was at full strength, equipped with Short Singapores. No. 230 Squadron re-formed here in December 1934 but had to borrow No. 210 Squadron's aircraft until it received its own complement of Singapores a few months later. The squadron left for the Far East soon afterwards.

No. 210 Squadron remained at Pembroke Dock with some intermittent periods overseas and came into the spotlight in 1938 when it became the first unit to re-equip with the Sunderland. When war came they immediately began patrols over the Western Approaches, and also detached aircraft to Scottish bases.

Originally a unit dating from the First World War, No. 228 Squadron had re-formed in December 1935 at 'PD' — as the base was now becoming known to its personnel. It was

This hangar is now hidden behind one of the modern port warehouses.

intended for the new Supermarine Stranraer but in November 1938 gave these up for Sunderlands. The war saw them taking up a routine of anti-submarine patrols and convoy escorts until a move was made to the Mediterranean in June 1940.

crews were lost on these and gradually problems arose because of a lack of spare parts for the aircraft. As a result, in October the squadron was transferred to nearby Carew Cheriton in order to re-equip with Ansons and later Hudsons.

The transformation in the dockside, and elimination of the RAF slipways, is clearly illustrated with these two views from 1946 and 2015.

The Officers' Mess was hit during a bombing raid in May 1941 but an even worse fate befell it after the war when it was summarily demolished in the 1980s. Relaxing on the lawn are members of No. 461 Squadron. L-R: Flying Officer Colin Bremner, Flight Lieutenant Dick Lucas, Section Officer Marion Angus, Flight Lieutenant I. V. R. Peatty and Flying Officer Alan Hannan.

The end of 1940 found the base without a residential operational squadron, although it did handle occasional detachments and weather diversions, as well as using its facilities for the maintenance of flying boats from elsewhere. A long-term lodger unit was the Fleet Air Arm's 764 Squadron which provided marine aircraft conversion training using Walrus and Swordfish aircraft as its original base at Lee-on-Solent on the south coast had become far too vulnerable to attack. It remained at PD from July 1940 until October 1941 when it moved to its own base at Lawrenny Ferry, further up the River Cleddau to the east.

Although there had been numerous air raids in the area, PD escaped damage until May 12, 1941 when a land mine destroyed the operations block, the armoury and clothing and barracks stores, as well as badly damaging the Officers' Mess. It was very fortunate that there was only a single fatality. At the end of May, No. 10 Squadron, RAAF, returned although at least three of its Sunderlands had already been stationed at PD for some weeks. The squadron often used Mount Batten as an advanced base for Biscay patrols.

Just across the road at the rear of the slipways — the Mess can just be seen through the trees on the left — more Australians from No. 10 Squadron enjoy a game of rugby. At first we could not understand how the Sunderland got on the playing field until John Evans of the Pembroke Dock Sunderland Trust showed us where the match had been played — now a concreted lorry park.

No. 461 Squadron launched Sunderland 'ANZAC' on February 16, 1944 but it was the previous year that one of its pilots performed a first.

On May 28, 1943, Sunderland T9114 was captained by Pilot Officer Gordon Singleton of St Kilda, Victoria, his mission being to rescue survivors from a Whitley and a Sunderland which had crashed in the Bay of Biscay. The 16 survivors from both aircraft were transferred to the French destroyer *La Combattante* by whaler. However, by the time this had been carried out, the heavy sea would have made a take-off dicey so the rescue aircraft was taken in tow. When Singleton finally took off the hull was ruptured leaving a 7ft by 4ft gash below the water line. Gordon Singleton returned to Pembrokeshire in June 2008 when he described what happened: 'In 1943 my Sunderland would have sunk immediately had I landed on water so I opted for an airfield, the nearest to Pembroke Dock being Angle. I did not aim for the runways but chose an area of grass which was much more forgiving. Lots of my squadron colleagues rushed out from 'PD' expecting to see a big crash — instead my CO filmed a smooth landing!' This was the only time that a Sunderland was successfully dry-landed. T9114 was recovered from the airfield and six hedges were removed to tow it to the nearby beach but it never flew again, becoming an instructional airframe.

In our comparison, the railway entrance into the dockyard can be seen on the extreme left although the track has since been lifted.

In 1943, Flight Sergeant Ross Woolhouse from Perth, Western Australia, was an air gunner with the eleven-man crew of Sunderland JM685, captained by Flight Lieutenant P. Davenport. When the aircraft was returning from a routine patrol down the Spanish coast on August 15, it was attacked by a formation of six Ju 88s west of Ushant and after repeated attacks the Sunderland was badly damaged. Flight Sergeant Woolhouse, who was operating the midships turret, was killed, and the wireless operator, Warrant Officer I. Jones, badly wounded. After violent evasive action the Sunderland reached the safety of a bank of clouds. The aircraft was now almost defenceless, the tail, midships and nose turrets all being unserviceable, the hydraulics shot away, and

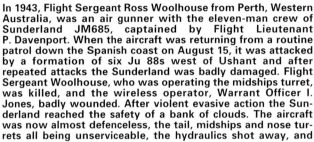

when the aircraft flew out of the clouds it had a further 300 miles to go to reach land. The captain elected to make an emergency landing at the nearest landfall on the Scilly Islands, 25 miles west of Land's End, and during the approach both inner engines cut out but it landed safely. However, this would not be end of the saga. The next day another Sunderland was sent from Pembroke Dock to pick up the crew but during its take-off it struck a reef that ripped a gash down the hull. After an eventful landing at Pembroke Dock the Sunderland was quickly hauled up the slipway but was so badly damaged it was written off. Flight Sergeant Woolhouse was buried on August 19 with full military honours in the Military Cemetery at Pembroke Dock.

No. 119 Squadron was based at Pembroke Dock from August 1942 but did not fly any patrols until November as it was converting from the Catalina to the Sunderland. The squadron disbanded here on April 17, 1943, with its Sunderlands being dispersed to other units. Its place was taken by No. 461 Squadron. On May 28 one of its Sunderlands attempted to land to pick up a crew adrift in a dinghy but the aircraft crashed, killing the captain. The rest of his crew escaped in their own dinghy and were picked up the next day by a fellow Sunderland but unfortunately it was hit by a huge wave during take off which tore a hole seven feet by four feet in the hull. As a result it had to be landed at Angle aerodrome, near base, relatively undamaged! In an epic and lengthy operation, a salvage team dragged it to a beach a mile away and began repairs but then decided to scrap it on site. The fuselage was taken to St Athan to be used for training flight engineers.

The US Navy's air arm now had a chance to play its part in the Battle of the Atlantic and the Catalina-equipped Patrol Squadron VP-63 arrived at PD in July 1943. The navy men called the station 'Blitzville', as damage was still very evident from the 1941 air raids on the port. They flew Bay of Biscay patrol along with the RAF Sunderlands and lost one aircraft to Ju 88s before moving to North Africa in December. A change of policy now transferred the US Navy's anti-submarine operations to land-based aircraft. These were the Liberators of Fleet Air Wing 7 based at Dunkeswell in Devon and operating under the control of No. 19 Group, RAF Coastal Command.

Returning to the exploits of No. 461 Squadron, on June 2 a running battle with eight Ju 88s resulted in the death of a gunner but the shooting down of three of the attackers. In July three U-Boats were attacked, one of which was destroyed. In August 1943, two Sunderlands were lost to Ju 88s and one U-Boat was 'shared' with No. 228 Squadron. Nevertheless, the battle continued; sometimes the Ju 88s being the victors, sometimes the Sunderlands. On January 28, 1944, a crew had the satisfaction of seeing the U-Boat they had depth-charged blow up.

At the end of that month the squadron transferred its area of operations from Biscay to the Western Approaches. On D-Day, the station's Sunderlands, which now included those of No. 201 Squadron, shared in a huge operation to prevent the enemy from moving its submarines into the Channel to harass the invasion craft. Patrolling aircraft criss-crossed the entire Bay of Biscay, making it virtually impossible for any U-Boat or surface vessel to remain undetected.

No further attacks were made by No. 461 Squadron until August when a U-Boat was

damaged at night and finished off by the Royal Navy, another being sunk a few days later. No. 201 Squadron, meanwhile, had sunk three U-Boats in a three-month period, beginning in June. It transferred to Northern Ireland in November and was replaced by No. 422 Squadron. The PD squadrons spent the rest of the war over the Western Approaches, where there was far less activity following the capture of U-Boat bases in France. No. 461 Squadron disbanded at PD on June 20, 1945 and the following month No. 422 Squadron moved out.

Pembroke Dock Military Cemetery . . . then and now. The Jewish grave in the background belongs to Private Heinz Schwartze of the Pioneer Corps who lost his life with a colleague, Corporal Heinz Abraham, on April 28, 1942.

No. 461 had been formed from a nucleus from No. 10 to become the second RAAF Sunderland squadron in the UK. On May 2, 1943, they took this beautiful photo of the docks area from 1,000 feet looking east. Two Sunderlands can be seen parked on the 'football field' and five more on the slipways. At least two more are standing outside the camouflaged hangars which look like housing.

ANZAC Day 1944; Air Vice-Marshal Henry Wrigley takes the salute to the march past. In 1921 he was a founding member of the Royal Australian Air Force but now he was the Air Officer commanding the RAAF Overseas Headquarters in London.

The RAF Station closed finally in 1959, ending nearly 30 years of flying boat history at 'PD' — one chapter in a fine military heritage spanning two centuries and involving all three Armed Services. The local ferry which linked both sides of the Haven Waterway ceased when a toll brodge was built, but Wales and Ireland are connected by a twice-daily ferry.

Then this un-named road was part of the RAF camp but now it is Meyrick Owen Way.

Sunderlands continued in service with the RAF but the days of the flying boat were numbered and no replacements were ordered.

Pembroke Dock hosted No. 201 Squadron from August 1945 until March 1946 when it moved to Calshot. The following month No. 230 Squadron brought its Sunderlands back from Singapore before moving to Northern Ireland in August. Nos. 201 and 230 Squadrons returned in January and February 1949, respectively. By the time they disbanded in February 1957, they had become the last UK-based Sunderland units. The station was then reduced to a Care and Maintenance basis. In March 1961 an-ex French Navy Sunderland alighted in the Haven and remained on static display until 1971 when it was transported to the RAF Museum at Hendon as a permanent exhibit.

The entrance to the station was one of the most unusual of any in the RAF, being merely a gate in a high dockyard wall. Today, the two flying-boat hangars still dominate the former RAF station, but the slipway used to bring flying-boats ashore has been removed to make way for new port facilities. The fine 1930s-style Officers' Mess was demolished in the 1980s but the former Sergeants' Mess located just inside the main gate was converted into a hotel.

So, on February 28, 1957, No. 230 Squadron was disbanded at Pembroke Dock together with its sister squadron, No. 201.

Photo taken in the twilight days of RAF Pembroke Dock when Sunderlands of both squadrons were awaiting disposal.

Soon all were gone but in March 1961 a machine from the French Navy arrived. ML824 was winched onto dry land and remained beside the station chapel as a static display until it was dismantled and moved to the RAF Museum at Hendon.

now the Heritage Centre — as well as other plaques on the dockyard wall relating to local military history. An RAF Pembroke Dock Memorial Window was dedicated in November 1945 in the former Royal Dockyard Chapel (then the RAF Church and Garrison Theatre) but removed to Plymouth in 1959 when the station closed. It is now displayed at the RAF Museum at Hendon. In Pembroke Dock's library is a smaller scale replica window, which differs from the original in that it includes the badges of every squadron based at PD in wartime (RAF, RAAF, RCAF, Dutch and USN, plus the RAF Station badge and that of the ASR/Marine Craft Section — 14 in all), whereas the original window only has six badges. There are plans to transfer the replica to the Heritage Centre in due course.

Finally, it is worthy of note that the station badge of RAF Pembroke Dock bore a very appropriate Welsh motto which translates as 'Watching the west from the air'.

Nearby is the Pembroke Dock Sunderland Trust's Heritage Centre, a very popular visitor attraction which tells the station's story.

The Trust plans to raise Sunderland Mk I T9044 which sank in a gale in the Haven in November 1940. They have already brought up two of the Bristol Pegasus engines and propellers, along with cockpit parts, the front turret and its Vickers 'K' machine gun and these are displayed at the Centre. On external display are a Sunderland float, with the badge of RAF Pembroke Dock painted on it. This was retrieved from New Zealand in the late 1980s and refurbished and painted up by No. 201 Sqn at Kinloss. There is also, a 200 class Seaplane Tender which is being cosmetically restored to wartime glory, complete with roundel and number.

A plaque in memory of Nos. 10 and 461 Squadrons is located alongside the entrance to the Pater Hall in Lewis Street. Inside, in the hallway, are plaques commemorating No. 422 Squadron, RCAF, and the US Navy's VP-63 Squadron. There are Coastal Command memorials at the Dockyard Church —

The wings went by road while the fuselage was loaded aboard a landing craft for unloading at Dagenham dock in East London.

By the 1990s the station chapel had fallen into disrepair and was badly vandalised. More than £1 million was raised for a

superb restoration and Her Majesty The Queen officially opened the Sunderland Trust's Heritage Centre there in April 2014.

PORTREATH

Built on Nancekuke Common close to the cliffs of north Cornwall, it was a multi-purpose station which for part of its life had Coastal Command squadrons as lodgers. Very unusually, it had four runways of 1,800, 1,300, 1,090 and 1,000 yards respectively. Two T2 hangars and eight blisters were made available, with two more T2s completed at a later date. Double blast pens were dispersed around the perimeter track. It was opened on March 14, 1941 under the control of No. 10 Group, Fighter Command, and within days, No. 263 Squadron's Westland Whirlwinds arrived from St Eval for convoy escort, soon being replaced by Spitfires of No. 152 Squadron.

The Luftwaffe made three small-scale attacks on the airfield during April with little result but a more determined effort made on May 9 resulted in the death of an airman and injuries to three others. Two aircraft, including a Blenheim, were destroyed and three others damaged. In mid-May, the permanent Operations Room for the Portreath Sector came into use, replacing a temporary arrangement in a bakery at Redruth. It was located at Tehidy Barton Farm, about two miles from the aerodrome. There was also a 'Q' site decoy at Tehidy, which presumably was withdrawn from use at this point! The substantial control bunker still stands.

Towards the end of June 1941, the arrival of a detachment of officers and men from the Overseas Aircraft Despatch Flight at Kemble in Gloucestershire heralded Portreath's main future role. Its three functions were to ensure that the aircraft were fully serviceable

Attempts were made to camouflage aerodromes and Portreath is a good example. Not only were field boundaries added, usually by a tractor spraying thin dark green paint, but at Portreath a road was added crossing the airfield. In some cases, the brilliant white concrete of newly-built runways was toned down by spraying them with tar and wood chips mixed with green paint.

This Vickers-Armstrong Wellington, Z1111, built at their Chester factory, and issued to No. 311 Squadron. It was later passed on to No. 7 (Coastal) Operational Training Unit and struck off charge on January 22, 1944. The photo is interesting because it was taken soon after a repaint from Bomber to Coastal Command camouflage (see also page 244).

and properly equipped for despatch to overseas destinations; to brief the crews of such aircraft for flights to Gibraltar or Malta and, lastly, to ensure that the aircraft took off on schedule. During the first month of operation, 62 aircraft were sent on their way. A succession of Spitfire squadrons maintained the convoy escort duties and on one occasion No. 152 Squadron provided close support for 18 Hampdens raiding Brest, losing two aircraft in the process. Offensive operations increased, including airfield attacks in France.

Towards the end of September 1941, four Beaufighters of No. 248 Squadron arrived at Portreath for an indefinite stay, tasked with carrying out Atlantic patrols off the Scilly Isles. A detachment of No. 276 Squadron's air-sea rescue aircraft formed the rest of Coastal Command's meagre presence, a response to the growing need for such a facility in the south-west. The rapid growth of the OAD Flight's workload resulted in its redesignation as the Overseas Aircraft Despatch Unit (OADU) in mid-December 1941. It was soon given the prefix No. 1 to

differentiate it from similar units being formed elsewhere by No. 44 Group, Ferry Command. A record number of 160 aircraft were handled by No. 1 OADU in January 1942, including 17 which departed from nearby St Eval.

Construction of a new Sector Operations Block began in August 1942 and on the 10th the station was allocated to the USAAF as a fighter base but this order was cancelled early the following month. However, many USAAF aircraft did pass through late in October and early November en route to take part in Operation 'Torch', the landings in French North Africa. Two RAF Mustang squadrons, Nos. 414 and 613, were based at Portreath during the summer of 1943, mainly for shipping escort and also to cover USAAF B-17s returning from raids on French targets. In June, the OADU dispatched no less than 409 British and 124 USAAF aircraft including Albemarles and Halifaxes towing Horsa gliders to North Africa in preparation for the invasion of Sicily.

The third and final Operations Room for the Portreath Sector came into use in July

1943, located on top of Trigea Hill, close to Portreath village. It still exists today, having been converted into apartments. At the end of August, the first major Coastal Command presence arrived in the shape of the Beaufighters of No. 235 Squadron. They were joined in mid-September by more Beaufighters from No. 143 Squadron. Pilot Norman Carr summed up numerous patrols from Portreath in these words: 'My main impressions of the time spent on this type of operation are of the long hard slogs of six-hour flights, bad weather, endless sea, and sheer relief when a good landfall was made. But at least pilots learned to fly, navigators to navigate, and operational hours mounted quickly.'

In a rather bizarre incident on September 10, a Halifax destined for the Middle East, swung off the runway on landing and struck a first floor window of the watch tower with its port wing with an engine cowling ending up on the flying controller's desk, ruining his cup of tea! Fortunately, no one was injured but the aircraft was wrecked and a corner of the tower had to be rebuilt.

A fine comparison taken by Flight Sergeant Al Williams, the Detachment Commander at Portreath today.

Crewmen from No. 235 Squadron — Alec Williamson, Jimmy Eaton, Harry Bibby plus an un-named navigator. Their Beaufighters carried a crew of two and mounted a formidable armament of four 20mm cannon and six .303 Brownings.

In September 1944, Nos 235 and 248 Squadrons were transferred to the Banff Strike Wing, and at this point the only Coastal Command activity at Portreath was reduced to air-sea rescue. No. 276 Squadron had already left for a French base, leaving only its Warwick aircraft, which were supported by a detachment of three Walrus amphibians from No. 275 Squadron. As far back as July 19, a Portreath-based Walrus had been summoned to investigate a report of 20 dinghies lashed together. It landed nearby and found that the occupants were 46 survivors from a sunken U-Boat. Unable to cope with this number, the Walrus flew the captain to Harrowbeer, near Plymouth, and was rewarded with two bottles of wine for his trouble while the Navy picked up the rest of his crew!

The station's rescue role ceased in mid-February 1945 with the disbandment of the two detachments. No. 1 OADU was left as the only resident and its operations inevitably began to wind down that summer, until disbandment on October 10. After a brief period of ground instruction, Portreath fell into disuse.

In 1950, Portreath — now renamed Nancekuke — was chosen as a centre for experiments with the large-scale production of chemical weapons. As an outstation of the Chemical Defence Establishment at Porton

No. 235 Squadron flew anti-aircraft patrols over the Bay of Biscay and when these were extended to the west coast of Ireland a Ju 290 was shot down in February 1944. No. 143 Squadron, meanwhile, was also patrolling the Bay and claimed several victories but suffered some losses before it joined the North Coates Wing in February. No. 248 Squadron was its replacement at Portreath, equipped with the first Mosquitos to be based here. Two Marks were operated; XVI-IIs to attack shipping with their heavy 57mm Molins cannon and FB.VIs to fight off any air cover. A sortie rate of over 100 per month was being maintained, building up in June 1944's invasion support to 274. One U-Boat was sunk, one was damaged and several aircraft were shot down during this intensive period. In September, five crews were lost on convoy attacks off the Gironde Estuary, before the squadron moved north to join the Banff Strike Wing.

No. 235 Squadron, meanwhile, had partly converted to Mosquitos during June and operated Channel blocking patrols and also covered aircraft strafing targets around the beach-heads. Two enemy aircraft were shot down and a U-Boat damaged. On July 21, two Do 217s were accounted for by Mosquitos.

Flight Sergeant Al Williams, the RAF Detachment Commander, at what is now RRH (Remote Radar Head) Portreath, with Squadron Leader Colin Pomeroy, stand in for the wartime crew.

Squadron line up in 1943 — the four nose-mounted cannons on the Mosquito show up clearly.

Down, Wiltshire, it was deemed to be far enough away from large centres of population to minimise any risk of contamination. Fifteen tons of the nerve agent known as Sarin was produced at Nancekuke between 1953 and 1956 after which the plant ceased to operate. However, large quantities of Sarin were stored there for many years to test its shelf life. The plant closed down in 1976 and the buildings and equipment were decontaminated and buried in five dumps in the immediate area, which included old mine shafts and quarries. The site was handed back to the RAF who continue to run it as a remote radar head known as RRH Portreath, providing air surveillance in the South-West Approaches.

Little remains of the wartime buildings at Portreath, with notable survivors including the squash court, ambulance shed, gymnasium, Sergeants' Mess, and at least 18 air raid shelters. On the coast side of the airfield some fighter blast pens are slowly decaying. From the air, the runways appear to be complete but, apart from the NE-SW strip, they are said to be in very poor condition. A memorial on the RAF site is surmounted by a bent three-bladed propeller and bears the inscription: 'In memory of those Glider Pilot Regiment crews and RAF crews who died ferrying gliders from Portreath to Tunisia, June-July 1943, and to those who died in the subsequent airborne assault on Sicily to which this was a prelude.'

Nevertheless, this firepower was trumped when the squadron received the Mk XVIII version of the Mosquito which mounted a Quick Firing 6-pounder anti-tank gun similar to the one depicted, minus, of course, its carriage. The aircraft version was fitted with an automatic loader and was known as the Molins gun after its manufacturer.

The machine was standing on the grass, facing the sea, so Aldon took this comparison while standing on the runway.

Today 'warfare' in the 21st century is waged by different methods and Portreath is now a Remote Radar Head for the RAF linked to their national radar cover for control and defence.

The scanner with its protective dome is located on the seaward side of the airfield at the western end. Nearby is the redundant bunker of the Control and Reporting Post, unused since 2004.

No. 307 was the first Polish night fighter squadron being formed at Kirton-in-Lindsey in September 1940. Although not nominally part of Coastal Command, it spent time at Predannack in 1943 when equipped with the Mosquito.

PREDANNACK

A stretch of rough moorland on Cornwall's bleak Lizard peninsula was chosen as the site for this satellite of RAF Portreath. The intention was to use it for night fighters defending the ports of Falmouth and Penzance, with accommodation for two squadrons. Four Teesside hangars and four blisters were planned but it appears that initially only a single Bellman was actually provided. Three T2s were added later, along with a dozen blisters. Very unusually for an RAF site, it was built with four runways, presumably to help pilots better cope with the strong winds in these parts. The original strips were fairly short but by 1944 the main was 2,000 yards, with three subsidiaries of 1,000, 1,380 and 1,520 yards.

The building project was extremely difficult because the underlying dense china clay was the worst possible foundation. Hardcore was brought in by streams of lorries which struggled through the mire, while the Cornish quarries had to supply huge quantities of stone before the airfield was finally completed. An unknown number of fighter dispersal pens were built off the perimeter track and some were probably engulfed by more than 30 loop hardstandings constructed later in the war. Two 'Q' site decoy airfields were laid out at Kynance, about two miles to the south, and Goonhilly Downs, some four miles to the north-east.

Far from complete, the station opened somewhat prematurely in May 1941 and some of No. 247 Squadron's Hurricanes were detached from Portreath in June for night intruding over France. Accommodation was found to be incomplete and much of the airfield a sea of mud. Most of the personnel had to be billeted all over the peninsula while work on the buildings went on that summer. The Polurrian Hotel at Mullion was taken over as the Officers' Mess. Use by fighter aircraft continued and several air raids occurred, the first attack being on the night of October 12, 1941 when a raider followed a Beaufighter on the approach and shot up the airfield. GCI (Ground Controlled Interception) in the area was covered by RAF Treleaver radar station.

Defence soon gave way to offensive operations with fighter sweeps and intruder operations over France. The airfield's southerly location made it also suitable for anti-shipping strikes over the Bay of Biscay. Westland Whirlwind and Beaufighter squadrons mounted many patrols, followed later by a number of Mosquito squadrons. Although the station remained in No. 10 Group, Fighter Command, nearly all the operations were maritime-orientated. With the US Eighth Air Force making many daylight raids over France, there were frequent

There were several of these twin-engine dispersals around the airfield but all buildings and blast walls were demolished many years ago.

Aldon Ferguson explored Predannack with airfield historian Peter Wearne, hosted by Lieutenant Commander Graeme

Stringer of the Royal Navy which now uses the airfield as a relief landing ground for the Royal Navy Air Station at Culdrose.

diversions. On May 1, 1943, for example, the 306th Bomb Group was heavily attacked by Fw 190s over St Nazaire and 15 B-17s landed at Predannack, some with severe damage and carrying dead and wounded crewmen. One of the airmen was ball-turret gunner Sergeant Maynard Smith who later received the Medal of Honor for his conduct that day. He had fought fires in the rear of the aircraft, thrown out ammunition boxes and given first aid to the badly wounded tail gunner.

After the runways were extended in 1943, continuous operation by larger aircraft types became more feasible. The Polish-manned No. 304 Squadron spent nearly three months here from December 1943 with its Wellingtons. Bad weather reduced U-Boat sighting opportunities but during January 1944 they were credited with sinking one of the three they attacked. They were replaced by the Liberators of No. 311 Squadron in February, now equipped with rocket projectiles. The aim was to attack submarines making the

final run home on the surface but there were no successes as their prey was becoming very wary.

In March, No. 151 Squadron's Mosquitos arrived and began shipping attacks. They were soon supported by a Wing of two Spitfire squadrons at Predannack for 'Instep' operations designed to intercept Ju 88s harassing shipping in the south-west. The Leigh Light Wellingtons of No. 179 Squadron joined No. 311 in May. Both took part in so-called 'Cork' patrols, intended to

In November 1943, No. 157 Squadron, commanded by Wing Commander J. Mackie, arrived to carry out shipping patrols over the Western Approaches and it was during a practice flight on February 26, 1944 that one of their Mosquitos — DZ707 —came to grief right on the aerodrome. The aircraft was being piloted by Flying Officer John Clifton with Flying Officer Scobie as observer when it piled in from 200 feet. The Mosquito burst into flames and as firemen covered the aircraft with foam, officers

rushed to the rescue. In this dramatic photo, Wing Commander Mackie can be seen with a Czechoslovakian RAF doctor attempting to release the crew but it was difficult as the observer had been thrown across the pilot making it very awkward to reach their harnesses in the excessive heat. On the right is the station padre, Squadron Leader Brown. The crew were eventually cut free, Flying Officer Scobie surviving though badly injured but tragically Flying Officer Clifton could not be saved.

It is therefore ironic that today the airfield is scattered with wrecked aircraft used for training by the Royal Navy Fire Fighting School.

In December 1941, No. 224 Squadron moved to St Eval, its Hudsons being replaced in July 1942 by Liberators when they moved to Beaulieu to continue their conversion training. On September 20, Flying Officer David Sleep in FL910 attacked a U-Boat but the explosion of his depth-charges damaged his elevators and the Liberator became so uncontrollable that the control columns had to be tied forward. All loose items were jettisoned to reduce weight and they just managed to make landfall in Cornwall, crashing at Predannack. (A plaque in his memory can be seen at Beaulieu — see page 77.)

block off the Channel and Irish Sea from U-Boats bent on attacking the invasion fleets. The Spitfire Wing was also flying continuous cover patrols over the ships massing in and around Falmouth.

The U-Boat war moved away from the Channel in the summer of 1944 and with it went Nos. 179 and 311 Squadrons. Predannack now became a rest and re-equipment base for fighter squadrons. Around that time, there was a tentative plan to rebuild the airfield as a VHB (Very Heavy Bomber Station) for the ultimately unsuccessful Vickers Windsor, but nothing came of this.

Predannack Down was unusual in that it was provided with four runways. Three of them were extended in 1943.

It appears that the full title of the airfield was only used in the planning stages and that the word 'Down' has now been discontinued.

On September 15, 1945, its gates were opened to the public and 4,000 visitors arrived for the Battle of Britain air display. A highlight was the return of No. 151 Squadron's Mosquitos after a mass flypast over London. This squadron lingered until May 1946 before moving out and a month later, the airfield was reduced to Care and Maintenance.

It now seemed likely to be reclaimed as heathland, but its very remoteness attracted the attention of Vickers-Armstrong and famous aeronautical engineer Barnes Wallis, later to become Sir Barnes. Although he did not invent the concept, Wallis did much pioneering work to make the variable geometry ('swing-wing') concept functional. This was demonstrated at Predannack by large 30ft wingspan models. Vickers eventually stopped work on the project and in 1954 the airfield was again abandoned.

Four years later helicopter training was being expanded at Royal Naval Air Station Culdrose and a relief landing ground was required for elementary pilot training away from the main airfield. As a result all four runways were now made serviceable, and since 1971 the Royal Navy Fire Fighting School has been based at Predannack. No. 626 Volunteer Gliding Squadron is another long-term resident.

Many of the airfield buildings have been demolished but notable remnants are the original Station Headquarters, the Gymnasium/Chancel and a parachute store but there is little left of the 'Blenheim' and 'Hurricane' type E dispersal pens. Out on the airfield are the remains of the long ramp once used to launch radio-controlled scale models for Barnes Wallis's test work. The wartime Explosives Storage Area survives, complete with most of its former road structure but only the bases of buildings. At the main entrance is a plaque commemorating all who served here which was unveiled on June 11, 2002.

Predannack Memorial: 'Like a breath of wind gone in a fleeting second, only the memories now remain'.

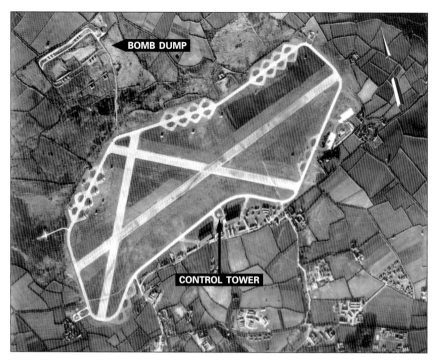

The brand new aerodrome of St Davids, photographed three months after completion in September 1943, its first permanent occupants being the Halifax squadrons, Nos. 58 and 502. The bomb dump with its sheltered revetments shows up clearly.

ST DAVIDS

The most westerly airfield in Wales, St Davids was planned to house operational squadrons of the US Navy equipped with the PB4Y Liberator. However, soon after it opened in September 1943 a change of plan resulted in the American units being allocated Dunkeswell in Devon. Now a station for No. 19 Group of RAF Coastal Command, it was still often used as a diversion airfield by the US Navy and now and again by USAAF aircraft on the southern ferry route via Marrakesh to St Mawgan.

Construction was by George Wimpey and Co Ltd at a cost of £1,262,656, with work beginning in August 1942. Three runways were laid down, the longest being 2,000 yards with two subsidiaries of 1,200 and 1,100 yards. Three T2 hangars were provided, plus the floor and foundations for a fourth which was never erected for reasons unknown. Thirty loop hardstandings were placed in five clusters around the perimeter track. The living sites were dispersed to the south, whilst the bomb storage area was in the marshy ground to the north.

The first RAF aircraft to be based at St Davids were detachments of Fortresses from Nos. 206 and 220 Squadrons at Thorney Island in Sussex, but rather more permanent residents arrived in December 1943. Their arrival was organised so that operations could be continued throughout the move, so on December 11 two Halifaxes of No. 58 Squadron and two from No. 502 took off from Holmsley South on anti-submarine patrols but on their return they landed at their new base the following morning. The remaining aircraft of the two squadrons soon did the same.

During January 1944 aircraft from St Davids sighted ten U-Boats at night and attacked nine of them although with no observed results. Retaliation came early in February when Ju 88 intruders shot down a returning Halifax over St Bride's Bay. Rescue craft found only a floating wheel. Another Halifax was warned by Flying Control to orbit clear of base but, with fuel running out, it was forced to make a nerve-wracking landing, expecting to be shot down at any moment. Fortunately by that time the raiders had departed.

There were now three squadrons crowding the airfield but the opening of a satellite at Brawdy in February 1944 resulted in No. 517 Squadron — which had been at St Davids since the previous November — moving its Halifaxes there immediately. Paradoxically, the satellite had longer runways which were arranged in a cross shape, rather than St Davids' standard triangular pattern. They were also better aligned with the prevailing winds so that if the cross-wind component at the parent station was unacceptable for a fully-loaded Halifax, the aircraft were flown to Brawdy with a light fuel load. The tanks were then filled up prior to an operational patrol.

Although most of these sorties passed without incident, constant vigilance was vital because the next radar contact could be a fishing boat, an enemy submarine or an E-Boat. Action, when it came, was swift and violent as shown by an incident which happened in the early hours of April 26, 1944. A radar contact was picked up nine miles ahead and flares were dropped at one and a half miles, silhouetting a U-Boat and a small ship. The Halifax dived through a terrific barrage and dropped four anti-submarine bombs, resulting in a vivid blue flash and clouds of smoke. Looking through the flare chute, a gunner saw what might have been the bows of a U-Boat sticking up out of the water as if its back were broken but confirmation of the kill was impossible in the darkness. The target may have disappeared from the radar but this could mean that it had merely crash-dived. The Halifax had sustained a hole in the wing two feet across but luckily no vital parts were hit.

On D-Day, three aircraft from St Davids flew a box patrol between Brest and St Nazaire, one of a specially-planned series of flights to provide a constant watch in case any enemy sea forces tried to interfere with Allied shipping in the Channel.

At the end of August, No. 58 Squadron moved to Stornoway and the following month No. 502 Squadron also departed. They were replaced by a detachment of No. 220 Squadron from Lagens in the Azores for a two-month conversion course onto Leigh Light Liberators, after which the crews flew the aircraft back to their Atlantic base.

Station headquarters was moved to Brawdy in November 1945 when St Davids was reduced to Care and Maintenance until both airfields were taken over by the Royal Navy in January 1946. It was then used as a Relief Landing Ground for Brawdy and from 1955 by a Fleet Requirements Unit equipped with Sea Hornets and Mosquitos. During this period, the three T2 hangars were dismantled and moved to Brawdy, where they could be better utilised.

After the RAF regained the station in 1974, St Davids served as an RLG again. All the airfield buildings were demolished and maintenance restricted to the main runway and associated taxiways. Flying ceased in 1992 when Brawdy closed whereupon much of the land was sold off. Stretches of the eastern and south-eastern perimeter track are now public roads and a handful of huts survive on dispersed sites.

This spectacular crash took place on July 20, 1944. The Halifax MkII (HX177) of No. 58 Squadron swung round on take off and ground-looped. The undercarriage collapsed and it came to rest alongside the control tower looking rather worse for wear.

The hangars were dismantled and moved to the nearby satellite at Brawdy although the runways were still maintained until the 1990s. Sadly we found that the control tower had also disappeared making the present-day comparison rather meaningless.

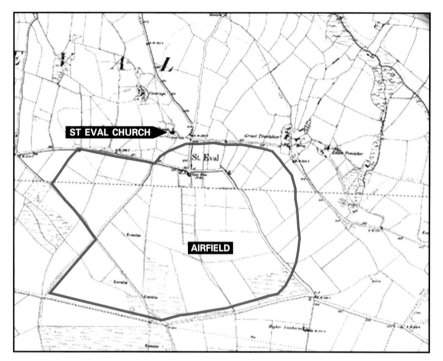

The great shame with St Eval is that where during the war it was one of the largest Coastal Command stations, today virtually every building has gone. It is all the more tragic as its construction involved the complete loss of St Eval village.

ST EVAL

Six miles north-east of Newquay and just inland from 300-foot high cliffs, this was an Expansion Scheme station planned specifically for Coastal Command. Work began in 1938, sadly resulting in the compulsory purchase and demolition of St Eval village, to bitter protest. Levelling of the airfield involved the removal of many dry stone walls and three ancient tumuli. Only the 13th century church, St Uvelas, the vicarage, and Trevisker Farm were spared but were effectively surrounded by RAF activity. During the war they were taken over for RAF use, with the church tower used as an observation post and serving as a distinctive landmark for aircrew, so much so that it became the centre-piece of the station's badge, with the apt motto: 'Faith in our Task'.

Although planned in the grand style of an Expansion Scheme site, with the aim of accommodating two General Reconnaissance squadrons, little progress had been made with buildings by the time the war started. Apart from four C Type hangars still incomplete, the rest of the station buildings were of temporary construction, including a watch office unusually made from wood. There were four grass runways, the longest being 1,200 yards.

RAF Station St Eval opened on October 2, 1939 with the arrival of No. 217 Squadron's Ansons from Dorset. They began to fly convoy escorts and anti-submarine patrols, reaching 94 sorties during December. For close inshore cover between Start Point and Land's End, No. 6 Coastal Patrol Flight formed here in January 1940 with Tiger and Hornet Moths but disbanded towards the end of May. No. 217 Squadron began to convert onto Beauforts in April 1940 but the Ansons continued to bear the brunt of operations, even bombing barge concentrations in French ports by night. By the end of the year, the Ansons were withdrawn and the Beauforts had taken over. These sorties consisted in the main of raids on the French Atlantic coast ports, using IMPS (Impact Magnesium Percussion Mines) and TIMS (Time Impact Mines).

After the fall of France, fighters were based at St Eval for inshore convoy protection. No. 234 Squadron's Spitfires shot down a Ju 88 over a convoy on July 8, having damaged another the day before. The station proved an attractive target and a series of air raids started in August 1940, one of the C Type hangars being destroyed on the 21st. The dummy flare path on the 'Q' site decoy at Trelow Down, three miles to the east, attracted numerous bombs on the night of the 26th/27th. Two other 'Q' sites were also in operation at Tregonetha Down, four miles to the south-east and at Colan, four miles south-west of the aerodrome. Two much needed concrete runways were constructed during 1940, one of 1,200 yards and the other of 1,000 yards, flying continuing around the work.

From August 1940, No. 236 Squadron's Blenheims flew convoy patrols and during September accounted for one He 111 and a Do 18. The major area of operation became the Biscay coast with such activities as the escort of St Eval's Beauforts. The squadron moved to south-west Wales in March 1941. Detachments from Nos. 220 and 221 Squadrons were also present well into 1941, the aircraft being Hudsons and Wellingtons, respectively. Almost nightly Luftwaffe attacks were mounted from January 1941 and on the 25th a shelter near the watch office took a direct hit, killing 21. As the raids intensified, hotels and guest houses in the area were requisitioned in an effort to get as many personnel as possible away from the

Work begins clearing the dry stone walls criss-crossing the site.

Tell-tale evidence of the many enemy attacks on the airfield, the white spots denoting the filled in craters from sticks of bombs.

The first arrival at the aerodrome was No. 217 Squadron which arrived with Avro Ansons in October 1939. They began converting to the Bristol Beaufort in April 1940. This clever arrangement of a canvas shelter permitted work to continue in inclement weather. This particular aircraft (L4463) named 'Sweet Pea' was shot down by flak near Vannes, France on December 17, 1940.

airfield. Two heavy raids in May 1941 resulted in the destruction of two Blenheims and damage to over a dozen other aircraft. The officers' and sergeants' messes were virtually demolished and two more of the C Type hangars were so badly damaged that canvas Bessonneau hangars had to be erected inside the roofless shells.

A satellite for St Eval was in the early stages of being adapted from the pre-war Newquay aerodrome. Now named Trebelzue, it was first used by Beauforts to disperse them away from the repeated night bombing of their base. Any not required for night operations would be flown over and parked overnight.

Two runways had been completed by September 1941 but it was little used until transferred to Ferry Command in December of that year. By mid-1943, it had been engulfed by the entirely new base known as St Mawgan and loop hardstandings were superimposed on its main runway to form a huge dispersal parking area for the USAAF ferry terminal.

A detached flight of No. 1 Photographic Reconnaissance Unit had been based since October 1940, with the main purpose of keeping camera watch on Brest and the other Biscay ports for any signs of German capital ships. If any of these vessels became loose in the Atlantic, they could massacre the convoys. In March 1941, the *Scharnhorst* and *Gneisenau* were identified at Brest and for almost a whole year, until their escape in the so-called Channel Dash, they were the most often photographed, and often bombed, targets in Occupied Europe. They were also the most ferociously defended, with seven PRU Spitfire pilots losing their lives as the price for the unceasing watch from St Eval. One of them was Flying Officer Michael Suckling who had found *Tirpitz* on a sortie from Wick in May 1941.

'B' Flight of No. 1 Photographic Reconnaissance Unit (PRU) was based at St Eval from October 1941 to October 19, 1942. On the latter date, 'B' and 'F' Flights of the PRU were combined at Benson to form No. 541 Squadron. Thereafter, the squadron kept a detachment at St Eval.

Michael Prendergast gave Aldon Ferguson this photo of a Spitfire from the photo-reconnaisance unit based at St Eval from No. 541 Squadron. Even though the airfield has now been flattened, Aldon was thrilled to find this fighter pen intact because they were supposed to have all been removed when the loop hardstandings were built..

Although the Treaty of Versailles limited Germany from building battleships of more than 10,000 tons, once Hitler came to power the restriction was ignored and in October 1936 the *Scharnhorst* was launched at Wilhelmshaven weighing in at over 30,000 tons. Her sister ship was the *Gneisenau*, launched two months later at Kiel. Both ships proved to be formidable adversaries and every effort was made to sink them. After a foray into the North Atlantic in early 1941, the two ships put into Brest where they were subjected to sustained attacks by Bomber Command. One bomb fell near the *Gneisenau* in the dry dock but failed to explode so the ship had to be quickly removed so that the bomb could be defuzed.

Now lying moored in the outer harbour, the *Gneisenau* was vulnerable to an attack by torpedoes and an operation was quickly put into place for April 6 using six Beauforts of No. 22 Squadron from St Eval. The plan was for three advance machines to be armed with bombs to be followed by the others with torpedoes. However, unbeknown to the three torpedo crews, two of the bombers had become bogged down and failed to take off and the third lost its way. Two of the Beauforts reached Brest. Flying Officer Kenneth Campbell dropped his weapon from 50 feet having just crossed the outer mole. With 500 yards to run to the target, his aim was true although his aircraft was shot out of the sky by concentrated anti-aircraft fire.

On April 5, 1941, PRU photos showed that *Gneisenau* had left dry dock and it was decided that a torpedo strike should be attempted from St Eval by a detachment of No. 22 Squadron's Beauforts. Six aircraft were to be sent on the raid but two became bogged while taxiing on the rain-soaked aerodrome and two got lost in the bad weather. Flying Officer Kenneth Campbell's aircraft was left as the only one equipped with a torpedo (four of the others had been carrying bombs) so he decided to make a lone attack. After a near perfect approach, he dropped his torpedo as he crossed the mole of the inner harbour. Flak hit the aircraft as it turned away and the Beaufort fell into the harbour. Nevertheless *Gneisenau* had been severely damaged and eight months later was still under repair. Campbell was posthumously awarded the Victoria Cross.

In October 1941 the whole of No. 22 Squadron concentrated at St Eval but came off operations by the end of the year prior to a posting to Ceylon. In 27 months of operations from various bases, it had sunk over 100,000 tons of enemy shipping. No. 53 Squadron had also been based there between February and July 1941 operating Blenheims against such targets as Brest, with consider-

able losses. For the second half of 1941 the squadron's base was in Northern Ireland but a detachment of Hudsons was maintained in Cornwall for anti-submarine patrols. Hudsons of No. 206 Squadron were also detached here for raids on the French Atlantic ports in the summer of 1941 and a U-Boat was claimed as a 'probable' on July 4.

Citation: **The King has been graciously pleased to approve the posthumous award of the Victoria Cross to Flying Officer Kenneth Campbell in recognition of most conspicuous bravery. This officer was the pilot of a Beaufort aircraft of Coastal Command which was detailed to attack an enemy battle cruiser in Brest Harbour at first light on the morning of 6th April 1941. The aircraft did not return but it is known that a torpedo attack was carried out with the utmost daring. The battle cruiser was severely damaged below the water-line and was obliged to return to the dock whence she had come only the day before. By pressing home his attack at close quarters in the face of withering fire on a course fraught with extreme peril, Flying Officer Campbell displayed valour of the highest order.'**

St Eval was featured in the film *RAF Coastal Command* and, although individual bases are not named, the tower of the parish church is a dead giveaway. There were fears that it might be lost when the airfield was under construction . . .

No. 224 Squadron in its entirety was resident from December 1941 to February 1942. Using Hudsons, its main duty was flying anti-shipping patrols along the French coast. No. 233 Squadron was yet another St Eval unit, being based from August 1941 until January 1942. Its Biscay operations saw attacks on four U-Boats and a surface vessel during September for the loss of one Hudson. Part of No. 86 Squadron, equipped with Beauforts was here for a few months early in 1942 and claimed two ships torpedoed and sunk during February.

In the spring of 1942 the U-Boat threat in the Atlantic reached a new peak so Nos. 53 and 58 Squadrons were sent to St Eval to cover the Bay of Biscay. The former had Hudsons and the latter Whitleys, and were soon joined by detachments of pupil crews from No. 10 Operational Training Unit based at Abingdon, Oxfordshire. Using Whitleys and bearing in mind the inexperience of the aircrew involved, this was hardly an effective force but indicative of the desperate measures thought necessary at this stage of the Battle of the Atlantic. No less than 33 Whitleys were lost before the OTU involvement was withdrawn in July 1943.

. . . but it survived to become a welcoming landmark to returning crews. As the church played such an important part in the life of the station it now contains a number of memorials.

No. 61 Squadron of Bomber Command was twice loaned to Coastal at St Eval during the summer of 1942. On July 17, a Lancaster crew brought back photographic evidence of a U-Boat sinking. No. 502 Squadron's Whitleys were also based for most of 1942 and were credited with a U-Boat sinking on July 17.

Even the members of 'B' Flight of No. 541 Squadron grouped themselves in front of the church for this photo.

In October 1942 a squadron of Liberators from the USAAF's 93rd Bomb Group had been attached to gain experience in anti-submarine work. Several other American units followed. The invasion of North Africa in November 1942 put immense pressure on the station, so much so, that most anti-submarine aircraft were detached to New Forest airfields but continued to use St Eval as a forward base. Halifaxes appeared in March 1943 now flown by No. 58 Squadron and focused on anti-submarine patrols and convoy escort. During May, 11 U-Boats were attacked, of which two were sunk and two seriously damaged. Combats with Ju 88s resulted in several losses before the squadron moved to Holmsley South in December 1943. The 479th Anti-Submarine Group's Liberators spent July 1943 at St Eval, sinking *U-558* on the 20th. They moved to Dunkeswell, Devon, early in August, straight into an ongoing dispute between the USAAF and US Navy over which service should conduct anti-submarine operations by land-based aircraft. Within weeks the Navy had prevailed.

Like most coastal airfields in the south-west, St Eval suffered from sea fog which drifted in on a 10-15mph wind, so in April 1943 Coastal Command requested that it be equipped with FIDO so that round the clock patrols could be maintained. They also requested it for Ballykelly in Northern Ireland but this was turned down. FIDO stood for Fog Investigation and Dispersal Operation but was sometimes interpreted as Fog Intense Dispersal Of. In a nutshell, it was a way of literally burning off fog from a runway by pumping thousands of gallons of petrol through lines of burners placed on each side of the strip. It coped well in the windless conditions accompanying normal radiation fog, but sea fog presented great dif-

And in come the Yanks! This US Navy PB4Y Liberator, almost certainly operating out of Dunkeswell, was filmed overflying RAF Culdrose which lies 30 miles south of St Eval.

ficulties. The St Eval installation required extra lines of burners to cope with the greater water content of sea fog as well as problems with cross-winds. Take-offs were considered to be easily achievable but land-ings were likely to be much more difficult unless coupled with GCA (Ground Controlled Approach) radar. In fact, trials of GCA were transferred from Davidstow Moor to St Eval for a short period.

One of the first tasks the Americans undertook was to take a series of photographs of their new base. This shot was taken on December 6 from 11,000 feet.

No. 224 Squadron had been detaching aircraft here from its Hampshire base at Beaulieu for some time but the whole squadron moved in during April 1943. Its Liberators mainly flew anti-submarine patrols and May produced seven attacks with obviously severe damage to one U-Boat. This pace was maintained throughout the summer and a definite kill was achieved on July 3. From October the squadron began to use rockets and at the end of the year intensive Leigh Light training took place. The Liberators then concentrated on the transit routes in and out of the French Atlantic ports, scoring at least one kill in June, but losing two crews that month. A move was made to Scotland in September 1944.

No. 53 Squadron was also based from January 1944 providing 24-hour cover of the Western Approaches. Many attacks were made but results were inconclusive until the night of June 6/7 when a U-Boat was sunk although one Liberator was lost. On July 30, the squadron shared in the first aerial sonobuoy sinking of a U-Boat. This floating device, dropped from an aircraft, picked up underwater sounds and transmitted them to its parent. It relied upon the ability of the human ear to differentiate man-made noises from the almost overwhelming oceanic background. Thus it was only of limited effectiveness until the concept was perfected with the aid of electronic advances many years after the war.

No doubt Captain Swayne Latham, the unit S-2, Lieutenant Colonel James H. Rothrock, the Executive Officer, and the S-4, Major Wilkie A. Rambo, were none too pleased with the state of their hangar!

Taken over as the headquarters for the 1st Anti-Submarine Squadron, which was commanded by Lieutenant Colonel Jack Roberts, a canvas Bessoneau hangar had to be erected inside

to give some measure of shelter from the elements. Today, nothing remains save for the overgrown base where the hangar once stood.

Bombing up on January 23, 1943. The American Liberators moved out to Holmsley South in December that year.

After the war, Coastal Command adopted the Lockheed Neptune for maritime patrols. His Royal Highness the Duke of Edinburgh inspected the very first of the type to enter service at St Eval in May 1952.

No. 53 Squadron moved to Iceland in September 1944. A third Liberator unit, No. 547 Squadron, had been at St Eval since January 1944 and scored a U-Boat sinking during March. With the U-Boats ousted from their French ports, the squadron moved to Scotland in September. In April 1944, a fourth Liberator Squadron — No. 206 — had arrived in preparation for Operation 'Cork'. This was a massive undertaking which, as its name implied, was designed to block U-Boat access to the Channel during the build-up and execution of the Normandy invasion. Former Liberator pilot Jim Glazebrook in his book *Someone to Watch Over Me* (Roper Penberthy Publishing, 2005) described it thus:

'Crowded onto St Eval were four Liberator squadrons. Most of the crews were billeted in the surrounding countryside. Blocking the western end of the English Channel was achieved by setting up three "endless chain" patrols between England and France, so spaced that a U-Boat would not be able to cross all three from west to east without surfacing. Each aircraft flew to a strict timetable, so that an observer at any point on each of the three chains would see a Liberator pass every 30 minutes. This was maintained day and night for six weeks. Nos. 206 and 547 Squadrons flew through the daylight hours, being relieved at Night by Nos. 53 and 224 Squadrons, which had been equipped with Leigh Lights for night attacks. On the only two days when fog blanketed St Eval, the patrols were covered from Northern Ireland.

'The Germans, of course, knew of our patrols and made no attempt to run the gauntlet of the Liberators in daylight hours. They did, however, try to break through at night, and one crew of No. 224 Squadron made history by sinking two U-Boats in 22 minutes. Next morning, the Navy picked up survivors from both. Unfortunately, there was another hazard to be faced at night. A number of flak ships, no bigger than a surfaced submarine but bristling with anti-aircraft guns, slipped into the Channel at night to decoy the patrolling Liberators. On one occasion the tactic proved successful.'

The first Warwicks to be used for anti-submarine work arrived in November 1944 in the shape of No. 179 Squadron which had just re-equipped with them. The first attack took place on February 24 when a 'probable' was claimed but no further action was seen before the war ended. No. 304 Squadron's sonobuoy-equipped Wellingtons were the other final operational aircraft, based here from March 1945 until moving to Essex in July. Rescue squadron detachments had been based for many years but from September 1944 the whole of No. 282 Squadron was present until the unit disbanded on July 19, 1945.

St Eval seems to have been in a constant state of development to meet ever-changing operational requirements. At an early stage some fighter dispersal pens were constructed but most were later obliterated by extensive loop dispersals intended for the Liberators. Runways were progressively lengthened by Canadian engineers and the FIDO installation was another major project. The C Type hangars lost to bombing were replaced by a Bellman, two T2s and seven blisters.

No. 228 Squadron re-formed at St Eval on June 1, 1946 to operate Liberator freight services to Northern Ireland, Gibraltar, the Azores and Morocco. It also had reconnaissance, air-sea rescue and meteorological tasks but disbanded on September 30, 1946. Also present around this period was No. 210 Squadron from June 1946, equipped with Lancasters for maritime reconnaissance. It became a long-term resident until moving to Yorkshire to re-equip with Lockheed Neptunes in September 1952.

A succession of maritime squadrons followed, equipped first with the Lancaster and from 1952 with its successor, the Shackleton. When the Mk 3 version of this aircraft began to come into service, it was considered too heavy for operational flying from St Eval. Thus the station closed on March 6, 1959, with the existing squadrons moving to nearby St. Mawgan. Air Training Corps gliding continued until 1964, after which two of the taxiways became public roads. The RAF presence now became a communications centre with the old airfield site eventually covered with tall aerials. Over the years, those C Type hangars that survived the wartime bombing were demolished, leaving only the concrete bases. Almost all the other original buildings have gone too, save for some bomb stores just to the south of the airfield.

Although Lancasters were first issued to maritime squadrons, its successor was the Shackleton MR2 but its days at St Eval were numbered as operations were transferred to nearby St Mawgan.

In May 2015, Squadron Leader Colin Pomeroy made a nostalgic tour of St Eval with Aldon. Here he bids a final farewell to the airfield which closed its doors on March 6, 1959.

St Eval Church still overlooks the forlorn remnants of what was once one of the most distinguished stations of RAF Coastal Command and contains a number of memorials. On October 1, 1989, a stained glass window was dedicated depicting aspects of the station's history and a Book of Remembrance was raised for all air and ground personnel who lost their lives while serving here. The church also displays plaques with the badges of many of the squadrons based here. Just outside the church gates is a memorial dedicated on April 10, 2005 to all who served at St Eval. Finally, it should be remembered that the poet and author John Pudney served at RAF St Eval and wrote some of his best poems here. Perhaps one of them was the poignant 'Missing' whose last verse reads:

'For Smith, our brother,
Only son of loving mother,
The ocean lifted, stirred,
Leaving no word.'

September 1982 — Paul Francis photographed the dismantling of the hangars.

CHURCH

It was announced in August 1941 that the paint scheme for Coastal Command aircraft was to be changed to Dark Slate Grey/Dark Sea Grey on the upper surface with white fuselage sides but this obviously took time to be changed on all aircraft. Unfortunately this photograph of a Czech crew of No. 311 Squadron is undated, but the first of the squadron's aircraft to be painted in the 'Temperate Sea Scheme' was Wellington Z1111 in September 1942.

TALBENNY

Talbenny in Pembrokeshire opened on May 1, 1942 in No. 19 Group, using Dale as a satellite and with a 'Q' site decoy at Marloes. Owing to terrain constraints, the three runways were built with a central intersection, rather than the standard triangular pattern. The latter was designed to reduce the effects of bomb damage or a crashed aircraft blocking all three strips. The main runway was 1,600 yards and the two subsidiaries were both 1,100 yards. Two T2 hangars were provided, along with 36 frying-pan hardstandings. Bleak in winter but a beautiful location in summer, the airfield overlooked St Bride's Bay. With two overwater approaches to its runways, the radio call-sign was appropriately 'Blue Sea'.

The Wellingtons of No. 311 Squadron, a Czechoslovak bomber squadron, arrived in June 1942, having been transferred from Bomber Command to carry out anti-submarine patrols in the Bay of Biscay. They were supported by No. 304 Squadron's Wellingtons based at nearby Dale. The Bay was a transit area for U-Boats heading out into the Atlantic or returning to their bases in western France. Long-range fighter cover for the Wellingtons was later supplied by detachments of Beaufighters from No. 248 Squadron based at Talbenny.

The squadron's first U-Boat kill occurred on July 15, 1942 when Flying Officer Bala's crew found one and almost certainly destroyed it. Sadly, another crew failed to return that day. Another major exploit occurred on August 5 when a high-level attack was mounted against a tanker in La Pallice harbour. All available aircraft of Nos. 311 and 304 Squadrons took part and all returned safely. The same month a Talbenny Wellington attacked a U-Boat although its destruction was unconfirmed. Late in August, the second anniversary of the formation of No. 311 Squadron was marked by an inspection by General Ingr, the Czechoslovak Minister of War who was representing the Minister of National Defence, Jan Masaryk.

In September a Wellington was engaged by two Arado Ar 196 floatplanes and limped back to Talbenny with a wounded tail gunner. One of the Arados was claimed as probably destroyed.

In May 1943 the squadron turned its attention to surface ships as well as submarines, with a bombing raid on Bordeaux in January and then attacks on Biscay shipping. These attacks were carried out at night and were attempts to catch blockade-runners.

No. 4 Armament Practice Camp, also part of No. 19 Group, had transferred to Talbenny from Carew Cheriton at the end of October 1942 and gave training in anti-submarine bombing, air-to-air gunnery and air-to-surface attacks, and it remained there for the remainder of the airfield's active life. By 1944 its duties extended to training Liberator crews of the US Navy's Fleet Air Wing 7 based in Devon. Talbenny also had a secondary role as a weather diversion aerodrome owing to its favourable location on the extreme south-western tip of Wales. Notable visitors included USAAF Liberators returning from raids on French targets, a USAAF C-47 from Marrakesh, and a BOAC Liberator.

On May 26, 1943, No. 311 Squadron left for Beaulieu, leaving the station to No. 303 Ferry Training Unit's Wellingtons which had been here since March. Crews were given training and preparation were put in hand to fly Wellingtons, Warwicks and Lockheed Venturas overseas. In June 1943, the RAF was urging the Fleet Air Arm to exchange their aerodrome at St Merryn in Cornwall for Talbenny so that the former might be used for the maintenance of Liberators based at adjacent St Eval. The plan was not

Talbenny hosted the Wellingtons of the Czechoslovakian No. 311 Squadron from June 1942, but as the Poles of No. 304 also used the airfield for servicing their aircraft, it is difficult to positively identify to which unit this machine belonged, although it does still bear Bomber Command camouflage.

taken up, however, probably because it was realised that St Merryn's runways were far too short.

In October 1943, Talbenny was transferred from Coastal to Transport Command, retaining No. 4 APC as a lodger unit. No. 303 FTU disbanded into No. 11 Ferry Unit in September 1944. Replacement Wellingtons and Warwicks continued to be the main types handled, with crews being made conversant with the demands of overseas ferrying and converting on to other types of aircraft as necessary. In August 1945, No. 11 FU was transferred to Dunkeswell in Devon at which point Talbenny was reduced to Care and Maintenance under Pembroke Dock, to be finally closed in December 1946.

Most of the airfield buildings have gone and Talbenny presents a somewhat desolate aspect, although the operations block and many other buildings survive on the dispersed sites. Unfortunately a brick-built emergency field kitchen, which lay just outside the airfield perimeter and was a unique wartime relic was recently demolished. Nearby, an upright section of sewer pipe served as an ad hoc defence position.

After being de-requisitioned at the end of hostilities, the airfield was returned to the pre-war landowners, and now encompasses three farms. We were fortunate that our guide and local historian Malcolm Cullen knew the layout of the 'drome intimately. The tower, since demolished, lay on what is now Bert George's Cross Farm.

While the airfields themselves were a vital part of the system, so were the myriad number of buildings which comprised the dispersed sites. Talbenny possessed a dozen such sites containing over 250 individual buildings and we were thrilled to find many still standing even though there have been three proposals since the war to demolish them. Probably the most important is the Operations Block, still standing on what was Glebe Farm.

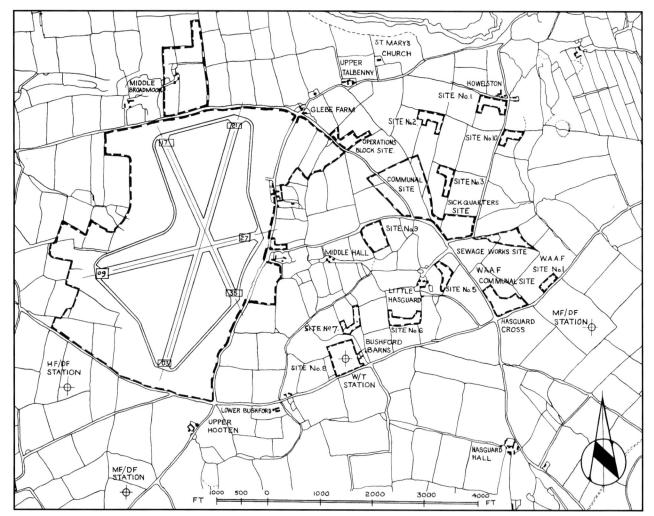

The sick bay — now owned by Redlands Farm.

The WAAF site is now Hasguard Cross Caravan Park.

The dining hall on the Communal Site is now a cold store for Pembrokeshire Foods Ltd. *After the Battle* Editor-in-Chief, Winston

Ramsey, was keen to visit Talbenny as his father was based there in 1943 and he had re-visited the airfield with him in 1956.

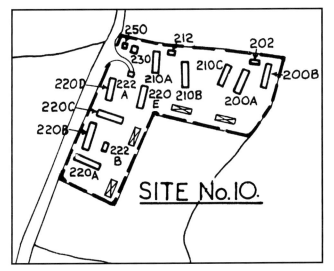

Winston's father had taken him back to Talbenny ten years after the war, driving in his old Vauxhall Wyvern to his quarters only to burst out laughing when he found the barrack hut now occupied by chickens! Winston still clearly remembered driving along a narrow lane and, by studying the wartime plan and

Google Earth, realised that they had visited Site 10 as his Dad's hut lay parallel to the road, which did not occur at any of the other accomodation sites. Even more amazing, he found that several of the huts in Site 10 still remained. 'To walk in my Dad's footsteps was a very special moment', said Winston.

He remembered that his father had gone to the first hut inside the entrance and Andrew Davies of Redlands Farm kindly came to unlock the door, since converted from the original 'porch' to

allow the access of farm machinery. 'My father told me that his bed was right here', Winston told Andrew, 'and today you have made a dream come true'.

An incredible photo with a couple of dozen aircraft dispersed around the aerodrome.

The hedge line crossing the airfield clearly denotes separate farms: to the north the ownership is split between Fred Hiam Ltd; Mr R. Reynolds and Mr Bert George, and to the south between Mr A. Mathias; Mr W. George and Mr W. Richards.

No. 311 Squadron had been formed
using Czech personnel in July 1940 at
Honington as a unit in No. 3 Group of
RAF Bomber Command, but it was transferred to Coastal Command in April
1942. For two months it was based at
Aldergrove in Northern Ireland but it
then moved to south Wales in June. On
the 25th of that month it was 'seconded'
back to Bomber Command to help make
up the numbers for a 1,000-bomber raid
which had been scheduled against Bremen that night. Churchill had insisted
that the Admiralty allow Coastal Command to participate and the command
provided 102 Hudsons and Wellingtons
which raised the total to 1,067 aircraft —
more than the first 1,000 bomber raid on
Cologne at the end of May.

In September that year, Air Vice-Marshal Geoffrey Bromet, the
Air Officer Commanding-in-Chief of No. 19 Group of Coastal
Command, visited Talbenny to decorate four members of the
squadron. Shown standing (L-R) they are: Squadron Leader
Jindrich Breitcetl, Flying Officer Václav Korda and Flight
Lieutenant Alois Sedivý who were all awarded the Distin-
guished Flying Cross, while Flight Sergeant Karel Mazurek
received the Distinguished Flying Medal. Breitcetl, by then a
Wing Commander, was lost over Biscay in Liberator BZ780 on
August 28, 1943.

OVERSEAS

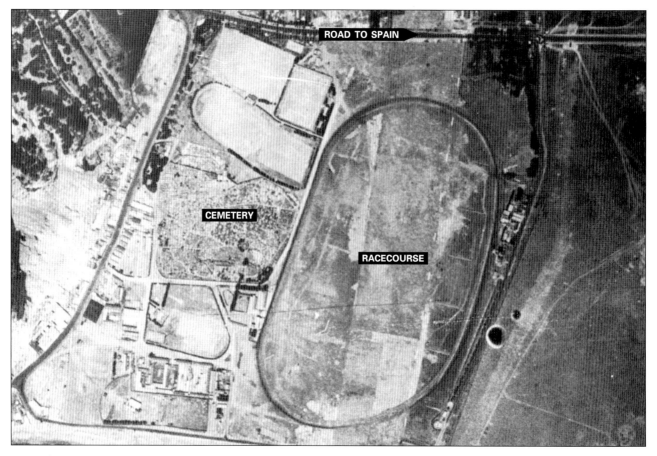

ROAD TO SPAIN

CEMETERY

RACECOURSE

When Gibraltar was ceded to Britain under the Treaty of Utrecht which ended the War of the Spanish Succession in 1713, no map was provided to delineate the border. Instead a 1,450-metre strip of the battlefield was declared neutral ground based on the range of cannons at the time. However, by 1881 the British occupation of the neutral zone extended to 800 metres from the rock face encompassing a racecourse which also served as a landing ground.

GIBRALTAR

The RAF station, sometimes known as North Front, owed its origins to a short-lived pre-war civilian airport which shared its site with a racecourse. Mussolini's activities in Abyssinia were causing some concern, so much so that early in 1932 the War Office passed on a recommendation to Gibraltar's Governor that plans should be worked out for the establishment at short notice of an airfield at Gibraltar. Local discussions were held and the conclusion was that the racecourse was the only acceptable site. However, apart from the fact that this was, in Spanish eyes, on 'neutral ground', the British Army also used the racecourse as a rifle range. Objections from this quarter were fended off by declaring that this would be an Emergency Landing Ground only. Construction work by the Royal Engineers began in September 1934. All the rails, posts and other paraphernalia of the racecourse had to be made removable to allow aircraft room to land. This would enable horse racing to be quickly restored and cause minimal disruption to the Army's equestrian sports.

In the event of a true emergency landing, for example when there was no time to take precautions on the ground, it was agreed that a pilot making a forced landing would do so as nearly as possible in the middle of the racecourse. Both pilots and army personnel were made aware of this. By March 10, 1936, the 'emergency landing ground' was fully available for the first time. The whole affair was conducted with a great deal of chicanery and a very full account of the goings-on can be found in *After the Battle* No. 21. Franco's Spanish Nationalist Government was not impressed with the scheme either but the British persisted with the ELG cover story. A proper runway had been constructed by the time the war began but it was far too short for the safe operation of Hudsons and Wellingtons.

By the 1930s it was realised that plans should be drawn up for the establishment of a permanent airfield on the Rock in view of Mussolini's activities in Abyssinia. The only acceptable site was the racecourse although the Colonial Office privately expressed doubt as to the international validity of using it, stating that the Spanish had always claimed that the neutral ground began at the foot of the Rock — not 800 metres to the north. However, as can be seen in the top photo taken in May 1940, there were already a considerable number of buildings plus a cemetery occupying the area so construction work was authorised in September 1934. Royal Engineers arrived to begin tunneling operations within the Rock to provide bomb-proof facilities while utilising the spoil to extend the runway westward into Algeciras Bay.

The runway extension crossed the Spanish Road. Meanwhile, the harbour, bottom left, was used by seaplanes.

The previously mentioned Hudsons had been detached from No. 233 Squadron in southern England since around August 1941. Early in 1942, the squadron's base was Thorney Island but most of its operations were being flown from Gibraltar. This was obviously a clumsy arrangement, so in June 1942 the whole unit settled at North Front. Here its task was to cover the convoys up the Portuguese coast, look for U-Boats and also operate over the western Mediterranean. In the autumn of 1942 it was reinforced by Hudsons from No. 608 Squadron in an effort to provide cover for the large convoys bringing the invasion force to North Africa in November. No. 179 Squadron based its Leigh Light Wellingtons from that month, attempting to bar the western end of the Mediterranean to submarines.

Gibraltar proved to be the pivotal point of the whole 'Torch' operation, its naval base and army fortress now mightily supported by the RAF aerodrome. It was only from here that aircraft could be provided to guard the convoys in their passage of the Strait and to their assault positions off the North African shore, as well as flying the anti-submarine patrols. It also provided a location for the assembly of fighter aircraft to be flown to captured airfields, and to act as a staging post for reinforcements after the landings. The following examples show the extent of the undertakings.

Work began in December 1941 to extend the runway to the west into the sea, with the aim of increasing its length to 1,550 yards using enormous quantities of spoil blasted from the Rock or dug from the defensive tunnels being prepared. An average of 7,500 tons per day was transported to the shore and then dumped into the sea to form the basis of the runway extension. The racecourse had by now been obliterated and the longer term policy, urged by Coastal Command, was to stretch the runway to 1,800 yards. By mid-January 1942, it was still only 985 yards but an undertaking was given to the Air Council that it would reach 1,150 yards by the end of April. By now, the runway crossed the road running towards the Spanish frontier, with traffic on it being controlled by the police. Petrol storage had reached a massive 5,400 tons, plus potential stowage for 10,000 tons of bombs. Aircraft parking was described simply as 'anywhere off the runway'!

The scale of air attacks on Malta was beginning to cause heavy casualties to aircraft staging through en route to the Middle East and India. The planned remedy was for aircraft to fly from Britain to Gibraltar and thence direct to Egypt. It would mean taking off from North Front with a very heavy load of petrol although this would be impossible until the runway had been extended to 1,150 yards which, after a huge effort, was achieved 27 days earlier than the original estimate. After that, the next target was the 1,550 yards required to accommodate aircraft supporting the Allied landings in North Africa. Operation 'Torch' was planned for November 1942 but of course this was a secret known only to those at high command level.

Meanwhile, a steady stream of transit aircraft had been passing through and Fleet Air Arm squadrons were based for varying periods. Coastal Command land-based types had been limited to Hudson detachments, but its flying boats had been using Gibraltar as a base since September 1939 and visited frequently before that. No. 202 Squadron began its war by covering the security of the Strait of Gibraltar, using Saro Londons. Swordfish were soon added to strength for short-range patrols, enabling the Londons to range farther afield. This obsolete type was replaced by Catalinas in May 1941. Aircraft moorings were in the north part of the harbour.

Freddie Parody, who took our comparisons, explains that the wartime flying boat base would now be several dozen yards inland due to the land that has since been reclaimed to provide a marina.

On October 28, 1942, 116 Spitfires and 13 Hurricanes in crates were shipped in. All these were erected and made operational by November 6. During that month the station's Operations Record Book noted that the following aircraft were accommodated or operated from the airfield: 450 fighters, 60 Hudsons, 36 Fleet Air Arm aircraft, 15 photographic reconnaissance aircraft, 10 amphibian Catalinas (US Navy VP-63 Squadron), eight Leigh Light Wellingtons, 20 large communications aircraft, and two meteorological Hudsons. No. 233 Squadron mounted 229 sorties during November, making eight attacks on U-Boats but losing six aircraft. No. 608 Squadron made 14 submarine attacks that month. The total air effort from Gibraltar amounted to more than 3,700 flying hours and resulted in 95 sightings and 64 attacks, causing the destruction of four U-Boats and damage to 19 others. This played a decisive part in frustrating the enemy's attempts to cripple the fleet that landed the Allied force in North Africa and its follow-up supply convoys.

With the approach of Operation 'Torch' there was an urgent need for more parking space. Here Royal Engineers work on the area east of the road to Spain.

A Hudson raises a cloud of dust from the graded dispersal park before undertaking a reconnaissance flight in August 1942.

From December 1942, No. 48 Squadron's Hudsons flew escort for the convoys to and from the forces in North Africa, as well as keeping watch on the western end of the Mediterranean, and by June 1943, rockets were being used in the attacks on U-Boats and surface vessels. The Hudsons were also having combats with Condors on the Atlantic side of their duties. As the North African campaign drew to its close and the Allies invaded Sicily, so the level of operations reduced, although there were occasional submarine attacks even in early 1944. The squadron returned to the UK in February of that year. There was then a short stay by No. 52 Squadron, equipped with Martin Baltimores. Anti-submarine patrols were flown until the unit disbanded at the end of March.

Yet another Hudson Squadron, No. 500, had been at Gibraltar covering the convoys heading for North Africa. During November, it had sunk two U-Boats and damaged another, as well as patrolling the assault beaches as the troops went in.

The road has now been widened to four lanes while in the distance lie the RAF facilities, including hangarage, workshops and the headquarters building.

In December 1941 orders were issued to extend the runway to 1,550 yards but by January the following year it was still over 500 yards short of the target length. With the landings in North Africa just months away, an undertaking was given that it would reach 1,150 yards by April and be completed to 1,550 yards by November. By July 1943 it had been extended to 1,800 yards and was now 150 feet wide.

Throughout the whole of 1943, the nominal base remained Gibraltar although most sorties were made from advanced locations along the African coast as the front line moved eastwards. No. 233 Squadron was still at Gibraltar but detached aircraft to many African locations and even some as far as the Azores to provide anti-submarine cover in the South Atlantic. In February 1944 it became non-operational and personnel left for the UK, leaving their aircraft behind. No. 179 Squadron's Wellingtons, meanwhile, had extended their night Leigh Light patrols to daylight operations. The pattern changed during 1943 to convoy escorts along the North African coast and out into the Atlantic but there were few sightings and a return was made to the UK in April 1944.

Anti-submarine patrol was now left to No. 202 Squadron that had been operating from the flying boat base since the beginning of the war. Its Catalinas had sunk at least two U-Boats and damaged many more before it moved to Northern Ireland in September

Coastal Command at Gibraltar. Crews relax on Eastern Bay — reserved for men only — as a Ventura takes off.

255

The North African operation had brought the North Front airfield to breaking point. In this picture taken at Christmas 1942 Lockheed Lightnings are crammed in with Wellngtons, Hudsons, Liberators, Mosquitos, Spitfires, Hurricanes, Marauders, Mitchells and even an Auster. A Swordfish, Argus, Halifax and Walrus can also be identified.

1944. Gibraltar's final wartime operational unit was No. 458 Squadron that arrived from an Italian base in April 1945. Regular patrols were maintained until the war ended, with enemy targets becoming few and far between, the squadron being disbanded on June 8, 1945. This left only No. 520 Squadron at North Front, a met reconnaissance unit that had formed here in September 1943 and by this time was operating Halifaxes, Spitfire and Hurricanes. Warwicks were added before it disbanded in April 1946.

The runway extension to its planned 1,800 yards had finally been completed in July 1943 and it was on the 4th of that month that General Sikorski was killed in a Liberator which crashed into the sea seconds after take off from Gibraltar. The circumstances have

remained controversial ever since and have given rise to conspiracy theories (see *After the Battle* No. 20).

From May 1948, a detachment of Halifaxes from No. 224 Squadron were based at Gibraltar for weather flights. Now equipped with Shackletons, the whole squadron moved here in August 1951, its main duty being to keep watch on naval vessels moving through the Strait but reductions in RAF strength led to the squadron disbanding in 1966. Since than there have been no based units but RAF and aircraft of other NATO nations periodically arrive for transient stopovers, exercises, or other temporary duty. Administered by British Forces Gibraltar, the station is a joint civil-military facility which also functions as Gibraltar Airport. The civilian

airport's passenger terminal building and apron facilities are located on the north side of the runway while the apron and the two re-clad wartime T2 hangars of RAF Gibraltar are located on the south side.

As an interesting footnote, US Navy Fleet Air Wing 15 based at Port Lyautey in French Morocco coordinated its anti-submarine warfare operations with RAF Gibraltar and assigned a liaison officer to Gibraltar. From the summer of 1944, Goodyear K Type non-rigid airships conducted night patrols, searching for U-Boats around the Strait of Gibraltar using Magnetic Anomaly Detection (MAD). Based at Craw Field, Port Lyautey, they were operated by Blimp Squadron ZP-14 (Blimpron 14, in USN terminology).

This picture taken in July 1944 shows a K Type non-rigid blimp of the United States Navy at North Front.

Today the eastern beach is fenced off below the flight paths, and the runway has been further extended to the west with an extra 200 yards beyond the circular radar mole. In January 1966, Spanish restrictions to the airspace around Gibraltar began when member countries of NATO were informed that any of their aircraft would not be allowed to fly over Spanish territory if bound for Gibraltar. In August the ban was extended to apply to all British military aircraft and was followed in September and October by a number of complaints about the alleged violations of Spanish airspace north of the frontier fence. A line of buoys, extending southwards across Algeciras Bay, marked the limit of Spanish waters meaning that aircraft landing from the west were required to approach from the south and make a very steep turn to line up on the runway. Most jet aircraft were forced to land off a curved path as no straight-line Instrument

Landing System approach was possible from this direction. Instead a measure of control was effected by a circular sweep radar. Approaches from the east were more normal and could be monitored by ILS although an additional hazard to aircraft landing from this direction was the Spanish TV mast erected in 1970 close by the frontier fence. The huge mass of Gibraltar can create some unusual weather phenomenon, one being caused by a southerly wind which is split by the Rock giving air currents from both ends of the runway at the same time. The unique result is that the two windsocks at either end of the airfield can point towards each other! The road to the frontier still crosses the runway and is controlled by traffic lights from the control tower. Its original name was Inundation Road, later just referred to as the Road to Spain, but now renamed Winston Churchill Avenue.

LAGENS

As early as 1941, the British Government had requested from their Portuguese counterpart information on subjects ranging from the possibility of building aerodromes in the Azores to detailed surveys of ports, highways and other infrastructure. There are nine inhabited islands in a chain stretching about 370 miles and located about 850 miles west of the Portuguese mainland. Although ostensibly neutral, Portugal was mindful of the Treaty of Peace, Friendship and Alliance with England signed in London in 1373 and renewed at intervals thereafter into the 20th century. Major examples of co-operation included Portuguese soldiers fighting with Wellington's Army in the Peninsular War and in France in the First World War. Not for nothing is Portugal known as Britain's oldest ally.

Even before Pearl Harbor, the Americans had realised the military importance of the Azores as a staging post for their bombers and transports when looking for alternatives to the winter routes to Britain. Overtures to Antonio de Olivera Salazar, the Portuguese Prime Minister, came to nothing because the US failed to realise the significance of the Anglo-Portuguese Alliance. It was not until the end of December 1943 that the Americans — to use their own words — 'came in through the back door' when Salazar agreed to them using the islands, provided the bases remained under the control of the British.

Returning to 1942, secret discussions continued throughout that year, by which time Coastal Command had become very concerned that it was unable to cover the Sierra Leone convoys for the whole of their route to England. From West Africa the Sunderlands and Hudsons could give protection for some 500 miles but then there was a gap until Catalinas from Gibraltar could meet the ships. In the final stages, once again there was a gap until the Liberators from Cornwall at 750 miles' range, and lastly the Bay patrols could give the necessary cover. A base in the Azores would solve the problem.

After long negotiations, an accord was established between Portugal and Great Britain on August 1, 1943, which conceded the facilities at Lagens for use by British forces to base their North Atlantic anti-submarine patrols. In exchange, the Portuguese received six squadrons of Hawker Hurricanes. Many more aircraft, including around 50 Spitfires, were handed over as the war progressed.

Lagens was located on Terceira, the third largest island in the group and which had a reasonable port at Angra. There was already a landing strip of packed earth and a small group of support facilities built by the Portuguese. Work started almost immediately

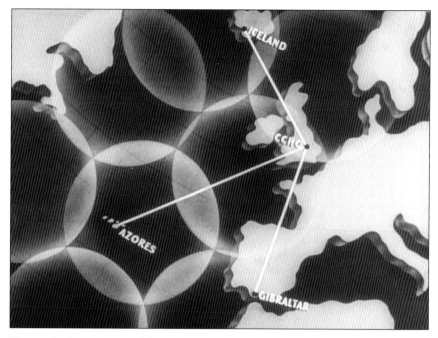

The gap in the coverage of the North Atlantic — schematically illustrated in this still from the 1944 film *RAF Coastal Command*, was solved when Portugal agreed (under the Peace Treaty signed with Britain back in the 14th century), to permit an airfield to be built in the Azores.

A site was selected in a natural valley on the island of Terceira.

The construction was a combined Portuguese-British operation with the help of local labour to 'pave' the surface of the runway with pierced steel planking.

on improving the airfield. Air Commodore R. E. Vintras describes the official opening in his book *The Portuguese Connection* (Bachman & Turner, 1974):

'By the end of October 1943, the runway on which all our hopes were pinned had been competed and its splendid 2,000 yards of pierced steel planking, put into place by all arms of the British services and the local Portuguese inhabitants was opened by His Excellency Brigadier Tamagnini Barbosa. At a signal from Air Vice-Marshal G. E. Bromet one red and one green flare was fired (the Portuguese national colours — fortunately the only colours this Verey pistol could produce) and the Governor cut with a mallet suitably painted, a tape which had been held by men of the Royal Air Force and Portuguese Army, each holding the colour of the opposite nation. A Fortress aircraft piloted by Wing Commander P. E. Hadlow, the Officer Commanding No. 220 Squadron, sealed the matter with a display of low flying.'

This squadron settled down to a routine of about 50 sorties per month, building up to an average of around 100 by the summer of 1944. It was largely monotonous patrolling, but a definite U-Boat kill was achieved on September 26, 1944, although one aircraft

The aerodrome was formerly opened by the Portugese Governor Brigadier Tamagnini Barbosa.

and crew had been lost two weeks earlier. The following month, crews were detached to the UK to convert to Leigh Light Liberators. They brought aircraft back with them to re-equip, the first Liberator operation taking place on December 4, 1944. The Fortresses were gradually replaced and by April 1945, the squadron was mounting mostly air-sea rescue sorties. With the end of the war in Europe, it returned to the UK in June.

The other long-range squadron at Lagens was No. 206, which also arrived during October 1943. Its Fortresses found some targets early in 1944 but results were inconclusive, apart from encouraging the U-Boats to stay submerged. In April 1944, the squadron returned to the UK to convert to Liberators. Also at Lagens until March 1944 for further South Atlantic coverage was a detachment of No. 233 Squadron's Hudsons from their base at Gibraltar. From March 1944, No. 269 Squadron was in the Azores taking on a composite task of anti-submarine, weather reconnaissance and air-sea rescue. The mix of types consisted of Walrus amphibians, Hudsons and Spitfires. Hudsons operated the primary weather flight function and the Spitfires, rather bizarrely, were used for submarine hunts! The Hudsons also carrried airborne lifeboats and successfully dropped one to a downed Liberator crew in July 1944.

In October, Warwicks replaced the Hudsons for the ASR work and also flew anti-submarine operations. The Spitfires now carried out twice daily meteorological flights which continued into 1945. Because of the amount of transatlantic flying immediately post-war, the squadron remained on ASR and met duties until May 10, 1946 when it disbanded at Lagens.

Also worthy of mention are two Wellington detachments, the first from No. 172 Squadron and the second from No. 179 Squadron for roughly the same period between November 1943 and April 1944.

Going back to December 1, 1943, British and US military representatives had signed a joint agreement outlining the roles and responsibilities for the United States Army Air Forces (USAAF) and United States Navy (USN) at Lagens. The agreement established guidelines and limitations for the ferrying of aircraft and use by transport aircraft to the United Kingdom via Lagens. In return, the US agreed to assist the British in improving and extending existing facilities. US Air Transport Command C-54 Skymasters began staging through soon afterwards.

Then as now, Lagens strategic location midway between North America and Europe performs a vital role for NATO. Officialy renamed Portugese Air Base No. 4, the main runway has since been extended to over 10,000 feet.

By the end of June 1944, more than 1,900 American aircraft had passed through the Azores. Using Lagens — or Lajes Field, as the Americans preferred to call it — the flying time relative to the usual transatlantic route via Brazil and West Africa was nearly cut in half from 70 to 40 hours.

Lajes Field was one of the two stopover and refueling bases for the first transatlantic crossing of non-rigid airships (blimps) in 1944. The US Navy sent six Goodyear-built K-ships from Naval Air Station South Weymouth in Massachusetts to their first stopover base at Naval Station Argentia, Newfoundland, and then on to Lajes Field in the Azores before flying to their final destination at Port Lyautey in French Morocco.

Robert Chandler, in his memoir of an aircraft radio operator *Off the Beam* (David Rendel, 1970) wrote: 'We landed at Lagens about midday; it was a fine, wide airfield, completely equipped with all the then known radio aids and with accommodation to handle plenty of transient crews. The single runway was laid with PSP and the aircraft were parked along taxiways parallel with this. Several of us decided to do the tiny town of Angra. We loaded up on a jolting bullock cart and set off. The town had a small square and a few shops but you could sense we were far from welcome. The whole island was desperately poor and seemed numbed from the catastrophic impact of this big base being dumped in their midst.

Ted Hedges, a 19-year old Fortress Flight Engineer with No. 220 Squadron formed a different opinion: 'For the next nine months I met and lived amongst a very poor but happy and kind people. Terceira is a very beautiful island and we found that in the midst of such people and the beauty surrounding us it was possible to do our operational duty despite the stresses and strains of our flying.'

Local living standards vastly improved once the military presence became more established. For the people of Lagens, a new village was created, with its own public laundry and in its village square a drinking fountain bearing the inscription in Portuguese: 'This fountain is erected for the people of Aldeia Nova de Lagens by the British and American Forces, 1945'. The Lajes War Cemetery is maintained in the usual superb condition by the Commonwealth War Graves Commission. Of its 46 graves, 42 are of Royal Air Force personnel.

By war's end, the airfield had three concrete runways and became a base for the Portuguese Air Force, along with the USAF and a US Navy Air Facility as tenants. During the Cold War it supported rotational detachments of US Navy maritime patrol aircraft that would track Soviet attack, guided

From wartime . . . to peacetime . . . to the present day.

missile, and ballistic missile submarines in the region. Lajes handled the large airlift during the Gulf War and on the first day of the deployment over 90 aircraft passed through. The civilian terminal also plays an important role for passenger and cargo airliners and private jets flying to the island or beyond.

US Marine Corps F/A-18 Hornets from Marine Fighter Attack Squadron 115 stopover to refuel in October 2013.

REYKJAVIK

German interest in Iceland in the 1930s, previously almost non-existent, began with friendly soccer matches and culminated in 1938 with a team of German gliding enthusiasts arriving on the island with gliders and a tow-plane. This was a perfect ploy, in British eyes, for compiling maps and discovering suitable landing grounds. A 'suspicious' number of German anthropology teams also arrived to survey the island and Lufthansa airlines attempted — unsuccessfully — to establish an air service. U-Boats visited Reykjavik, as did the cruiser *Emden*. Commercial trade between the countries also increased dramatically. By the time the war started, the British government had become increasingly concerned that Germany would soon try to establish a military presence in Iceland which would obviously have presented an intolerable threat to British control of the North Atlantic. At the same time, Britain was eager to obtain bases in Iceland for maritime patrol, so pre-emptive plans were drawn up.

On May 10, 1940, British military forces began an invasion of Iceland when they sailed into Reykjavik harbour in Operation 'Fork'. The force — consisting of 746 marines, ill-equipped and only partially trained — was obviously insufficient to defend an island of Iceland's size and a week later, 4,000 British Army troops arrived to relieve the marines. They were soon reinforced by Canadian Army units. The Government of Iceland issued a protest against what it called a 'flagrant violation' of Icelandic neutrality and an infringement of its independence. The British promised compensation, favourable business agreements, non-interference in Icelandic affairs, and the withdrawal of all forces at the end of the war. On the day of the invasion, Prime Minister Hermann Jónasson read a radio announcement telling Icelanders to treat the British troops with the politeness due to guests. A year later, the Americans offered to take over the defence of Iceland and this was eagerly accepted by Churchill. The Allied occupation of Iceland was destined to last throughout the war.

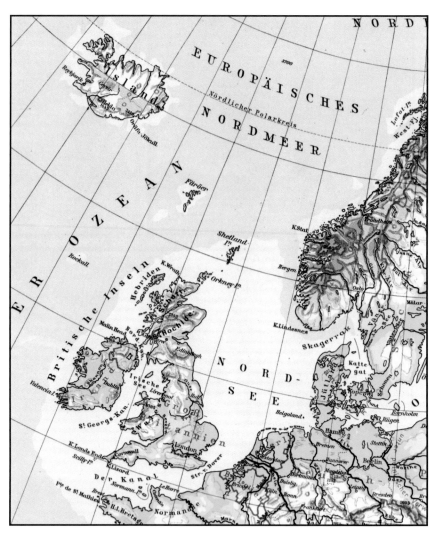

In May 1940, when attacks by Germany on France, Belgium, Denmark and Norway broke the eight-month hiatus of the 'Phoney War', Britain was already looking at the wider picture to obtain bases in Iceland which would give a huge strategic advantage in the coming war against the U-Boat.

On May 10 British forces landed in Reykjavik, the capital of Iceland. The existing airfield there was boggy grass so work began immediately on constructing hard runways, two of which finished up extra wide at 100 yards.

In August 1941, Winston Churchill travelled to Newfoundland to confer with President Roosevelt, a meeting which motivated the 'Atlantic Charter', a statement between Britain and the United States which defined Allied goals for the post-war world.

On his return voyage in the battleship HMS *Prince of Wales*, Churchill broke his journey at Iceland. Here he inspects British troops *(left)* and American Marines *(right)*, the latter still wearing their WWI-style uniforms and helmets.

Construction of naval facilities at Hvalfordhur began soon after the occupation and these gradually grew into a large and important complex. As such, it served as a well-defended base for Allied escort and anti-submarine forces. The British air presence on Iceland began with Walrus amphibians of 710 Squadron, Fleet Air Arm, which were stationed at Reykjavik. The city's grass-surfaced airport had a troubled history with boggy ground and would need considerable development. Work began in October 1940 when the Black Watch Regiment built the first runway, constructing a concrete surface over sunken oil barrels. Three more were added later, the lengths being 1,570, 1,110, with two of 1,000 yards. Although one had the standard width of 50 yards, the other three were 100 yards wide, perhaps to reduce the possibility of straying off the paved area and bogging down. In the early days, the sole hangarage was a large blister, 250ft by 110ft.

Nissen huts in various sizes served for technical and administrative purposes, barracks, mess halls and other communal buildings. For insulation, the barrack huts were lined with half-inch thick wood pulp panels. A veteran recalled: 'Much of our off duty time was spent in the hut where we would write letters home and play cards. We had a radio driven by a car battery and during the winter months we could receive medium wave stations from both the UK and America, but in summer only Radio Reykjavik and short-wave stations could be received. We had a free cigarette ration of 200 a month, along with some chocolate. The food in camp was not wonderful with porridge occasionally tainted with paraffin and Icelandic mutton alternating with Maconochie's tinned meat and vegetable ration, by no means our favourite dish. Occasionally there was Icelandic rhubarb and when the bread ran out, as it often did, we were fed hard biscuits.'

Until more progress was made with runway construction and the creation of an entirely new base at Kaldadarnes, a flying boat base was established on Skerjafjordur.

This is a stretch of water immediately adjacent to the perimeter of Reykjavik airport, where the remains of a wooden slipway can still be seen. Mooring rings were available near the airfield and also in the two sheltered inlets at the head of the fjord. In July 1940, Nos. 204 and No. 210 Squadron detached Sunderlands to Reykjavik. The whole of No. 204 Squadron moved to Iceland in April 1941 in order to patrol the gap between the island and the Denmark Strait. The Sunderlands also flew a survey of the country for landmarks and possible alighting areas. The stay was a short one, however, and the squadron moved to Gibraltar in July.

The MV *Manela* and her sister ship *Dumana* had been purpose built for RAF flying boat maintenance on the Indian coast during the pre-war period. Now *Manela* found herself moored up in Iceland for similar duties. When her ballast tanks were flooded, the ship sank low enough in the water to enable aircraft equipped with beaching gear to be towed and secured in the

Reykjavik Airport today still uses the wartime runways. Note the T2 hangar.

Armstrong Whitworth Whitleys were the backbone of No. 612 Squadron when it alternated between Reykjavik and St Eval in 1941-42.

aft part of the vessel — similar in layout to a dry dock. When the tanks were pumped out, the vessel rose sufficiently out of the water to enable major aircraft servicing to be carried out as if it were on dry land. The personnel, equipment, and the various sections of No. 204 Squadron were all provided with quite reasonable working quarters, throughout the ship, sleeping in hammocks being a new experience for the airmen.

The next squadron to be posted in was No. 209, one of whose Catalinas accounted for a U-Boat on August 25. Two more attacks took place with no definite result before the squadron returned to the UK in October 1941. Going back to that year, No. 330 Squadron had been formed at Reykjavik from Norwegian personnel who had escaped and trained in Canada. They were to be equipped with 18 Northrop N3-PB seaplanes ordered by the Norwegian Government before the war. First operation took place on June 23, a night convoy escort. A rapid build-up resulted in 'B' Flight forming and moving to Akureyri Harbour on the north coast. At the end of August a U-Boat was depth-charged with unknown results but a day later another crew did the same and had the satis-faction of seeing it surrender to a destroyer. 'C' Flight formed in December and moved to the port of Budareyri on the east coast.

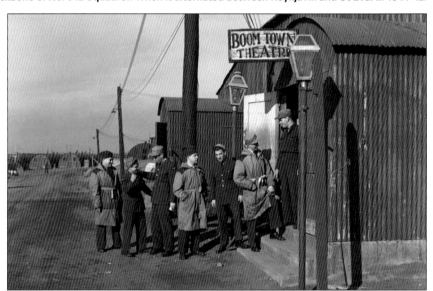

The Canadian No. 162 Squadron was seconded to Coastal Command in January 1944 to cover the mid-ocean portion of the North Atlantic from what they called Camp Maple Leaf in Reykjavik. These men are queuing to see the latest American film in the cinema inherited from the US Navy's 'Camp Quitcherbeliakin'.

The Cansos were sheltered from the violent storms which assail Iceland in this T2 hangar.

A recent highlight was the arrival of the Avro Lancaster owned by the Canadian Warplane Heritage Museum when it staged through Iceland on its visit to Britain in August 2014.

Reykjavik airfield, also known as Corbett Camp, had been occupied by Hurricanes of No. 1423 Fighter Flight since June 1941. By September it was ready to accept larger aircraft, the first being Wellingtons of No. 221 Squadron from Northern Ireland. Five attacks on submarines were made during August and one was claimed as damaged. No. 221 Squadron returned to the UK in December 1941, handing over anti-submarine duties to No. 612 Squadron's Whitleys. Little action took place and the squadron moved to southern England in August 1942. No. 330 Squadron had continued to operate but, from Coastal Command's point of view, the Northrops were considered unsuitable for operations and conversion to Hudsons was planned. However, it was decided that the squadron should receive Catalinas instead, but few were available so the Northrops had to soldier on for the moment alongside the two Catalinas that were allocated. Apart from the Northrop Flight which remained in Iceland until April, the bulk of the squadron moved to Scotland in January 1943.

'Iceland was hardly a health resort', as Air Chief Marshal Sir Philip Joubert de la Ferté wrote in *Birds and Fishes* (Hutchinson, 1960). 'On one occasion a gale blew up that had remarkable consequences. On Reykjavik airfield a number of Whitleys were parked. Firmly anchored down to heavy weights, and with their controls locked, they seemed safe enough. As the wind increased further precautions had to be taken. First thirty men per aircraft were assembled as anchorage. Then the engines had to be started to keep the machines from being blown backwards. Meanwhile the watch hut had left its moorings and was last seen proceeding airborne out over Reykjavik Bay. A letter from the Group Commander to the C-in-C recorded that, at the moment of writing, large sheets of corrugated iron, petrol cans, and other heavy objects were literally flying past his office window.'

Nature struck again on a much larger scale when early in March 1943, a river flood engulfed RAF Kaldadarnes, forcing a mass evacuation to Reykjavik. The refugees included No. 269 Squadron which, even after their station dried out, decided to stay put! May proved a record month for the squadron with a total of 13 submarine attacks. In August, the Hudsons began to carry underwing rockets and this bore fruit on October 5 when they were used to sink a U-Boat. No. 269 Squadron returned to the UK in January 1944.

A detachment of No. 120 Squadron's Liberators had been here since September 1942 and in April 1943 the whole squadron moved in from Northern Ireland. U-Boat sightings proved relatively few until October, which was a record month, with 20 attacks and three definitely destroyed. In January 1944, the first Leigh Lights were introduced on Liberator Mk. Vs and the squadron turned primarily to night attacks. A move was made back to Northern Ireland in March 1944, the replacement being No. 86 Squadron whose Liberators took over anti-submarine and escort sorties. On May 4, Pilot Officer J. C. Green scored the squadron's first U-Boat kill.

After No. 86 Squadron moved to Scotland in July, No. 53 Squadron was its successor, again using Liberators for mid-Atlantic patrols. There was comparatively little action and in March 1945 the Leigh Lights were removed and the unit reverted to solely daylight operations. April brought 107 operational sorties with two U-Boat attacks, after which it was mainly tasked with searching for surrendered U-Boats along with Greenland weather reconnaissance.

A long-term resident was No. 1407 Meteorological Flight, which formed in October 1941 with Hudsons for North Atlantic weather flights. Hampdens were added later but proved unsuitable so were replaced by Venturas. The flight was re-designated No. 251 Squadron on August 1, 1944 and it had a secondary role as an air-sea rescue unit. It disbanded in October 1945. A dedicated rescue squadron, No. 279, had kept detachments here at various times between 1941 and 1944. RAF Reykjavik's last resident unit was a detachment of No. 280 Squadron's Warwicks from January until June 1946, after which it returned to the UK for disbandment.

The airfield was handed back to the Icelandic Government on July 6, 1946, being developed into a fine airport for the city. Unfortunately, the urban area has grown around it, which is considered inconvenient by many for noise and safety reasons and because it takes up a lot of valuable space in a central location. However this central position is also the reason why many others want to keep the airport where it is, as it is a vital link between the capital and the sparsely populated regions in the rest of the country. The alternative international airport at Keflavik is 31 miles away. And so the debate continues.

Although replaced by a modern building, the wartime control tower still exists as office accommodation. An original T2 hangar houses aircraft on the southern perimeter, close to the remains of the slipway. In this area, there is also what looks like a watch office for the flying boat base. Just to the east of the airport, in the Fossvogur Cemetery, the Commonwealth War Graves plot has a memorial to two crews of No. 251 Squadron who failed to return from weather reconnaissance flights. There is also a memorial to all British and American forces stationed in Iceland during the war. It was unveiled by the Duke of Kent on September 12, 2007.

KALDADARNES

On August 27, 1941, Squadron Leader James Thompson, captain of a Hudson of No. 269 Squadron based at Kaldadarnes, claimed a unique first when he captured a U-Boat 80 miles south of Iceland.

Perhaps the bleakest of all Coastal Command stations, Kaldadarnes was located on the southern bank of the River Ölfusá, about 25 miles south-east of Iceland's capital, Reykjavik. When British forces occupied the country in May 1940, pre-empting any German attempt to do the same, the existing Reykjavik airfield was found to be entirely inadequate without reconstruction. While the work was going on, Kaldarnes was identified as one of the very few possible makeshift landing sites in the south of the island. Preparation and construction began almost immediately and on August 27, the Battles of No. 98 Squadron landed on the far-from-complete airfield, having been escorted from Scotland to Iceland by two Sunderlands.

A single runway had been finished and eventually there were three, their lengths being 1,200, 1,026 and 1,000 yards. The work was a combined effort by Army units, including the Royal Engineers and Pioneer Corps. On June 5, 1941, RAF Kaldadarnes was formally established but it was not until the end of July that all three runways were operational. A description of the base in official records dated December 1, 1942 states that 'the ground at the sides of the runways has not been prepared and aircraft which leave a runway are in danger of being bogged. The site is subject to flooding during the winter months on an average of once in two years, due to the river backing up when ice becomes jammed in its mouth.' This cautionary note proved true, as we shall see.

In June 1941, No. 269 Squadron moved in from Wick and began to patrol the Atlantic gap with its Hudsons. These aircraft were able to provide cover for convoys following a great circle track from Halifax, Nova Scotia to the UK. They were able also to escort convoys for the first 150 miles from Reykjavik to Murmansk and Archangel. All Hudson aircrews crossing the Arctic Circle were presented with a 'Blue Nose Certificate' by Coastal Command.

U-Boat attacks began almost immediately and on August 27 Squadron Leader James Thompson made RAF history by becoming the first aircraft captain to have a U-Boat — in this case U-570 — surrender to him. After severe damage was inflicted by a depth-charge, it seems that the inexperienced crew

U-570 had been launched from the Blohm & Voss shipyard in Hamburg in April 1941, being commissioned the following month. On her maiden voyage, Kapitänleutnant Hans-Joachim Rahmlow was ordered to patrol the area south of Iceland. Thompson caught the submarine semi-submerged and straddled her with four depth-charges. The U-Boat promptly surfaced and the crew raised a white flag. Rahmlow radioed his situation to

Germany whereupon Admiral Dönitz ordered other U-Boats to the rescue but, at the same time, Admiral Percy Noble at Western Approaches Command despatched several ships while a Catalina from No. 209 Squadron kept watch overhead. After much difficulty, the U-Boat was boarded, taken in tow and beached in Iceland. The exploit earned both Thompson and his navigator, Flying Officer John Coleman, a Distinguished Flying Cross.

The *U-570* was commissioned into the Royal Navy as HMS *Graph* on September 19 and, after having been made seaworthy, was sailed to Barrow-in-Furness to be repaired in the Vickers dry-dock. However, due to the damage she had suffered, four torpedoes were found to be trapped in their tubes, Lieutenant Martin Johnson being awarded the George Medal for rendering them safe. The Kriegsmarine had no idea of the fate of the U-Boat, that is until the press reported its arrival in Britain on October 3. They also could not be certain if the Enigma code machine had been captured so new code-settings were issued in November. In actual fact, the machine had been thrown overboard although important encryption signals with their corresponding plain language texts were recovered and were of great value to British code-breaking efforts. Following its repair, an exhaustive examination was carried out to determine every apect of the performance of the U-Boat — a Type VIIC — one important discovery being the maximum depth she could dive — some 60 metres below the setting of Royal Navy depth-chargers.

The *Graph* carried out three war patrols before being laid up for lack of spare parts. In March 1944, while being towed to the Clyde for scrapping, the tow parted and she ran aground on the Isle of Islay. The wreck was finally salvaged in 1947.

panicked, believing that poisonous chlorine gas from overturned batteries was about to kill them. The watertight door to the engine compartment was sealed and the U-Boat had no choice but to surface. As soon as it did so, the hatches were flung open and the crew ran to the guns. Amidst the heavy seas rolling the submarine, they quickly realised that they could not effectively defend the boat. The Hudson was already coming round for another run and the U-Boat captain knew that another attack would finish them off although, unbeknown to him, the Hudson had already used all its weapons. A white sheet was waved from the conning tower and seeing this the Hudson crew radioed for additional aircraft and for a ship to come to the scene. A Catalina soon arrived and then a naval vessel which towed the U-Boat to Iceland and beached it to prevent it sinking. (Thompson and his navigator/bomb-aimer, Flying Officer John Coleman, were subsequently awarded the DFC.)

Ice reconnaissance was also part of the squadron's duties — keeping an eye on the extent of the icebergs for shipping information. For the first part of 1942, bad weather hindered operations and it was not until July that the next U-Boat attack took place that was claimed as a probable. At the end of that month, anti-submarine 'fan' patrols were begun, so called because they fanned out south-eastward from Iceland to link up with similar patrols working north-westward from Scotland. This enlarged the scope of the Northern Transit Offensive which now extended from the narrows between Shet-

land and Norway right round to a line joining Iceland and Ireland. In September three U-Boats were found and attacked but two Hudsons and crews were lost. On October 5 a U-Boat was confirmed destroyed.

Despite the weather in January 1943, 159 sorties were flown and a detachment was sent to Bluie West One on the west coast of Greenland, in an attempt to close the Atlantic gap still further. Known today as Narsarsuak but with its wartime code-name commemorated by the international designation BGBW, this was — and still is — a very challenging airfield. Situated at the head of a lengthy fjord, with a uni-directional runway because of high ground at one end, a wireless operator with No. 269 Squadron described it as 'a ghastly place'. The treacherous weather caused the loss of two Hudsons which were trying to get back into Bluie West One on March 1 and the following month the detachment was withdrawn to Iceland.

Andrew Hendrie wrote in *Seek and Strike, the Lockheed Hudson in World War II* (William Kimber, 1983) 'At Kaldadarnes, the accommodation for crews was in Nissen huts which were anchored down with hawsers and by earth which was banked halfway up the sides to provide additional stability and insulation against the winds which could reach 120 mph. Heating was provided by the usual RAF stove, but fuel was rationed and insufficient. Some crews were able to obtain a "pot belly" stove with a load of fuel from the American Army and some RAF personnel bartered spirits for additional items of food. There were no laundry

facilities and washing was done in peaty, brackish water. By 1942 a cinema had been constructed using petrol tins filled with earth. Special clothing had been issued for non-flying wear, including double-lined coats and boots which were designed to withstand the harsh conditions.'

Early in 1942, No. 5021 Airfield Construction Squadron, RAF, formed in Iceland to take over from the Royal Engineers all civil and mechanical engineering works required by the RAF on the island. One of their minor jobs, a Nissen hut extension to the Officers Mess at Kaldadarnes, was due to be opened by Air Commodore HRH The Duke of Kent, but he was killed on August 25, 1942 in a Sunderland crash en route to Iceland from Oban. The Duke was in the Welfare Section of the RAF Inspector General's Staff. In this role he went on official visits to RAF bases to help boost wartime morale.

On March 6, 1943 the nearby river overflowed and flooded the airfield to a depth of two feet or more. The USAAF, which by now had taken over the air defence of Iceland, flew its local detachment of P-39 Airacobras back to base and No. 269 Squadron relocated to RAF Reykjavik. Although Kaldadarnes dried out after a few weeks and was declared operational, No. 269 Squadron remained at Reykjavik. It was found later that the floodwaters had undercut one of the runways and done other damage. Reconstruction was not considered a cost-effective option so the airfield was to be abandoned and on November 30 RAF Kaldadarnes was officially closed.

Shots of Kaldadarnes were included in *Coastal Command*, directed by Jack Holmes of the Crown Film Unit, which was released to cinema audiences in Britain in November 1942. Although predominantly featuring the Sunderlands at RAF Bowmore (see page 34), a second camera unit was sent to Iceland to film with the Hudsons of No. 269 Squadron.

One particular machine was a Mk III serial T9465, coded N-UA, also being identified by the legend on its fuselage: *Spirit of Lockheed and Vega Employees*. She joined the squadron in May 1941, staying with them for 13 months before being transferred to No. 161 (Special Duties) Squadron at Tempsford. She was written off in a crash in July 1943.

We also get a glimpse in the film of the American participation at Kaldadarnes with shots of Curtiss P-40C Warhawks.

The RN Air Section Kaldadarnes had been shut down some months earlier. Its purpose was to hold a strategic reserve of replacement aircraft to replenish squadrons on the American-built escort carriers. Atlantic convoys were now covered by naval aircraft for the whole of the crossing. The section's two hangars could accommodate 12 Swordfish, and up to 100 ratings and six officers could be accommodated on site. It had seen relatively little use, apart from a few short stops by aircraft flown ashore from carriers.

In 1943 Icelandic labour was used to dismantle many of the airfield buildings, including a hangar, and move them to Meeks Field, Keflavik. The runways continued to be used during the early years of Icelandic aviation before being abandoned. It is now a scene of desolation with a few ruined buildings and lengths of rusty PSP sticking out of the ground. From the air the runways can be made out but are covered with a very thick layer of grass and moss.

Kaldadarnes in its heyday . . . a bleak, barren landscape battered by icy winds and frequent storms.

At the small flying club airfield at Selfoss a few miles east of the remains of Kaldadarnes is a memorial to No. 269 Squadron. It was financed by Air Atlanta Icelandic and was unveiled by the British Ambassador in the presence of ten ex-members of the squadron and various Icelandic dignitaries on August 10, 1999. The memorial itself is a carefully selected dolorite rock with a copper wind-vane sculpture depicting the three runways at Kaldadarnes. Each of the ten veterans then planted a semi-circle of Sitka spruce around the memorial.

Mention should be made of two Emergency Landing Grounds (ELGs) prepared for use by Coastal Command at Hofn and Oddi. The former, on the south-east coast, was a level area of grey volcanic dust with the landing area marked by white painted petrol tins along the boundaries. Transport to Hofn town was by means of a motor launch! A small single runway airport is now on or near the wartime site. Oddi, about 20 miles south-east of Kaldadarnes had three runways, the longest being 1,000 yards, of 'rolled natural lava dust', again marked by white petrol tins.

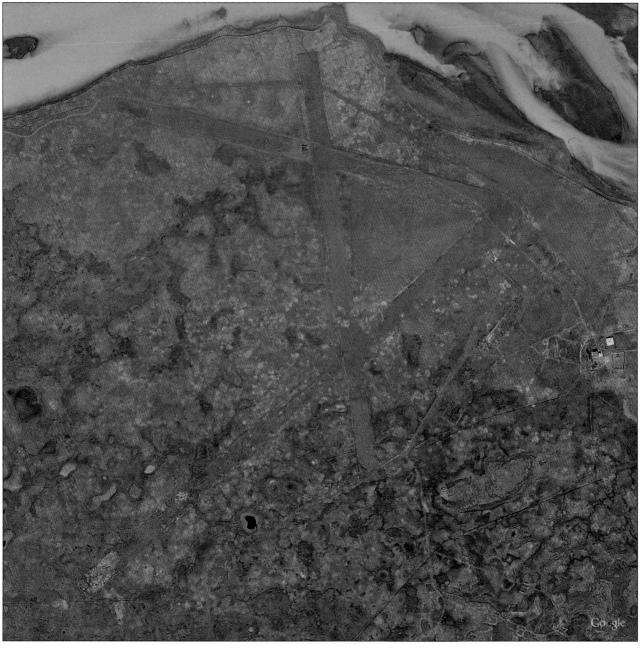

Nature is now claiming back what was rightfully hers as the outline of the airfield steadily merges into the landscape.

With six years of war coming to an end, for those who had come through a group photograph was a bitter-sweet memory with so many friends and colleagues lost along the way. Squadron associations might keep the memories alive but because of the multi-national make up of the Scottish strike wings, the members dispersed to the four corners of the world, seldom to meet up again. *Above:* **This is the Banff Strike Wing, poignantly captioned in the squadron records: 'Some of those who took part'.**

POSTSCRIPT

They pushed their way forward, hoping to find seats. Piles of equipment of all kinds barred their passage. Soldiers were jammed with airmen, ATS, Marines, WAAFs, and WRENs; Home Guard, Civil Defence. They passed through a corridor of Poles; a coach of Dutch, and mixed carriages of English, French, Scots, Welsh, Czechs. There were Canadian troops and Newfoundland foresters; New Zealand and Australian pilots and Norwegian air crews; and Rhodesian cadets, Greek sailors, Belgian airmen. They came to a car of Americans. They could tell, by the shaking of the train, that they had reached the end of it. 'There's no hope of a seat, the train's crammed. We'll have to stand.'

There were farms, lanes, fields. The train intermingled with the country like a stave of music. The bars of the line made a rhythm of their own. The railway forked, joined, and the train moved on.

At Birmingham they changed. They had seats in the new train. From the Y.M.C.A. they had bought sandwiches, rolls, buns; tea, matches, cigarettes. Their funds were low, but they still had a few shillings.

Members of No. 455 Squadron of the Royal Australian Air Force based at Dallachy pictured just after VE-Day. Ian Murray, standing directly behind the airman in the light-coloured RAF uniform in the centre of the picture, sent this photo from Australia. He notes in his caption that his navigator Don Mitchell stands on his right.

Now war is over and the time has come to go home. Kitbags have been packed and airmen await the train on Spey Bay Station, Dallachy. Then, the line along the coast was run by the London and North Eastern Railway, but the line closed on May 6, 1968. The track was lifted soon after but rather fortunately the station building survived as a private dwelling. With the removal of the LNER-style passenger foot-bridge, John Gray had to picture it from ground level.

The train kept chattering to the country as it passed by. There was a great migration of wings with lights and flares. He saw his footsteps walking, their imprints fading while the sun peeled back the clouds from the sky. His youth had ended. He had lived so thoroughly that a century's growth had bloomed.

The train rattled on. Now the suburbs swelled. There was a rapid concentration of buildings as the country disappeared.

They stepped out of the train and passed through the station into a yard. Here buses were lined up. The bus was quiet. It was still empty on top. They went up the High Street. A crater gaped in the shops, they were sliced like cheese. There were other holes. 'They've copped it there! That was Boots, the Chemists . . . that was the Town Hall.' Small shops had fallen down, there were boarded windows. Houses were propped by stays.

They turned a corner, this was the road. Gingerly we walk through the gate and ring the bell and wait. Will she think it a telegram? What will she say, do, think? She will come to the door and Mother will wish to know more than we can tell. She will ask questions yet she will know only that we are safe . . . and have returned.

ARTHUR GWYNN-BROWNE, 1945

The crew of a Bristol Beaufighter of No. 144 Squadron based at Tain, Ross-shire. The 'Torbeau' was armed with the Mk XII aerial torpedo.

Photographic Credits

Australian War Memorial: 2-3, 98 top, 213 centre, 214 top and centre, 215 top left, 219 top left, 220 top, 221 top left, bottom left, 222 bottom. **Author's Collection:** 24 top. **Steve Branley:** 59 bottom. **Deric Brock:** 186 top. **Robin Brooks:** 88 top and centre, 90, 228 top and centre. **Bill Charlton:** 169 bottom left. **Construction Industry Training Board:** 83 top left. **Malcolm Cullen:** 198 top, 199 top left and right. **Tom Dolezal:** 244 top and bottom, 249 top and bottom. **Roy Dunstan:** 236 centre. **Aldon Ferguson:** 28 top, 41 bottom, 61 top, 62 top, 68 top, 70 centre, 77 top and bottom left, 78 top and bottom left, 80 top left and centre, 81 top left, 95 top left and right, 102 top and bottom, 104 top, 105 top and centre, 106 bottom, 107 top, 109 top, 112 top, 114 top and centre, 119 top, 120 top left, 122 bottom left and right, 123 top, 126 top left, 134 top, centre and bottom left, 136 top, 137 centre, 139 top, 140 top, 141 top left, 142 top left, centre, bottom left, 144 top, 148 top, 150 bottom, 151 centre, 154 top, 159 bottom left, 172 bottom, 176 top and centre, 177 top left and centre left and right, 178 top and bottom left, 179 top left, centre and bottom left, 191 top and centre, 227 top, 231 top left, 239 bottom, 242 top and bottom, 243 top left, 272, 273, 280. **Paul Francis:** 243 centre. **Friends of New Forest Airfields:** 210 top, bottom left and right, 211 top and centre. **Ken Galloway:** 56 top. **Wing Commander Hugh Garlick:** 162 top, 163

top. **John Gray:** 271 bottom. **P.H.T. Green:** 103 top. **Peter Gunn:** 83 bottom, 84 top right and bottom, 85 both, 86 top and bottom, 87 top right, 92 bottom right, 93 top right, 96 bottom, 98 bottom. **Geoffrey Hall:** 91 both. **Google Earth:** images reproduced under licence. **Hooton Park Trust:** 44 bottom. **Imperial War Museum:** Front Cover (TR1082), 8 top left (HU 84645), 10 bottom left (CH20397), bottom right (CH10674), 22 top (CH9612), 24 bottom (CH18031), 30 bottom (CH11101), 58 top (CH14814), 59 top (CH14815), 62 centre (CH2446), 76 top (CH8089), 82 bottom (CH283), 83 top (ATP10574-B), 96 top (HU81248), 100 bottom (CH1854), 108 bottom left (CH4772), 110-111 (HU91255), 124 top (CH17876), 125 top (HU90824), 135 bottom (CH17422), 146 bottom left (CH864), 148 centre (CH859), bottom (CH840), 158 centre (C5355), 172 top (CH62), 173 bottom (CH41), 180-181 (HU91262), 187 top (CH1079), 192 top (CH12779), 209 top (CH10434), 213 top left (H254), 217 centre (HU91251), 219 centre (CH4355), 229 top (CH18219), 231 centre left (CH18732), right (CH18734), 232 top (CH7710), 233 (CH7709), 237 top (CH1599), 253 centre (CM6527), 261 top (CH9), 263 top left (A4976), right (A4962), 264 top (CS249), 266 top (CS112), 272 (CH9765). **Colin Jeffries:** 118 bottom. **Jozef Krzywonus:** 196 bottom, 197 top. **Greg Morss:** 31 bottom, 33 bottom. **Ian Murray:** 270 bottom, 271 top right. **Bobby Nelson:** 166 top right. **No. 304 Squadron:** 193 top left and right, centre left. **Neil Owen:** 147 all. **Freddie Parody:** 253 bottom, 254 bottom. **Picture Partnership:** 7.

Plymouth Yacht Haven: 212 bottom. **Poole Flying Boats Celebration:** 204 bottom, 205 top left, centre left, 206 bottom left, 207 top right, centre and bottom. **Public Archives of Canada:** 5, 19, 20-21, 40 top, 42 top and bottom, 92 top, 108 top left, top right, 164 top, 200 top, 238 centre left, centre right, 264 centre and bottom. **John Quinn:** 51 centre and bottom. **RAF Museum:** 64, 65 top, 133 top, 212 top, 215 bottom left, 258 bottom left and right, 259 top and centre, 268 bottom. **Samuel Sjoberg:** 156 top, 157 top, 158 top left and right, bottom, 159 centre and bottom right, 162 bottom, 163 bottom. **Ian Smiles:** 168. **Brian Stafford:** 100 top, 102 centre, 103 centre and bottom. **Sunderland Flying Boat Trust:** 217 top left, 218 top, 222 top, 224 top, 225 centre left and right, bottom left and right. **William Sutherland:** 174 bottom. **Wojtek Szczepanik:** 201 top left, centre, bottom left. **Les Taylor:** 116 top, 117 top, 118 top and centre, 121 top right. **The SCAPE Trust:** 63 all, 126 bottom, 131 bottom left. **David Thompson:** 170 both. **Thornaby Town Council:** 171. **Tiree Historical Centre:** 66 bottom. **Robert Truman:** 47 top left, 48 bottom left, 66 top, 69 bottom left, 84 centre left and right, 92 bottom left, 104 bottom left and right, 116 bottom left, 126 top right, 183 top right, 187 bottom left, 195 top left. **Ken Tyrrell:** 203 centre. **Ulster Aviation Society:** 23 top, 25 top, bottom left and right, 27 top, 29 top left, 38 top and bottom, 48 top, 50 top, 52 top, 53 top left. **US National Archives:** 241 top, centre left and bottom. **Vauxhall Motors:** 47 top right. **Peter Wearne:** 230 top.

We featured the Coastal Command Memorial in Westminster Abbey on page 7 but a second memorial stands on the seafront at North Berwick (see also page 280) as it was considered that the vital part that Scotland played in the campaign justified its own tribute. It was unveiled by John Cruickshank, VC, (see pages 158-159) on May 4, 2007 — the day traditionally set aside to mark the victory over the U-Boat threat in 1943 and now known as Batte of the Atlantic Sunday. Both memorials are named 'Constant Endeavour' after the motto of RAF Coastal Command.

INDEX

COMPILED BY PETER GUNN

Note: Page numbers in *italics* refer to illustrations. There may also be textual references on these pages.

**In memory of Leading Aircraftman Gordon Ramsey (1910-1988)
who served with No. 311 Squadron at Talbenny and No. 248 Squadron at Banff.**

PORTREATH